MANAGING REAL ESTATE PORTFOLIOS

MANAGING REAL ESTATE PORTFOLIOS

Edited by
Susan Hudson-Wilson, CFA
and
Charles H. Wurtzebach

IRWIN

Professional Publishing
Burr Ridge, IL 60521
New York, NY 10001

Project editor: Denise V. Santor
Assistant production manager: Jon Christopher
Art manager: Kim Meriwether
Compositor: Alexander Graphics Limited
Typeface: 11/13 Times Roman
Printer: Book Press, Inc.

Library of Congress Cataloging-in-Publication Data

Managing real estate portfolios / edited by Susan Hudson-Wilson and
    Charles H. Wurtzebach.
      p.   cm.
    Includes bibliographical references and index.
    ISBN 1-55623-363-9
    1. Real estate investment.   2. Portfolio management.   I. Hudson
-Wilson, Susan.   II. Wurtzebach, Charles H.
    HD1382.5.M278   1994
    332.63'24—dc20   93–10847

Table of Contents

INTRODUCTION

We edited this volume on real estate portfolio management because we feel that it is a subject whose time has come and that has tremendous relevance for today's institutional and individual investors. In the 1980s, investors were real estate investment "accumulators" and now are left with a "collection of deeds." For most investors, this approach resulted in less than satisfactory portfolio performance. The day of reckoning has now arrived. Investors, consultants, and managers are now asking— "What are the characteristics of this real estate 'collection?' " or "What role will real estate fulfill in a multiasset portfolio?"

Practitioners have long asked for a volume that would help them become more familiar with the status of the developing field of real estate portfolio management and the many issues still unresolved in it. While we cheerfully acknowledge that we have failed to accomplish the assemblage of a complete exposition on real estate portfolio management, we feel that we have succeeded in focusing on the parts of the field of portfolio management that are of the greatest interest to us and to many of our friends and colleagues in the industry and in academia.

On a personal note we would observe that it has been immensely gratifying to work both with each other and with some of our finest associates in the business and academic communities in compiling this collection. We thank them and hope that you are well served by their efforts.

The cooperation represented in these pages between real estate investors, managers, and consultants, exemplifies all that is "right" in the real estate investment community. Viewed from the perspective of a human life cycle, collective understanding of how to efficiently design and build real estate portfolios is akin to that of the condition of a toddler. We keep falling down, but we always get up and try to take another, longer step. We have a lot to learn and are committed to the continuing exploration of the applicability of financial theory to the real estate investment process.

An Overview

Chapter 1, "Real Estate Markets: A Historical Perspective," evolved from a monumental work authored by Blake Eagle and his colleagues at the Frank Russell Company. Susan Hudson-Wilson, CFA was charged with shaping it into a historical accounting which should be obligatory reading for all new entrants into the field of real estate investing. Historically, real estate was regarded strictly as a factor of production—not as an investment medium. Real estate had "use" value only. Property markets and their associated capital markets operated locally and, it was believed, idiosyncratically. Real estate was nonfungible, markets were fragmented, pricing was private, large barriers to entry characterized the marketplace, and there was much uncertainty about performance and its measurement.

Only in the 70s, principally with the advent of the Prudential Insurance Company of America's PRISA fund, was real estate given serious consideration as a meaningful part of an institutional investment portfolio. The passage of the Employment Retirement Income Security Act (ERISA) of 1974 was a very important contributor to the notion of the usefulness of real estate within a multiasset portfolio. In this act, the principle of diversification was sanctified and real estate was soon to be introduced to many portfolios as an important diversifier.

During the late 1980s and early 90s real estate's role in the multiasset portfolio has come under great pressure as performance has severely lagged expectations. Yet still, investor interest in the asset class continues and, given real estate's share of total world wealth, it is not likely to wane.

In Chapter 2, "Commercial and Multifamily Real Estate Investment Vehicles," Mark P. Snyderman, CFA offers a very thorough "catalog" of the myriad real estate investment vehicles available to institutional and individual investors. Mr. Snyderman places real estate vehicles in the familiar context of corporate securities and explains real estate in terms of financial asset counterparts. Bonds are analogous to mortgages, convertibles are like hybrid debt, stock securities are similar to fee simple equity, growth stocks behave like leveraged equity, and options are like options! Futures do not currently have a financial asset relative in the real estate market, but they will, they will.

Snyderman hypothesizes that property is not different from an operating business. The property's manager is selling space and tenant services as the corporation's manager is selling a good or service. The property's owner must decide how to finance the property as must the corporation's owner. One possible difference is that the corporate manager can more easily expand or contract the business or product line, while this is more difficult for the manager of an individual property.

Chapter 3 is jointly authored by Mark Coleman, Susan Hudson-Wilson, CFA, and James R. Webb and is titled "Real Estate in the Multiasset Portfolio." On average, pension funds currently hold only 4 percent of their aggregate portfolio in real estate, but this average disguises the wide variance in levels of participation. Many smaller funds hold no real estate at all, while others are invested at a 10 percent level. This chapter describes the various reasons why an institution or a person might want to include real estate among their holdings (of course, more than 50 percent of all individuals are homeowners and so have included real estate in their personal portfolios). The chapter is coldly analytical and studies the empirical veracity of each of the typical rationalizations: diversification, inflation hedging, and high absolute returns. In addition, the characteristics of real estate are reviewed and the response of real estate to various macroeconomic forces is studied. The bottom line is that real estate has a valid place in a well-diversified portfolio—it is simply more difficult to accept this in times of poor real estate performance.

S. Michael Giliberto and Sandon J. Goldberg authored Chapter 4 entitled "Real Estate in a Capital Markets Context." They have sought to clarify the linkages between the "hard" asset, real estate (the space market) and the "investment" asset, real estate (the capital market). The misunderstanding of the inextricable ties between these markets caused the sustained and highly destructive space and capital market disequilibria that has plagued the real estate market since the mid-1980s. They trace the linkage from rents, created in the space markets by the relationship between supply and demand, to capitalization rates created in the capital markets by the demand for and the supply of investments of all kinds. The key to the appropriate equilibrium solution is the correct reflection of capital market pricing in the property valuation process. The authors point out that other traditional capital market analytics may sensibly and helpfully be applied to the real estate markets and cite duration as an example.

Valuation is a constant theme and nemesis in real estate portfolio management and so Chapter 5, "Real Estate Appraisal" authored by Jeffrey D. Fisher, is devoted to a critical exposition of the techniques currently employed. Dr. Fisher points out the limitations of the appraisal process including a reflection on the difference between the value of a property and the value of a portfolio of properties. The difference between the value of a property in abstract from the value of a property in a portfolio context is discussed as well as the true uniqueness of each property. Again the contrast to, and coincidence with the public market is explored.

Chapter 6, entitled "Real Estate Portfolio Management," is the heart of the book. It is a collection of pieces organized into Parts; each seeks to "get real"; that is, to integrate the theoretical tenets of modern portfolio theory with the practical challenges of managing real estate portfolios. Charles H. Wurtzebach opens with a discussion titled "Financial Theory Replaces Anecdote." This discussion reviews how real estate portfolio management "used to be" and how it "needs to be." A true investment revolution has occurred, and this book is a reflection of it. Dr. Wurtzebach reflects the fact that the typical institutional real estate portfolio was built one "good deal" at a time. This approach suggested that the primary factor which affected the success of a portfolio's performance was the selection of individual properties. Investors and portfolio managers have now come to the realization that while it was a necessary condition that each deal be "good," it was not a sufficient condition. It was equally important that the portfolio's exposure to risk and return be actively managed. We believe that decisions made at the portfolio composition level are more important to the production of *favorable portfolio performance* than are decisions made at the property level. This is certainly confirmed in public market studies of stock selection. Does the idiosyncratic behavior of real estate dominate the market-related behavior of real estate? Does artful portfolio creation add value?

Dr. Wurtzebach proposes that real estate investments are comprised of systematic, diversifiable, and idiosyncratic risks—he proposes that there is enough diversifiable risk to make it well worth managing.

Part II of Chapter 6 is authored by Charles R. Lightner and is entitled "What Saved PRISA? A Case Study." Mr. Lightner recounts the history of the PRISA portfolio and the recognition of how the application of modern portfolio theory was used to improve portfolio performance. This is a real-life case study in which the results of actual investment decisions are documented and open to the investment community's judgment. The restructuring of PRISA has to be one of the most important portfolio events in our industry.

Part III of Chapter 6, "SampCo: A Hypothetical Portfolio Analysis," is authored by Susan Hudson-Wilson, CFA and offers a second example of a different approach to the same problem as was experienced by PRISA. The approach is different, but the message is the same—develop and apply a rigorous, objective, systematic approach to portfolio analyses and diagnostics. A composite portfolio analysis is presented as it was to the investors. The portfolio risks associated with property type, property location, and property financial structure are analyzed in a systematic fashion. Without this discipline, we will continue to assemble "collections of deeds" without taking advantage of the information imbedded in the marketplace.

In Chapter 7, Stephen E. Roulac presents "Real Estate Investment Performance Measurement." This is another very difficult and evolutionary topic in real estate portfolio management. We do not present answers, but rather a catalog of the central performance measurement issues confronting our industry. Dr. Roulac differentiates performance measurement, benchmarks, and attribution analysis. In the "Performance

Measurement Purposes" section he focuses on the reality of different uses, users, and levels of sophistication among users. He notes the difficulties in the mere calculation of returns. Again, the public market analog is used to illustrate several points. Dr. Roulac addresses the performance benchmark field as a source of frustration—benchmarks must be specific and ought to be investable in order to function as well as possible. Both specificity and investibility are a problem in today's real estate markets. Finally, the issue of performance attribution is presented as a topic with a future, but not much of a past in the real estate investment community! This area is of particular concern to those interested in "proving" the contribution of portfolio theory to real estate portfolio performance.

Charles H. Wurtzebach and Andrew E. Baum coauthored the final Chapter 8 on "International Real Estate." The chapter looks both from Europe toward the United States as well as from the United States to the range of international markets. So far the flow funds have been primarily dominated by international investors looking to the United States. The U.S. institutional investors have not invested aggressively in international real estate. The authors examine the rationale for domestic and international real estate investment and find that there are some very legitimate and similar justifications. In particular there is evidence of considerable variation among market cycles across the property markets of the world. They also note the complexities and the added risks of allocating one's portfolio around the world—a lack of local knowledge, political risks, currency risks, and small-scale markets are of concern. The authors conclude with cautious optimism that global real estate investment will grow as its value to portfolio performance is better understood.

This then is our offering. We hope that you find it useful and thought provoking.

Finally, this book of readings could not have been completed without the considerable contribution of many of our friends and colleagues. Each of the authors obviously contributed their own special perspective. Beth Peterson and Susan Brennan of Aldrich, Eastman & Waltch, and Pat McVay of JMB Institutional Realty helped keep this project on schedule and organized. Without their help this book would not have been completed in timely fashion. Finally, the Pension Real Estate Association graciously permitted our inclusion of the bibliography assembled and published by PREA.

Susan Hudson-Wilson, CFA
Charlie Wurtzebach

CHAPTER 1

REAL ESTATE MARKETS: A HISTORICAL PERSPECTIVE

Blake Eagle
Frank Russell Company

Susan Hudson-Wilson, CFA
Aldrich, Eastman & Waltch

INTRODUCTION

No one knows exactly how much institutional-quality commercial and multifamily real estate there is in the United States. Estimates range from $815 billion to $4.7 trillion.[1] This real estate is held by corporations for their use in production and by insurance companies, pension funds, and individuals for investment purposes. Pension funds provide a fascinating embodiment of the development of the theory and the practice of the use of real estate in an investment portfolio.

While pension funds' use of real estate will be profiled in this chapter, the discussion will also cover banks, insurance companies, syndicators, and foreign investors participation in commercial and multifamily real estate markets. This discussion focuses on private market transactions and discussion of government agency activity is limited.

Prior to the mid-1970s, pension funds were concentrated almost exclusively in stock and bond investments. Both economic and political circum-

---

[1]Mike Miles, "Estimating the Size of the Real Estate Market in the U.S." *Real Estate Review* (1990).

stances have encouraged a strong look at alternative classes of investments. By 1990, pension funds had expanded their interests in real estate to comprise 4.5 percent of the average plan's assets. This average disguises a wide range of participations by individual plans, with small funds remaining at close to 0 percent and larger funds in the 10 to 15 percent area.

The purpose of this chapter is to detail the history that characterized the evolutionary growth of pension funds' participation in the real estate asset class. The history is instructive because it repeats similar themes to those experienced in the stock market, and possibly foreshadows themes to be experienced by other, now "nontraditional," asset classes. As our knowledge of the behavior and role of real estate improves and as the flexibility of investment vehicles grows, we can expect the asset class to assume an ever-expanding role in a well-managed portfolio.

PRE-1975

Pension funds in the United States, historically, avoided any major investment commitment to commercial and residential real estate for several reasons:

- For most of the post–World War II era, institutional investor portfolios that were constructed of high-quality financial assets produced total rates of return that equaled or exceeded expectations. Plan sponsors had no compelling reason to explore alternative investment forms.
- The investment characteristics of real estate that separated it from other asset classes were not compatible with the objectives set by plan sponsors. Such factors as nonfungibility, market fragmentation, infrequent pricing, lack of an auction market, and woefully inadequate information access and delivery systems were all perceived as barriers to entry.
- Tax-exempt investors questioned whether they could effectively participate in a marketplace that clearly favored taxable investors. Plan sponsors could not justify competing for investment product that involved paying for an investment benefit offering no clear economic value.
- The generally accepted perception of the real estate investment market was that it displayed a risk profile much higher than that

acceptable to pension funds. Further, the industry's major participants—developers, brokers, and financial packagers—were deemed "too entrepreneurial."

Additionally, portfolio managers entrusted with pension fund investment decision-making responsibilities were trained in the analysis and evaluation of stocks and bonds. Most had no investment experience in real estate and no compelling reason to gain such knowledge. In the 1960s and early 1970s, the capital markets clearly had a strong stock and bond bias. Real estate was viewed as nothing more than a distant peripheral player. To the mainstream capital market participants, real estate finance belonged to the life insurance and banking industries. Life insurance companies were the commercial mortgage lenders, and banks were active in community commercial and residential lending. Large properties were owned by their primary corporate tenants—regional malls had not yet been invented.

Attitudes began to change in the late 1960s when Wall Street underwrote the real estate investment trust (REIT) industry. REITs were introduced as the vehicle by which both individual investors and institutions could participate in U.S. real estate through publicly traded companies. Institutional investors began to view direct property investment with a more interested eye in the late 1960s when inflation suddenly increased. The level of interest accelerated in the mid-1970s and was affected by two events—one economic and one political:

- Inflation's negative impact on stock and bond investment performance.
- The congressional passage of the Employee Retirement Income Security Act (ERISA).

Two other factors contributed to the interest of institutional investors in broadening their portfolio horizons to include other classes of investment assets, particularly real estate. Both factors emerged from research work in academia:

- The recognition that real estate, as an asset class, represented the largest single store of wealth in the world. Investors seeking participation in a "market portfolio" of investable assets, should, therefore, hold some component of real estate.
- The increasing application of modern portfolio theory (MPT) in managing total portfolio risk. MPT was quite a departure from the

conventional wisdom which stated that risk was specific to individual assets or securities. It argued that the interrelationship among the asset classes is as important as their respective expected average returns.

Inflation's Impact on Stock and Bond Investment Performance

If inflation had not reached the levels exhibited in the late 1960s and early 1970s (levels were much higher than anticipated), it is doubtful whether U.S. pension funds would ever have displayed much interest in real estate. The 6.1 percent annual inflation rate reported for 1969 was the highest reached since 1947. The inflation of the late 1960s was only a harbinger of rates in evidence during the first half of the 1970s. By 1974, the impact of inflation on the investment performance of stocks and bonds was devastating.

Table 1–1 provides annual rates of return for common stocks and bonds during the 1960s. These data are also compared to the annual percentage changes in the consumer price index (CPI) and converted into real rates of return; that is, inflation adjusted returns.

From 1960 through 1964, common stocks produced annualized total rates of return of 10.6 percent. When adjusted for inflation of 1.2 percent, annualized common stock real rates of return were 9.3 percent. There were very few five-year periods since 1945 when common stocks produced any better inflation-adjusted results. For the same period, bonds produced annualized real rates of return of 3.8 percent. With this level of return, there were no convincing portfolio arguments to support a shift to the property sector, or to any other nontraditional investment medium. However, during the second half of the 1960s, inflation rates accelerated steadily upward from 1.9 percent in 1965 to 6.1 percent in 1969.

For the five-year period ending December 30, 1969, the annualized total rate of return for common stocks dropped to 5 percent. When adjusted for inflation, the real rate of return was a paltry 1.1 percent. As poor as common stock real returns were, the inflation-adjusted, five-year compounded return for bonds was an abysmal negative 6.4 percent.

Financial experts were quick to acknowledge that the increases in the inflation rates of the late 1960s were directly responsible for the substantial decline in the investment returns of both common stocks and bonds.

TABLE 1–1

Stocks, Bonds, and Inflation: 1960 through 1969 (One-Year Periods Ending December 31)

	Nominal Returns			Real Returns	
Year	Stocks	Bonds	CPI	Stocks	Bonds
1960	0.3%	8.6%	1.5%	(1.2%)	7.0%
1961	26.6	3.5	0.7	25.8	2.9
1962	(8.7)	7.3	1.2	(9.8)	6.0
1963	22.8	1.8	1.6	20.8	0.1
1964	16.5	4.6	1.2	15.1	3.3
1965	12.5	(0.9)	1.9	10.3	(2.8)
1966	(10.1)	(0.3)	3.4	(13.0)	(3.6)
1967	24.0	(5.0)	3.0	20.3	(7.8)
1968	11.1	(0.2)	4.7	6.0	(4.7)
1969	(8.5)	(7.7)	6.1	(13.8)	(13.0)
Annualized Returns					
5 yrs. 1964	10.6%	5.1%	1.2%	9.3%	3.8%
5 yrs. 1969	5.0	(2.9)	3.8	1.1	(6.4)
10 yrs. 1969	7.8	1.1	2.5	5.1	(1.4)

Source: Frank Russell Company, "Capital Market History and Asset Allocation: 1900–1989," Tacoma, Private Publication, 1990.

The near-perfect correlation between the two events was very convincing evidence. As inflation increased, total rates of return on financial assets decreased. Over the next five years, the situation worsened.

This time period was as dismal as any investor could possibly have imagined (see Table 1–2). Common stock returns experienced two incredibly bad years in 1973 and 1974, which, in fact, comprised the worst two-year period for common stocks since 1940 and 1941. A − 14.7 percent total rate of return in 1973 was the worst single year in common stock performance since 1937. When 1974 reported a pathetic − 26.5 percent return, it came as no surprise that investors became extremely disillusioned with equities. The U.S. economy had been impacted by global, political, and economic events. The Arab oil embargo was a bitter lesson in geopolitics. Inflation jumped to 8.8 percent in 1973 and 12.2 percent in 1974.

This period also alerted those with real, rather than nominal, liabilities to the enormous additional costs incurred as a direct outgrowth of unanticipated increases in inflation. For example, plan sponsors were

TABLE 1–2
Stocks, Bonds, and Inflation: 1970 through 1974 (One-Year Periods Ending December 31)

| Year | Nominal Returns | | | Real Returns | |
	Stocks	Bonds	CPI	Stocks	Bonds
1970	4.0%	18.4%	5.5%	(1.4%)	12.2%
1971	14.3	11.0	3.4	10.6	7.4
1972	19.0	7.3	3.4	15.0	3.7
1973	(14.7)	1.1	8.8	(21.6)	(7.0)
1974	(26.5)	(3.1)	12.2	(34.5)	(13.6)
Annualized Returns					
5 yrs. 1974	(2.4%)	6.7%	6.6%	(8.4%)	0.1%
10 yrs. 1974	1.2	1.8	5.2	(3.8)	(3.2)

Source: Frank Russell Company, "Capital Market History and Asset Allocation: 1900–1989," Tacoma, Private Publication, 1990.
For bonds, from 1970 forward, the Salomon Brothers *High Grade Corporate Bond Index* is used.

quickly learning that the inflation sword revealed two very distinct and sharp edges. First, because investment returns fell far below expectations for a sustained period of time (1970 to 1974) corporations and public entities with defined benefit retirement plans were required to plan for a substantial increase in the levels of contributions to cover investment return shortfalls, or else witness the rise of their unfunded liabilities to uncomfortably high levels. The equally sharp, second edge of the sword was the automatic increase in pension liabilities, because pension benefits are a direct product of wages, and wage increases are substantially driven by increases in inflation rates.

During the five-year period from 1970 to 1974, the annualized rate of inflation was a staggering 6.6 percent. The impact on the investment returns of stocks and bonds was severe. When adjusted for inflation, stocks produced compounded real rates of return of − 8.4 percent. Bonds faired somewhat better, but were only slightly on the positive side of the ledger at 0.1 percent.

During this same time period, the spread between the present value of pension assets and the present value of pension liabilities shifted from positive to negative. In time, the difference became enormous. Unfunded pension liabilities emerged as the single most critical pension industry problem to resolve. The nation's primary retirement system's pool of assets were under an inflation onslaught and the erosion could be measured in the hundreds of billions of dollars.

The inflation of the late 1960s and the first years of the 1970s had a material impact on the real estate capital markets as well. However, there were both winners and losers. The big winners were virtually every property owner in America (e.g., homeowners, businesses, investors, and developers) who had acquired real estate by financing its purchase with a high loan-to-value ratio, low-cost, fixed-rate mortgage payable over 20 to 25 years. The more leverage, the greater the "wealth transfer" from the banks and insurance companies (capital sources) to the borrowers. Conversely, the losers in the inflation game were the capital sources which lent mortgage money to property developers, owners, and investors at low, fixed-rate costs for 20 to 25 years. As inflation consumed unpaid principal, fixed repayment schedules fell sharply in real value.

For most of the post–World War II era up to 1980, banks and insurance company lenders chose to ignore the role of inflation, or viewed each unanticipated upward spike in inflation as a temporary market aberration. Capital suppliers continued to be willing to lend at fixed, relatively low-interest rates and to accept repayment of principal over 20 years or more. Their primary concern was that the money should be paid back at a faster rate than the collateral property was depreciating on the books of borrowers. Generally accepted accounting principles (GAAP) accounting was the basis for monitoring loan-to-value controls. There was also an assumption that property assets maintained market values at least equal to, and probably greater than, book values during the repayment period. Lenders were more concerned about collateral value, debt service coverage ratios, and loan-to-value ratios than the erosion of capital as a result of inflation.

For the borrowers, the situation was the proverbial "free lunch." The higher the ratio of debt to equity, the higher the percentage of investment return on the wealth transfer from lender to borrower. It was not unusual for a homeowner with a 10 percent equity position to rather quickly experience a three- or four-fold increase in equity purely as a function of a reduction in the value of the underlying mortgage debt. Leveraging real estate investments during an inflationary period with virtually no cost of capital is a superior way to create wealth. The wealth creation can occur in a relatively short period of time with little, if any, risk assumed.

The owners of real estate were the recipients of a second component of wealth transfer due to inflation's effect on the costs of land, building materials, and construction labor. As a result of the rising replacement costs, leveraged owners or investors in property had the best of both worlds. As the value of the underlying debt diminished, replacement costs increased, both at rates at least equal to inflation. In the majority of cases, appreciation rates exceeded inflation because investor demand for real estate also accelerated, thereby driving up prices.

The inflation impact of the mid-1960s and early 1970s on those portfolio investors heavily committed to financial assets was disastrous. However, the money management community was well aware that property values had increased during these inflationary periods. Corporate officers were also aware of inflation's impact on the value and replacement costs of corporate real estate assets. Virtually all categories of real estate assets had increased in value after adjustment for inflation.

The goals of conservative investors such as pension funds have always been (1) to preserve capital, (2) to achieve reasonable returns, and (3) to provide inflation protection. From 1965 through 1974, neither common stocks nor corporate and government bonds met these investment objectives. It is not difficult to surmise why the investment community— both taxable and tax-exempt—began to seriously consider alternative investments.

Congressional Passage of ERISA

In 1974, Congress passed the Employee Retirement Income Security Act (ERISA), also known as the Pension Reform Act of 1974.

The purpose of this act was to impose fiduciary guidelines to legally ensure that the private pension system was responsibly managed by plan sponsors. Several specific events led to this congressional act. In 1964, the Studebaker Corporation closed its manufacturing plant in South Bend, Indiana. Many of the employees, believing their pension dollars to be intact, were stunned to learn that the plan, which covered some 7,200 plant employees, would not be fully funded until 1989—25 years away! As a result, only 1,100 were eligible to receive a pension. Since the average age of the plant workers was 54, hundreds of people were not only left unemployed, but were stripped of their retirement dollars as well. Situations such as this prompted Congress to correct the weakness in the private pension system in an effort to protect the "nest eggs" of future retirees.

In establishing the standards for fiduciaries, the specific language of Section 404 of ERISA states: ". . . a fiduciary shall discharge his duties

with respect to a plan solely in the interests of the participants and beneficiaries, . . ." All ERISA fiduciaries are subject to the "prudent man" rule
and must invest accordingly. Further, a fiduciary must also "diversify the
investments of the plan so as to minimize the risks of large losses, unless
under the circumstances it is clearly prudent not to do so." ERISA made
no attempt to specifically define the meaning of "diversify the
investments."

New portfolio management concepts were incorporated in ERISA,
not the least of which emphasized the "total portfolio." As a result of this
legislation, nontraditional assets such as real estate and international equities could be considered as prudent pension fund investment alternatives
to the traditional outlets—stocks and bonds.

ERISA caused dramatic changes in the composition of institutional
investment portfolios. During the 1970s, real estate emerged as the first of
the nontraditional asset classes to be added to U.S. pension funds in any
meaningful amount. This occurred for two reasons: (1) the inflation of the
1960s and early 1970s revealed that a large commitment to financial assets
automatically exposed the portfolio to the impact of high rates of unanticipated inflation, a situation that was not in the best interests of plan beneficiaries or sponsors; and (2) recognition of the need to further diversify the
portfolio in an effort to reduce risk.

Real Estate Wealth

An understanding of the absolute dollar magnitude of various investment
markets can assist investors in not only improving their options for selection, but also in assigning specific asset class weightings. There is, however, no precise measure of the total value of all investment assets in the
world. Further, the value of all the subcomponents constantly changes.
However, this much is known: real estate, in the form of land and land
improvements, represents the largest piece of the world's wealth portfolio. Some experts estimate that real estate equities may account for more
than 50 percent of U.S. wealth.

In the mid-1970s, a common way to estimate the size of the U.S. real
estate market was to compare outstanding mortgage instruments against
other types of debt securities such as corporate bonds and government
fixed-income securities.

Table 1–3 provides a breakout of annual net increases for each major
classification of credit securities for the years 1971–76.

TABLE 1–3
Annual Net Increase in Amounts Outstanding
(dollars in billions)

	1971	1972	1973	1974	1975	1976	Amounts Outstanding
Privately held mortgages	$44.3	$68.8	$68.7	$42.8	$38.5	$61.3	$690.6
Corporate bonds	24.7	18.9	13.5	27.5	32.7	27.6	310.2
State and local securities (tax-exempt)	21.7	12.8	14.1	14.5	15.7	13.7	225.4
Privately held Treasury debt	19.0	15.2	(2.0)	10.2	75.8	61.8	357.2
Privately held agency debt	2.7	9.0	21.2	17.9	7.7	13.1	100.9

Source: Salomon Brothers, Bond Market Research, *Prospects for the Credit Markets in 1976.*

The data revealed the enormous size of the U.S. mortgage market. Outstanding, privately held mortgages were more than double the value of the corporate bond market and exceeded the Treasury debt by almost two to one. Since mortgages are secured by improved real estate and the land on which the improvements are situated, then the total value of all real estate (debt and equity) is obviously immense, and could easily be more than double the value of the underlying mortgages. The data disregarded real estate assets unencumbered by debt.

Table 1–4 provides a breakout of the distribution of the mortgage market by type of borrowing. Single-family housing was by far the largest borrower in the nation's mortgage markets. Commercial real estate was second.

By assuming that commercial mortgage loan-to-value ratios were no more than 70 percent of value, the total worth of commercial real estate financed by mortgage debt was in the $500 billion range. An investment market with an aggregate value of at least $500 billion is clearly one that commands attention relative to the other segments of the capital markets. To disallow inclusion of this market on the grounds that is too complex or underresearched is, in all probability, not valid.

Another broad indicator of the magnitude of real property value is the total amount of dollars invested annually in new construction. Historically, the total value of all new construction, private and public, had typi-

TABLE 1–4
Mortgage Borrowing by Type
(dollars in billions)

	1971	1972	1973	1974	1975	1976	Amounts Outstanding
1–4 family nonfarm residential	$30.8	$43.8	$44.1	$33.0	$42.3	$58.3	$483.3
Multifamily residential	9.7	12.8	10.3	7.0	(0.5)	1.0	97.9
Commercial	9.9	16.8	19.0	15.1	11.2	11.0	58.2
Farm	1.9	3.6	5.5	5.1	4.9	6.0	50.8
Total	$52.3	$77.0	$78.9	$60.2	$57.9	$76.3	$690.2
Less federal agency holdings	8.0	8.2	10.2	17.4	19.4	15.0	99.6
Privately held mortgages	$44.3	$68.8	$68.7	$42.8	$38.5	$61.3	$590.6

Source: Salomon Brothers, Bond Market Research, *Prospects for the Credit Markets in 1976.*

cally accounted for between 8 percent and 11 percent of the gross national product. Annual new construction volume includes everything from housing to dams, so not all new construction necessarily added incremental value to the nation's real property asset base. However, certain public projects, such as new highways and water and sewer systems, can be indirect contributors to increasing property values. Table 1–5 presents new construction for the years 1975 and 1976 by residential, nonresidential, and public sectors. The figures highlight that some $40 billion of new industrial and commercial development occurred during these two years. These are sizable annual additions to the existing stock.

By using selected economic data plus commercial mortgage underwritings per year, then extrapolating total commercial mortgage investments outstanding into a commercial property value for standing inventory, and adding new construction data as a proxy for additions to the country's stock of income property assets, it is possible to derive estimated aggregate values of commercial real estate to compare with other major asset classes.

Assuming an investor would want a "market portfolio" in an effort to be perfectly diversified, a 27 percent commitment to real estate equities (commercial and multifamily property) would be required (based on the data in Table 1–6).

TABLE 1–5

New Construction in Place by Major Types

(dollars in billions)

	1975	1976
Residential	$46.5	$60.5
Industrial	8.0	7.2
Commercial	12.8	12.8
Other nonresidential	5.6	6.2
Farm	2.3	2.5
Public utilities	17.3	19.3
All other private	1.1	1.1
	$93.6	$109.6
Residential	$0.7	$0.6
Nonresidential	14.6	12.6
Military	1.4	1.5
Highways	10.9	9.8
Sewer and water	6.6	6.9
Conservation and development	3.3	3.7
All other public	3.3	2.9
Total public	$40.8	$ 38.0
Total new construction	$134.4	$147.6

Source: U.S. Department of Commerce.

TABLE 1–6

Investment-Grade Assets: December 31, 1976

	Value (billions)	Percent
Corporate equities	$1,051	41%
Open-market paper	72	3
Corporate bonds	334	13
U.S. Treasury debt	407	16
Commercial real estate	500	19
Multifamily real estate	201	8
Total	$2,565	100%

Source: Frank Russell Company and Salomon Brothers.

   The methodology used in conjunction with this data to establish commercial real estate value aggregates is not statistically strong; these are estimates. However, one can conclude that commercial property represents a significant percentage of the total investable assets in the United States. The primary issue is not whether the percentage number is 10 percent or 50 percent. What is important is that the asset class is significant.

Modern Portfolio Theory

In the 1950s, Harry Markowitz published a paper describing the basic premise of what is now known as *modern portfolio theory (MPT)*. Markowitz studied the changes in relationships between individual asset classes and the subsets of a given asset class. His research recognized the inherent relationship between risk and return. Markowitz introduced the concept of the importance of a given investor's total portfolio, rather than that of a single entity of the portfolio. Markowitz's research concluded that the interrelationship of individual securities, or classes of investment assets, is as important in determining risk as any other established risk measure.

   Markowitz focused on mathematically measuring the impact of diversification on a portfolio of investments. There was nothing "new" about the concept of diversification as a strategy to reduce risk. Historically, investors wanting to reduce risk have always followed the same basic principal: don't put all your eggs in one basket. Markowitz knew, as all students of capital markets and investor behavior know, that in order to earn the highest return possible, the asset of choice will be one with the highest expected return. Implicit in any such decision is the investor's willingness to assume a commensurate level of risk.

   Clearly, implicit in an investor's decision to diversify is a decision to reduce risk. Markowitz introduced the concept of the covariance of returns of individual assets as a mathematical tool to more efficiently construct diversified portfolios. He developed a mathematical description of a portfolio's construction with a specific set of expected returns and standard deviations (risk) from an assemblage of multiple assets, each with its respective expected returns, standard deviations, and correlation coefficients. Markowitz demonstrated that portfolios can be constructed in such a way that the overall risk of the total portfolio is less than the weighted average of the standard deviation of the individual assets. In other words, by optimally combining individual assets into "efficient portfolios," investors could expect to earn the highest level of return at an overall lower level of risk.

The original work of Markowitz was followed by works authored by a number of academics including William Sharpe, John Linter, Eugene Fama, Roger Ibbotson, and Stephen Ross. In the mid-1960s, two University of Chicago professors, Lawrence Fisher and James Lorie, contributed significantly to information on historical investment returns of common stocks. Among their study's many findings, it was revealed that investors in the common stocks of the New York Stock Exchange during a majority of the time since 1926 received continual positive rates of return. Additionally, common stocks consistently out-performed long bonds and, over any meaningful period (e.g., 10 years), common stocks delivered annualized rates of return of 500 basis points over those of long bonds.

The study also highlighted that there were periods when long bonds outperformed stocks and that this should be expected during the course of a normal market cycle. The research also revealed that, although investors would earn superior rates of return from common stocks, they would have to accept an increase in their assumption of risk in order to do so. Total returns were negative in approximately 20 percent of the years. The returns displayed a standard deviation in the range of 19 percent, an indication of their relatively wide variability.

As a result of the work of Markowitz in the 1950s, the practice of investment management experienced radical changes. The academic world not only accepted, but began teaching MPT. The 1960s business school graduates brought the new finance technology to the investment management community. It proved to be simply a matter of time before investment managers shifted their focus from analyzing individual invest-ment risk to determining the risk characteristics of the entire portfolio. Within the investment management community, "diversification" became the key word of the decade.

This combination of MPT and research into historical stock market returns contributed to the increase of investment in equities by corporate pension funds in the mid-1960s, and the subsequent reduction of the com-mitment to fixed income. At the conclusion of the 1960s, the dominant asset class in the portfolios of most institutional investors was common stocks.

The passage of ERISA in 1974 further reinforced the notion of diver-sification. The math of MPT was available to help to implement the prin-ciple. The institutional investors had grown their stable of options to include common stocks, and were increasingly aware of the size and inflation hedging capacity of real estate. Between the demand for a greater array of investment vehicles and certainty on the concept of, and the mandate for, risk management real estate became an obvious solution for a multiplicity of problems.

Performance Results

Table 1–7 displays both nominal and real rates of return for stocks, bonds, and real estate for the five years 1975 through 1979.

Common stocks produced superior annualized total rates of return for the five-year period. However, as inflation rates increased, the real rate of return for common stocks moved countercyclically. Common stocks also displayed volatile one-year real returns, ranging from a high of 28.2 percent to a low of − 13.1 percent. Bonds failed to deliver positive five-year annualized real rates of return. Real estate, while not exhibiting any banner years, delivered positive real rates of return each year.

Those U.S. pension funds which added real estate to their portfolios during the second half of the 1970s were rewarded. As a result, most pension funds which had been more cautious in their overall response to real estate in the 1970s were preparing to diversify into this asset class in the 1980s.

TABLE 1–7
Stocks, Bonds, Real Estate, and Inflation: 1975 through 1979 (One-Year Periods Ending December 31)

	Nominal Returns				Real Returns		
Year	Stocks	Bonds	Real Estate	CPI	Stocks	Bonds	Real Estate
1975	37.2%	14.6%	8.8%	7.0%	28.2%	7.2%	1.7%
1976	23.8	18.7	10.3	4.8	18.1	13.2	5.3
1977	(7.2)	1.7	15.2	6.8	(13.1)	4.8	7.9
1978	6.6	(0.1)	16.0	9.0	(2.3)	(8.4)	6.4
1979	18.4	(4.2)	20.7	13.3	4.5	(15.4)	6.6
Annualized Returns							
5 yrs. 1979	14.8%	5.8%	14.1%	8.1%	6.1%	(2.2%)	5.5%

Source: S&P 500, Salomon Brothers, Russell-NCREIF.

Table 1–8 compares real and nominal returns for stocks, bonds, and real estate and changes in the annual percentage rates of the CPI for the nine-year period from 1971 to 1979.

During this nine-year period:

- Common stocks produced negative real rates of return in four of the nine years. Further, these returns evidenced a very wide range of values—from a high of 28.2 percent to a low of − 34.5 percent. For the nine years annualized, the common stock return, adjusted for inflation, was − 2.4 percent.
- Bonds produced negative real rates of return in five of the nine years. While not displaying the same variability of returns as did common stocks, the swings between the high of 13.2 percent and the low of − 15.4 percent were much greater than anticipated. Prior to the decade of the 1970s, bonds were expected to provide a dampening effect on common stocks' propensity for higher volatility. Not only did bonds fail to deliver as anticipated during the 1970s, for the nine-year period bonds produced a negative annualized real rate of return of − 1.4 percent.

TABLE 1–8

Stocks, Bonds, Real Estate, and Inflation: 1971 through 1979 (One-Year Periods Ending December 31)

	Nominal Returns				Real Returns		
Year	Stocks	Bonds	Real Estate	CPI	Stocks	Bonds	Real Estate
1971	14.3%	11.0%	5.3%	3.4%	10.6%	7.4	1.8%
1972	19.0	7.3	7.2	3.4	15.0	3.7	3.7
1973	(14.7)	1.1	11.0	8.8	(21.6)	(7.0)	2.0
1974	(26.5)	(3.1)	9.6	12.2	(34.5)	(13.6)	(2.3)
1975	37.2	14.6	8.8	7.0	28.2	7.2	1.7
1976	23.8	18.7	10.3	4.8	18.1	13.2	5.3
1977	(7.2)	1.7	15.2	6.8	(13.1)	(4.8)	7.9
1978	6.6	(0.1)	16.0	9.0	(2.3)	(8.4)	6.4
1979	18.4	(4.2)	20.7	13.3	4.5	(15.4)	6.6
Annualized Returns							
9 yrs. 1979	6.1%	5.0%	11.5%	7.6%	(2.4%)	(1.4%)	3.6%

Source: S&P 500, Salomon Brothers, Russell-NCREIF, U.S. Bureau of Labor Statistics.

- Equity real estate experienced a negative real rate of return in only one year. For the nine years annualized, real estate produced a real rate of return of 3.6 percent. What truly set this asset class apart from stocks and bonds was the narrow band of real return ranges: from a low of −2.3 percent to a high of 7.9 percent. Based on the real estate return data for the period 1971 through 1979, the asset's major contributions to the total portfolio were twofold: (1) it lowered overall portfolio risk, and (2) produced a positive real rate of return.

During the 1975 to 1979 period, investors did not raise any serious concerns about: (1) the subjectivity of the appraisal process; (2) the relatively high asset management fees charged by the investment managers; or (3) whether portfolios were being structured to maximize returns at the lowest level of risk. This prevailing attitude was probably due to the fact that real estate returns equaled or exceeded expectations. Also, investors were far more concerned with the extremely disappointing results of stocks and bonds; particularly given the sizes of their allocations.

The high inflation rates of 1978 to 1980 created chaos in the real estate capital markets. Once again, long-term mortgage lenders were learning the bitter lesson about mismatches in asset/liability maturities when inflation rates unexpectedly surge upward. Portfolios of long-term mortgages financed with short-term capital were getting hammered. Traditional commercial real estate mortgage lenders, primarily life insurance companies, could no longer issue long-term fixed-rate mortgages with 20- to 25-year maturities. To developers, investors, and packagers of real estate investments, this was a precursor of forthcoming problems. Long-term mortgage rates moved from 9.5 percent to 13.5 percent in less than two years. At these higher rates, no proposed new commercial real estate development could demonstrate economic feasibility, even under the most favorable conditions. Traditional long-term capital sources shortened their maturities and raised interest rates to double-digit levels in order to offset the inflation erosion in their older portfolios. Borrowers either paid higher prices for real estate debt or they looked elsewhere for capital.

As the decade came to a close, savings and loans and mutual savings banks were experiencing heavy disintermediation. Life insurance company general accounts were hemorrhaging badly. A little known and scarcely used clause in whole-life insurance policies was discovered which allowed policyholders to borrow against their whole-life cash values at 4.5 percent to 5 percent. When interest rates shot up to double-digit levels, policyholders borrowed back their own "savings" at very low interest rates and immediately reinvested these funds elsewhere at higher yields. The life insurance companies were left with billions of dollars of low-yielding, illiquid mortgages, while being forced to borrow in the capital markets at double-digit interest rates to fund policy loan demand.

Response to Inflation: 1980 to 1984

In 1980, the long-term outlook called for continued high rates of inflation. This projection was based upon the previous decades' annualized inflation rate of 7.4 percent, and the 13.3 percent level reached in 1979. While forecasts varied, the general consensus was that inflation would average about 8 percent throughout the decade.

Prospects for continued higher than normal inflation caused investors to seriously reconsider their past and present asset class weightings. Inflation was not discriminating; it negatively impacted both individual and institutional investor portfolios—taxable as well as tax exempt, foreign and domestic, large and small. As such, real estate equities were viewed in a much more favorable light in 1980 than at any time during the previous 30 years. The need to add an asset class capable of positively impacting investment returns during continued high inflation became a priority among investors. Real estate was selected as the asset class which would outperform high rates of inflation.

Investors did not raise major objections to real estate's inherent drawbacks of illiquidity, asset lumpiness, lack of capital market performance history, or the appraisal process. The trade-offs seemed advantageous. Rather, investors were focusing on what types of real estate investments to acquire, how much capital to invest, how to better source investment product, and the identification of experienced professional advisers.

Investors were shortening the time frame of the decision-making process. The marketplace had handsomely rewarded investors who had elected to participate in real estate during the 1970s. Thus, for those investors anxious to add real estate to the asset mix, 1980 seemed to be a timely starting point for these reasons:

- Real estate market fundamentals were very strong; vacancy rates in both office and industrial real estate were at all-time lows. User demand was increasing; supply shortages were causing rents to increase, particularly in the office sector.

- Sustained high inflation rates had significantly increased the cost of land, building materials, and construction labor, thereby driving up replacement costs. Market values of existing properties generally increased.
- Long-term mortgage rates reached record high levels, effectively resulting in a near total withdrawal from the market by traditional capital suppliers. This was a factor that only exacerbated supply and demand imbalances.

While U.S. pension funds, such as risk-averse "market investors," were planning to increase their level of investment in real estate, major financial intermediaries (thrift institutions, banks, and life companies) were reassessing their real estate investment strategies for the future. All had two common goals:

- To be more competitive in inflationary environments.
- To increase exposure to real estate and, in the process, to structure investments to protect portfolios against high rates of unanticipated inflation.

Foreign institutional investors, particularly European pension funds, were also increasing their commitment to real estate. Most intended to add U.S. real estate to their domestic portfolios for two reasons: (1) the U.S. market offered political and economic stability, and (2) they already had substantial exposure to property in their respective "home" markets.

The new sources of capital, cautiously invested in real estate in the 1970s, were now preparing to invest a substantial amount of capital during the 1980s. These investors cared little whether investments were in the form of straight equity, leveraged equity, or blended hybrid debt/equity structures. What they had in common was the determination to invest in real estate equities as opposed to straight real estate debt. These new sources of capital included pension funds and other pools of tax-exempt capital, individual investors through limited partnerships, and foreign institutional investors.

Pension funds had a major impact on the real estate capital market flow of funds during the 1980–84 era. Previously, their aggregate capital commitment had not made much of an impact. However, in a relatively short period of time, pension funds suddenly emerged as a formidable new source of funds. Investing upward of $30 billion between 1980 and 1984 provided ample replacement capital to offset the lack of capital from traditional sources due to high-interest rates, disintermediation, and inflation.

Public and Private Real Estate Syndications

In the late 1960s, packagers of real estate investments raised equity financing through the sale of limited partnership interests to individual investors. Money was raised through both public and private offerings.

Any entity seeking capital, be it a developer, entrepreneurial investor, or prospective asset manager, formed a limited partnership and then appointed itself general partner. Once the partnership was declared a legal entity, it would raise funds by selling investment units to local investors generally in $5,000, $10,000, or $20,000 increments. Monies raised were targeted for investment in specified properties or blind pools.

Once fully capitalized, the limited partnership would develop or acquire commercial real estate for investment purposes. Individual limited partners generally had priority rights to the lion's share of any investment cash flows, up to full recapture of initial capital contribution plus a modest cumulative preferred return. Thereafter, the limited partners and the general partner split the cash flows on some predetermined basis, usually 50/50. As an added inducement to commit capital, investors were entitled to receive most, if not all, of the tax-shelter benefits. During the life of the partnership, the general partner collected asset and property management fees.

As inflation accelerated in the late 1970s, a large number of small investors invested in real estate limited partnerships for tax-shelter purposes. During this period, many Americans were elevated into higher tax brackets as the by-product of inflation-driven wage increases. Since the majority of real estate limited partnerships offered a combination of current tax shelter and future economic benefits, millions of Americans became commercial real estate investors.

A number of successful local and regional real estate syndication firms eventually evolved into fully integrated real estate asset management businesses. As these firm's investor bases grew and their syndication activities expanded, it was only a matter of time before Wall Street took notice.

The leading syndicators began engaging Wall Street investment bankers to raise investment funds in the early 1970s. Some of the Wall Street firms that initially raised capital for the syndicators decided there was so much potential profit for those in the general partner role that they entered the business.

According to Questor Associates, a real estate consulting firm that tracked and monitored the real estate syndication activity, during the

1970s, approximately $2.5 billion of equity capital was raised in the public market for investment in real estate limited partnerships. Questor estimated that at least an equal amount of money was raised in the private market.

The amount of capital raised through public and private offerings of real estate limited partnerships in the 1970s was not significant when compared to the industry's total flow of funds. However, the syndication of equity capital played an important role. Often, the only source of equity capital to small, thinly financed developers was via the real estate syndication process. To the small "niche" developer trying to meet a specific need, syndicated capital was his or her only source of front-end equity.

When Congress passed the Economic Recovery Act of 1981, the underlying objective of the legislation was to improve the nation's economy through reduced taxes and increased incentives for savings and investments. Inflation was the key in Congress's recognition of the inadequacies of existing tax depreciation provisions. From inception, the U.S. tax system based depreciation allowances on the historical cost of assets. The tax system allowed taxpayers (investor, business, and industry) to recover these costs over the estimated useful lives of the assets. However, it did not permit owners of property assets (e.g., plant, buildings, equipment) depreciation allowances to replace worn-out assets at their inflated replacement costs.

The Tax Reform Act of 1981 provided accelerated write-off periods and simplified the various lives for different types of real estate investments. The primary objective of the act was to allow corporate America to recapture the cost of plant and equipment at much faster rates in order to adjust to the inflation-increased cost of replacement. What most legislators failed to recognize or foresee was that the act also substantially magnified the already favorable tax-shelter aspects of investment in commercial real estate. In fact, the act made real estate an immensely attractive tax shelter, particularly when the economic environment was one of increasing rates of both inflation and nominal wages. Real estate had always been accorded "favored nation" status under the previous tax codes. This time though, real estate was given virtually "universal" privileged status.

By 1981, millions of the Americans driven into inflation-induced, higher tax brackets were favorably disposed to new forms of investment that had the aspects of inflation protection and tax reduction. The Economic Recovery Act of 1981 and commercial real estate investment provided the means to achieve these objectives. Many who were involved in real estate syndication saw the opportunity to profit from investors wanting tax-advantaged real estate investments. In fact, investors were so focused on write-offs, many failed to observe the huge upfront and ongoing fees some of the more exploitative promoters were charging.

To develop a sense of the magnitude of investor capital committed to public real estate limited partnerships between 1980 and 1984, the following table is presented.

Sale of Limited Partnership Public Syndications: 1980 through 1984
(dollars in millions)

	1980	*1981*	*1982*	*1983*	*1984*
Oil and gas	NA	$2,884	$2,399	$2,972	1,696
Real estate	$1,988	3,587	2,471	4,448	5,685
Equipment leasing	NA	200	240	386	478
Other	NA	200	399	470	543

Source: Robert A. Stanger & Company.

During the decade of the 1970s, approximately $5 billion of equity capital was raised in the public and private markets for real estate limited partnership syndication investments. However, during the first five years of the 1980s, more than $18 billion was raised in the public market for real estate. At least another $18 billion was raised via private placements. Therefore, at least $36 billion of equity capital was raised from investors principally motivated to acquire tax shelters.

Assuming this equity was leveraged with two dollars of debt for each dollar of equity, then approximately $108 billion of investment purchasing power was created. In all likelihood, the debt-to-equity ratios could have been higher. The more debt-to-equity, the higher the tax write-offs. The high rates of inflation in the late 1970s and early 1980s, combined with shortened depreciation schedules and improved investment tax credits, caused taxable investors to focus almost solely on the tax-shelter aspects of real estate investment. Unfortunately, what most failed to realize was that good real estate tax shelters require bad real estate economics.

There are no precise statistics on exactly how much capital was raised for real estate investment through public and privately financed real estate limited partnerships. What is known for certain is that the amount was substantial. Compared to the 1970s, in absolute terms, the flow of small investor syndicated capital to real estate in the 1980s was staggering. 惊人，巨大

Savings and Loans

Inflation was the catalyst for financial deregulation, a process which began in the late 1970s and continued into the early 1980s. Once implemented, deregulation would eventually have an almost unbelievable impact on real estate capital formation.

In the late 1970s, rising interest rates, fueled by inflation, caused savers to seek higher investment returns than those that thrift institutions were regulated to pay. Another group of savers (buyers of life insurance policies) were also eager to earn higher returns, given the number of new investment options available to small investors and savers.

When interest rates rose to double-digit levels in the late 1970s, savers began to withdraw funds from thrifts and policyholders borrowed on the cash values of their insurance policies. Investments were made in Treasury bills, money market mutual funds, bond mutual funds, and other investments paying higher yields. In a relatively short time, savers had become investors.

To counteract the outflow of money from thrifts, the federal government authorized these institutions to offer a variety of deposit accounts which paid interest rates determined by the current market environment. Although this helped to reduce disintermediation, it increased the cost of doing business. Thrifts were paying higher interest rates on deposits, but were not generating higher returns on their investment portfolios. Thus, it was deemed imperative that thrift institutions be released from further government regulation in order to survive this period of high inflation, high interest rates, and capital disintermediation.

In January 1980, thrifts were allowed to introduce All-Savers certificates to inhibit deposit liabilities caused by depositors favoring money market certificates. Later in 1980, passage of the Depository Institutions Deregulation and Monetary Control Act permitted federally chartered thrifts to establish NOW Accounts, a form of interest-bearing checking accounts. Insured deposit limits were raised to $100,000. With the introduction of advanced electronic telecommunication and federal deposit insurance as a safeguard, savings and loans (S&Ls) were prepared to accommodate large depositors. Specialized deposit brokers materialized to raise money both nationally and internationally. Thrifts were able to raise a huge amount of capital by paying interest rate premiums and promoting federally insured deposit protection.

In 1982, to further enhance the thrifts' ability to compete for funds, the Depository Institutions Deregulation Committee was directed to allow federally chartered thrifts to establish deposit accounts which were the equivalent of money market mutual funds. The result, over a relatively short period of time, was the deregulation of the liability side of the thrift industry's balance sheet. Legislation passed in the late 1970s and early 1980s initiated deregulation of the asset side of the ledger as well. Initially, these efforts were aimed at the residential mortgage market by allowing thrifts to invest in graduated payment mortgages, adjustable rate mortgages, and other alternative mortgage instruments. These new powers included permission to invest in adjustable mortgages paying market rates of interest. Investment powers were subsequently broadened, allowing thrifts to invest a portion of assets in consumer loans, commercial paper, commercial real estate loans, corporate debt securities, and agricultural loans, as well as enabling the issuance of credit cards.

Prior to the 1980s, S&Ls were not major participants in the U.S. commercial property markets. After deregulation was in full effect, the S&Ls evolved into a major supplier of construction and development financing to commercial property developers. Financial Corporation of America (FCA), a California S&L, grew from $2 billion in assets in 1980 to $30 billion by 1984 (this figure includes a merger). The FCA followed a basic strategy of accumulating a substantial amount of short-term deposits through the use of brokers, with the intent of raising a huge amount of money for residential and commercial real estate loans.

Life Insurance Companies

Life insurance companies, not unlike S&Ls, experienced massive capital disintermediation in the late 1970s and early 1980s. The sale of whole-life and ordinary life insurance policies, which had been a major source of funds for investment in long-term commercial real estate first mortgages, declined when inflation increased. Financial deregulation created a multiple of investment opportunities for the small investor. As a result, individual purchasers of whole-life insurance either borrowed or cashed in their policies to reinvest into higher yielding money market funds, and so on. In the process, they replaced their old insurance with much lower cost term life insurance. This resulted in a major alteration in life companies' cash flows.

In order to remain competitive in the real estate capital market, life insurance companies targeted U.S. pension plans for two types of funds: (1) pension dollars earmarked for real estate equity investment, and (2) pension dollars targeted for guaranteed insurance contracts (GICs).

The GICs represent a form of uninsured fixed-income instruments backed by the assets in a life company's general account. Each issuing insurance company guarantees that interest will be paid when due and that principal will be paid in full at maturity. The GICs appeal to pension funds seeking high yields for a limited duration. The contracts are similar to bonds with terms of 3, 5, or 10 years.

The capital that pension funds invested in pooled real estate accounts, sponsored and managed by life companies, provided these institutions with a source of replacement capital as well as a major source of income in the form of asset management fees. If life companies were to continue to maintain large, vertically integrated real estate investment operations, replacement revenues were as important as developing new sources in capital. Although the pooled real estate equity separate account business was important to the life companies, their ability to continue to participate in the real estate market as a major capital supplier lay in the continuation of accessing new sources of capital through the regular issuance of GICs.

Not widely known is the fact that GIC investment proceeds are the life insurance industry's primary source of funds for making commercial real estate mortgages. Since the duration of GIC contracts have set maturities, investing requires careful asset/liability matching. Beginning in the early 1980s, as life insurance policy loan funds dissipated (which were the source of funds for long-term, self-liquidating commercial first mortgages), these institutions started issuing "bullet loans" with maturities to coincide with those of the GICs.

During the first five years of the 1980s, life companies were phenomenally successful in increasing their GIC business. When it initially appeared that they would be forced to cut back commercial real estate lending due to disintermediation, it turned out that the new funds raised through the issuance of GICs more than filled the void.

During the 1980s, life companies also made the decision to add and/ or increase the level of direct equity real estate investment for their general accounts. Prior to this period, about the only "equity" real estate a life company general account owned was in the form of long-term sale-leasebacks involving creditworthy tenants (U.S. Fortune 500 companies) or real estate acquired through foreclosure. However, to the extent that such assets were held in portfolios during the late 1970s and early 1980s, substantial gains in capital values were realized, which reinforced the argument that real estate offered inflation hedge benefits to portfolios. The capital losses in the fixed-rate mortgage portfolios only added more conviction. The "wealth transfer" from real estate lender to borrower caused life insurance companies to become more involved in real estate equities. In this regard, GIC sources of funds allowed life companies to become equity joint venture partners with developers, real estate co-investment partners with pension funds, and real estate mortgage lenders.

Foreign Investment

Historically, the media has focused a great deal of attention on foreign investment in U.S. commercial real estate. As a rule, the media has tended to exaggerate the dollar amounts involved. Yet, during the first half of the 1980s, foreign investors, both institutional and individual, probably invested more than $3 billion annually in U.S. property. Foreign investors have always been attracted to the economic and political stability of the U.S. Also, investment in U.S. property offers foreign investors additional investment capacity that is usually unavailable within their domestic markets.

Commercial Banks

Commercial banks have always been, and continue to be, the primary source of construction loans for the U.S. real estate development community. In this regard, banks provide construction loans to both the residential and commercial property sectors.

Banks are perennial short-term borrowers. Construction financing has generally been the type of lending activity where banks can match maturities of investments with the inherent short-term nature of their liability structures.

Construction lending can be, and usually is, a most profitable business. Banks have the capacity to raise a large amount of capital in the financial markets on very short notice. They almost always have the resources to make construction loans available to developers. Construction loan rates float with an established indicator, thereby assuring bank lenders a positive yield spread between cost of funds and the return on the construction loan investments. Banks also have the ability to underwrite major construction loans in their own backyard and then sell participations to "downstream" banks in other parts of the country.

Banks, like any other financial intermediary, compete to raise capital in the marketplace. The same deregulation which allowed savings and loans to compete for funds, and concurrently permitted broader investment parameters, also worked to the banks' advantage. All things being equal, investors would probably opt for bank-insured deposits over savings and loan-insured deposits.

At one time, banks could be severely exposed to disintermediation. Deregulation in the late 1970s and early 1980s not only provided much needed insulation, it also provided banks with a competitive advantage through deposit insurance increases to $100,000 and permitted multiple-capital accessing capabilities.

Banks were highly aggressive construction and development lenders in the late 1960s and early 1970s when the REIT industry was in full force. In fact, banks sponsored many of the REITs that specialized in short-term construction and development financing. During the late 1970s and early 1980s, their overall response to the real estate capital market's need for funds was somewhat indifferent. Possibly, banks were still gun-shy after their REIT experience. However, they finally began to accelerate construction and development lending in 1983 and 1984.

Table 1–9 presents data on year-end commercial real estate debt outstanding in the United States from 1977 through 1984. For the 1980–84 period, data are presented by major type of financial intermediary. The "other" category refers to real estate investment trusts, mortgage bankers, credit unions, pension funds, and so forth.

The year-to-year increases in commercial mortgage debt outstanding remained fairly consistent from 1978 through 1982. When adjusted for inflation, the annual incremental differences in the years 1980 to 1982 were actually increasing at decreasing rates. However, in 1983 the floodgates opened. The increases in commercial real estate mortgage debt in 1983 and 1984 were greater, in absolute terms, than the combined totals of annual increases from 1979 through 1982. In two years, banks added $53 billion in commercial real estate financings, an increase of more than 50 percent, while savings and loans added $42 billion, or an increase of 67 percent.

TABLE 1–9

Commercial Real Estate Mortgage Debt Outstanding: 1977 through 1984
(One-Year Periods Ending December 31)
(dollars in billions)

	1977	1978	1979	1980	1981	1982	1983	1984
Banks	NA	NA	NA	$81	$91	$100	$120	$153
Savings and loans	NA	NA	NA	61	62	63	80	105
Life companies	NA	NA	NA	81	88	92	103	111
Finance companies	NA	NA	NA	14	16	20	22	24
Other	NA	NA	NA	18	21	26	27	26
Total	$190	$211	$236	$255	$278	$301	$352	$419
		+21	+25	+19	+23	+23	+51	+67

Source: Federal Reserve Bulletin.

Commercial real estate mortgage debt outstanding increased from $236 billion at year-end 1979 to $419 billion at year-end 1984, a 78 percent increase. These data are not adjusted for inflation, but the $183 billion increase in this five-year period is only slightly less in absolute terms than the total of commercial mortgages outstanding on December 31, 1977.

Real Estate Performance

Given the huge increase in capital flows to commercial real estate between 1979 and 1984 from pension funds, syndications, savings and loans, life companies, foreign investment, and commercial banks the obvious question is, how did this affect investment performance?

Table 1–10 presents the nominal and real rates of return for stocks, bonds, and real estate, including annual percentage changes in the CPI, for the five years from 1980 through 1984.

During this five-year period, commercial real estate delivered compounded real rates of return of 7.1 percent. This was the best performing five-year period since pension funds began investing in real estate. The asset class produced 210 basis points per year of premium over the investment objective of a 5 percent annual real rate of return. Real estate equities far outperformed bonds, barely underperformed equities, produced positive real rates of return for each individual year, and displayed a much narrower range of investment returns.

TABLE 1–10
Stocks, Bonds, Real Estate, and Inflation: 1980 through 1984 (One-Year Periods Ending December 31)

	Nominal Returns				Real Returns		
Year	Stocks	Bonds	Real Estate	CPI	Stocks	Bonds	Real Estate
1980	32.4%	(2.8%)	18.1%	12.4%	17.8%	(15.4%)	5.0%
1981	(4.9)	(1.2)	16.9	8.9	(12.7)	(9.3)	7.3
1982	21.6	42.5	9.4	3.9	17.1	37.2	5.4
1983	22.2	6.3	13.2	3.8	17.9	2.4	9.1
1984	6.1	16.9	13.1	4.0	2.1	12.4	8.8
Annualized Returns							
5 yrs. 1984	14.7%	11.2%	14.1%	6.5%	7.7%	4.4%	7.1%

Sources: S&P 500, Salomon Brothers, Russell-NCREIF, U.S. Bureau of Labor Statistics.

Staunch proponents of real estate were quick to point out that: (1) real estate provided its best two years of real returns (1983 and 1984) when inflation rates dropped from 12.4 percent in 1980 to only 3.8 percent and 4.0 percent in 1983 and 1984, respectively, and (2) real estate delivered superior risk-adjusted returns when compared to stocks. During the first five years of the 1980s, real estate equities were perceived as displaying a lower risk profile than either stocks or bonds.

Many professionals who managed real estate investments were able to advertise that they were outperforming the Russell-NCREIF Property Index (RNPI). The message was clear: the better focused strategies (adopted at the beginning of the decade) were delivering higher returns. The implication was that these returns were earned without increasing risk.

Table 1–11 reports on returns for stocks, bonds, real estate, and inflation from 1975 through 1984. For the first time, investors could analyze and compare real estate returns with those of the financial assets over a 10-year period.

For the 10 years 1975 through 1984, real estate equities acquired for all-cash involving only tenanted, operating properties produced an annualized real rate of return of 6.3 percent which far outperformed bonds. Real estate equities underperformed stocks by 60 basis points after adjusting for inflation. However, in the process, more consistent annual rates of return were delivered. In 5 of the 10 years, bonds failed to deliver positive

TABLE 1–11
Stocks, Bonds, Real Estate, and Inflation: 1975 through 1984 (One-Year Periods Ending December 31)

Year	Nominal Returns			CPI	Real Returns		
	Stocks	Bonds	Real Estate		Stocks	Bonds	Real Estate
1975	37.2%	14.6%	8.8%	7.0%	28.2%	7.1%	1.7%
1976	23.8	18.7	10.3	4.8	18.1	13.2	5.3
1977	(7.2)	1.7	15.2	6.8	(13.1)	(4.8)	7.9
1978	6.6	(0.1)	16.0	9.0	(2.3)	(8.4)	6.4
1979	18.4	(4.2)	20.7	13.3	4.5	(15.4)	6.6
1980	32.4	(2.8)	18.1	12.4	17.8	(13.5)	5.0
1981	(4.9)	(1.2)	16.9	8.9	(12.7)	(9.3)	7.3
1982	21.6	42.5	9.4	3.9	17.1	39.2	5.4
1983	22.4	6.3	13.2	3.8	17.9	2.4	9.1
1984	6.1	16.9	13.1	4.0	2.1	12.4	8.8
Annualized Returns							
10 yrs. 1984	14.7%	8.5%	14.1%	7.3%	6.9%	1.0%	6.3%

Source: S&P 500, Salomon Brothers, Russell NCREIF, U.S. Bureau of Labor Statistics.

inflation-adjusted returns. Stocks did not produce positive inflation-adjusted returns in 3 of the 10 years. Real estate's annual real returns were positive each year.

For the 10 years 1975 through 1984, real estate, as an investment asset class, lived up to its advance billing. As early as 1984, however, there were changes in market indicators suggesting that all was not well.

Table 1–12 provides data on the value of new commercial real estate construction put in place each year from 1980 through 1984.

TABLE 1–12
New Commercial Real Estate Construction Put in Place: 1980 through 1984
(1982 constant dollars in billions)

	1980	1981	1982	1983	1984	Total
Industrial	$15.6	$17.7	$17.3	$12.4	$12.7	$75.7
Office	15.1	18.2	23.0	20.0	24.0	100.3
Commercial	18.8	17.5	14.2	14.5	20.6	85.6
Totals	49.5	53.4	54.5	46.9	57.3	261.6

Source: U.S. Department of Commerce, *Statistical Abstract of the United States* (Washington, D.C.: Government Printing Office).

Total new construction put in place did not change significantly from year to year. The change from 1980 to 1981 was 7.9 percent, a healthy one-year increase. In 1982, however, the increase was a modest 2.1 percent, and 1983 displayed a decline of 13.9 percent, followed in 1984 by a more than offsetting 27.2 percent increase. Although there were wide annual swings, for the five-year period the average value of new construction was $52.3 billion and individual annual output was near the average.

However, the value of new office building construction put in place changed significantly between 1980 and 1984. New office construction accounted for 30.5 percent of the total in 1980. It was 34.1 percent in 1981, 42.2 percent in 1982, 42.6 percent in 1983, and 41.9 percent in 1984. Both industrial and commercial additions declined as a percentage of the total.

The data in Table 1–13 represents office vacancy statistics for the downtown, or Central Business Districts (CBD), of selected urban markets.

The national CBD office market moved from 4.1 percent vacant in 1980 to 14.7 percent vacant in 1984. Virtually every urban market followed the same path. A relatively high percentage of increased vacancy

TABLE 1–13
Coldwell Banker Office Building Vacancy Rates: 1980 through 1984—
National Market and Selected Local Markets (Downtown Areas) (Periods Ending December 31)

	1980	1981	1982	1983	1984
National	4.1%	4.8%	10.3%	12.4%	14.7%
Atlanta	13.9	17.7	19.4	16.0	14.1
Boston	1.5	2.3	3.7	1.9	12.8
Chicago	3.7	4.0	8.3	11.3	10.4
Dallas	4.8	4.8	10.0	15.1	17.2
Denver	0.3	0.1	8.3	23.0	23.7
Houston	1.4	1.3	5.8	14.6	20.9
Los Angeles	0.2	0.8	9.5	12.3	11.8
New York (DT)	NA	.4	3.3	3.7	8.3
New York (MM)	1.5	2.4	4.3	7.2	6.9
Philadelphia	5.8	6.4	9.1	8.6	9.0
Seattle	6.0	6.9	8.7	14.3	14.5
Washington, D.C.	0.8%	2.7%	9.6%	11.7%	10.4%

Source: Coldwell Banker, "Office Building Vacancy Rates," 1985.

rates could be attributed to the severe economic retraction in the oil-producing states, but the problem transcended the regional recession.

In 1983 and 1984, suburban vacancy rates for the entire U.S. averaged above 18 percent. These unusually high levels of vacancy had little to do with the oil patch economy. The increase in suburban office building new construction was primarily capital driven. This was the result of: (1) a huge amount of tax-motivated equity capital in need of investment product, and (2) banks and savings and loans exercising their new regulatory freedom by making commercial real estate construction, development, and first-mortgage loans.

As the first half of the decade of 1980s came to a close, while the investment returns from commercial real estate remained very competitive, increases in the national office building vacancy rate and the additional billions of dollars seeking more investment in real estate were warning signs that the market was becoming overheated.

THE REAL ESTATE CAPITAL MARKET: 1985–1989

Capital continued to flow into real estate investments during the last half of the 1980s, even though early warning signs indicated the market was overheating. At times it appeared capital suppliers were oblivious to the increasing evidence of too much money chasing real estate. Ironically, many of the same capital sources which invested in commercial real estate between 1980 and 1984 put up most of the money during the last five years of the 1980s.

By the end of 1984, U.S. pension fund investment in real estate equities had reached $41 billion. Upon entering the second half of the 80s, most of the large defined benefit plans, including public sector and Taft-Hartley pension funds, had made the asset allocation decision to diversify into real estate. The majority followed their lead by routinely establishing minimum commitment levels of 10 percent of total assets.

U.S. pension assets reached $1.3 trillion by 1984. The decision made by an increasing number of plan sponsors to invest in real estate effectively sent a signal to the real estate industry that billions of additional investment dollars were queuing up. Even though pension funds had substantially increased their investment to real estate equities between 1980 and 1984, they were still as underallocated in real estate in 1985 as they were in 1980. This explains why a large sum of pension capital was committed to the real estate asset class during the last half of the 80s. The decision to invest capital was as much driven by a sense of urgency to meet allocation objectives as for any other reason.

Figure 1–1 presents annual changes in total pension fund investment in real estate equities between 1985 and 1989. U.S. pension funds had accumulated substantially more real estate wealth during the last 5 years of this decade than through the entire 15-year period from 1970 to 1984.

Between 1985 and 1989, U.S. pension fund investment in real estate grew from $41 billion to $112.9 billion, a net increase of about $71 billion. No more than $20 billion can be attributed to investment earnings (realized and unrealized gains). Thus, approximately $50 billion of the total was in the form of new investment capital.

The U.S. pension funds' mere presence in the market contributed to the overbuilding. Banks and S&Ls rationalized the expansion of speculative construction lending activities under the assumption that either tax-motivated syndications or pension funds would put up the money to take

FIGURE 1–1
U.S. Pension Fund Investment in Real Estate (1985–1989)

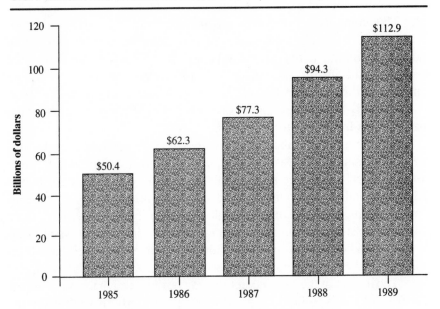

Source: Evaluation Associates, *Pensions & Investment Age.*

out unleased projects. They were financing real estate for the investor market, rather than the user market. Further, when pension funds invested capital, they effectively freed up nonliquid capital which could easily be recycled into new development. The velocity of the turnaround of capital in the real estate sector has never been tracked and measured, but one could conclude that money turns over at much faster rates than what is generally believed.

Public and Private Real Estate Syndication

Real estate limited partnerships continued to function as a vehicle through which millions of individuals channeled money into commercial real estate investments during the last half of the 1980s. According to Robert A. Stanger & Company, individuals put more than $30 billion into real estate limited partnerships between 1985 and 1989. This represented an enormous increase in real estate investment, particularly given the tax-shelter motivation of most individuals. In fact, the amount invested between 1985 and 1989 about doubled the investment by individuals in the 1980–84 period. If $30 billion was raised in the public market, then $60 billion was probably the real total assuming that $30 billion of privately placed limited partnership interests also took place, which is probable. This combination of public and privately raised investment capital created approximately $180 billion of real estate investment purchasing power, assuming a two-to-one leverage factor. Whatever the actual amount, millions of individual investors allocated disproportionate amounts of their net worth to real estate syndicated investments.

Table 1–14 provides annual sales data of publicly registered limited partnerships from 1985 through 1988.

In 1985 and 1986, the public invested more money in real estate limited partnerships than was invested in the five years from 1980 through 1984. In fact, these were record years in terms of commitment of public adviser capital to real estate. These decisions reflected the continued concern regarding inflation, even though high inflation rates had long since abated. Investor preoccupation with tax-efficient investment when inflation rates had declined is puzzling; however, money may well have been forced into the market knowing major tax reform was on the horizon.

The impact of the 1986 tax reform can be observed in the reduction of the flow of funds to limited partnerships, particularly in 1988 when tax reform took full effect on new issues. Money raised in 1988 was down 34

TABLE 1–14
Sale of Limited Partnership Public Syndications, 1985 through 1988
(dollars in millions)

	1985	1986	1987	1988
Oil and gas	$1,827	1,226	$1,346	$589
Real estate	8,062	8,461	6,955	5,304
Equipment leasing	—	812	1,175	1,119
Other	1,074	2,639	4,065	3,356
Total	$10,963	$13,138	$13,541	$10,368

Source: Robert A. Stanger & Company.

percent from 1984. The Tax Reform Act of 1986 eliminated all pre-1986 tax incentives for real estate investment. This effectively leveled the playing field for all categories of investors. However, between the two major tax reform bills (the 1981 bill, which made real estate a highly valuable tax preferred investment, and the 1986 bill) public and privately financed real estate limited partnerships attracted more than $100 billion of equity capital. Applying the two-to-one leverage factor, $300 billion of real estate was purchased, developed, or financed. In terms of real estate capital market flow of funds, individual investors provided more money to the real estate sector than anyone in 1980 could have possibly imagined.

In retrospect, individual investors provided far too much capital, and most was invested for the wrong reasons.

Savings and Loans, Banks, Life Insurance Companies

All three types of financial intermediaries substantially increased their role in real estate capital formation during the last half of the 1980s. All evolved into aggressive spread lenders. For decades, these institutions favored financing commercial and residential real estate primarily because of the perceived lower risk of the asset class. Real estate has always been deemed *lower risk* because loans are secured by land, brick, and mortar. Therefore, real estate lenders have typically accepted higher loan-to-value ratios and lower debt service coverage ratios when underwriting real estate investments than were considered prudent in most other lending activities. During the 1980s, all three categories of financial institutions significantly increased their speculative real estate financing activities far beyond that of their historical practices.

Commercial real estate lending activities of banks and S&Ls exploded. This can largely be attributed to financial deregulation. The Garn–St. Germain Act of 1982 allowed S&Ls to expand nonresidential lending far beyond previously imposed limits. Both banks (particularly the smaller regional and local banks) and S&Ls used their new legislative powers to raise huge sums of money in the capital markets that became the source of funds to expand commercial real estate lending portfolios.

In the process, underwriting standards were lowered. It was not unusual for these institutions to approve construction loans without requiring borrowers to make arrangements for permanent financing. These "uncovered" construction loans generated more fees (that was also borrowed money) and commanded higher interest rates. The borrowers accepted this. They were not taking on any risk because the banks and S&Ls were lending on 100 percent of value. They felt no need to line up permanent financing because the property could always be "sold to the syndicators or the pension funds." When loan underwriting required market studies or appraisals, apparently the inquiry and analysis focused on historical trends, and thus had no relevancy to current market realities. (Traditionally, real estate investment analysis has been historical rather than prospective. It is doubtful that banks and savings and loans were seriously concerned with such matters. Their concern was to "get the money out.")

Table 1–15 presents changes in mortgage debt outstanding for the major categories of financial institutions—banks, savings and loans, life insurance companies, and finance companies. Also included and classified as "others" are mortgage companies, real estate investment trusts, pension funds, credit unions, and so on.

On December 31, 1979, commercial mortgages outstanding in the United States stood at $236 billion. Ten years later, the commercial mortgage debt had grown to $747.3 billion, an increase of 317 percent, or, an annual compound growth rate in excess of 12 percent.

In retrospect, one question remains unanswered: How could so many ostensibly responsible managers collectively make so many bad decisions? As bad as the current problems are with the savings and loan industry, the commercial banks have contributed far more to the commercial property sector's overbuilt status than any other lender. The savings and loan industry was expected to experience severe problems as the result of deregulation. This was not the case for banks. Banks increased their commercial loan portfolios by more than 450 percent in 10 years, an annual

TABLE 1–15
Mortgage Debt Outstanding: 1985 through 1989 (Years Ending December 31)
(dollars in billions)

	1985	1986	1987	1988	1989
Banks	$176	$223	$268	$301	$344
Savings and loans	92	121	151	139	136
Insurance companies	127	149	168	186	191
Finance companies	31	34	40	45	51
Others	49	28	30	40	25
Total	$475	$555	$657	$711	$747
Increase from previous years	$56	$80	$102	$54	$36

Source: Federal Reserve Bulletin.

compound growth rate in excess of 16 percent. Banks nearly doubled their portfolios of mortgage debt outstanding from 1985 through 1989. There never was, and never could have been, enough capacity in the market to absorb that much money.

During the last half of the decade, the flow of funds to the real estate sector from banks, S&Ls, and insurance companies exceeded each previous year's output. Each year was almost invariably a record year of allocating additional funds to the real estate sector.

There is, however, some encouraging news. The net increases in commercial loan underwriting decreased by substantial absolute dollar amounts in 1988 and again in 1989. In fact, the net increase in 1989 was less than any single year since 1983. The thrift industry reported two consecutive years of reduction in commercial real estate mortgage loans outstanding. Unfortunately, the data speaks to the heart of the thrift industry problems. What portion of the "reductions" are actually transfers of assets to the Resolution Trust Corporation is not known.

Between 1985 and 1989, total net increases in commercial mortgage debt outstanding were greater than total commercial mortgage debt outstanding in 1983. To put it another way: the total value of commercial real estate debt outstanding more than doubled from $352 billion at year-end 1983 to $747 billion in 1989.

As would be expected, new construction put in place during the last half of the 1980s increased at very substantial rates. (See Table 1–16).

With respect to the previous data, it is important to note that all dollar amounts are stated in 1982 constant dollars. Between 1980 and 1984, the

TABLE 1–16

Commercial Real Estate; New Construction Put in Place: 1985 through 1988
(1982 dollars in billions)

	1985	1986	1987	1988	Total 1985-1988
Industrial	$14.1	$12.1	$11.6	$12.1	$49.9
Office	28.2	25.3	22.3	22.7	98.5
Commercial	25.0	24.9	24.5	24.4	98.8
Hotel	6.5	6.6	6.3	5.5	24.9
Totals	$73.8	$68.9	$64.7	$64.7	$272.1

Source: U.S. Department of Commerce, *Statistical Abstract of the United States* (Washington, D.C.: Government Printing Office).

dollar value of new commercial real estate construction put in place averaged $51.9 billion per year. The office component increased from $13.3 billion in 1980 to $25.0 billion in 1984, averaging $20.1 billion of new office building construction put in place per year. At an average finished building cost of $125 per square foot (excluding land), an average of 160.8 million square feet of new office building stock was added to the existing inventory every year. Office building construction put in place between 1980 through 1984 accounted for 38.7 percent of total new commercial real estate construction.

During the four years between 1985 and 1989, the dollar value of new commercial real estate put in place per year averaged $67.9 billion, an average annual increase of 31 percent over the 1980–84 period. New office building construction put in place averaged $24.6 billion per year, an average annual increase of 22.3 percent over the 1980–84 production. Once again, applying a finished cost per square foot average of $125, an average of 196.8 million square feet of new office building stock was added to the existing inventory each year. This represented an average annual increase of 27.5 percent.

The above data reveal that new construction put in place for commercial real estate classified as industrial had actually declined during the second half of the 1980s. Big increases in "commercial," which includes retail and all special-purpose real estate (ranging from restaurants to golf courses to marinas) were also recorded.

During the four years 1985 through 1988, the U.S. real estate industry continued on an unprecedented new property development binge that added huge amounts of commercial real estate structures to an existing stock that already was oversupplied, particularly in office, hotel, and research and development types of commercial property.

Foreign Investment

During the latter half of the 1980s, foreign investment in U.S. commercial real estate increased substantially. In a study published by Equitable Real Estate Investment Management, Inc., and Roulac Real Estate Consulting Group of Deloite Haskins & Sells, from 1983 through 1988 the value of foreign real estate equity assets in the United States increased by over 85 percent, from $17.2 billion to $31.9 billion. These numbers represent the actual equity component of foreign investment, and may not capture total value including leverage.

In the early 1970s, most foreign investment in U.S. real estate was by European institutions. However, since 1985 the influx of foreign money was from Asia, most notably the Japanese. Exchange rates for foreign investors improved significantly from 1986 to 1988, especially the yen/U.S. dollar rate.

National account surpluses have made large cash positions available to many foreign investors. Based on comparative current yields, U.S. commercial real estate has always been viewed as extremely attractive on a relative basis. Most real estate in foreign countries trades on a 3 percent to 5 percent current yield basis. In many foreign nations, investment in real estate represents long-term commitments. New development is constrained by rigid land-use policies. Turnover of high-quality real estate is infrequent. For these reasons, many foreign institutional investors (pension funds and insurance companies, in particular) have always been comfortable with investing a component of their real estate portfolio in U.S. property.

A contributing factor in terms of increases in the flow of foreign investment capital to U.S. real estate has been the relaxed regulatory environment in the United States and overseas. These changes have helped to facilitate cross-border property investment. The U.S. tax laws make U.S. real estate attractive to foreign investors because of shorter depreciation schedules. The 1986 Tax Reform encouraged sale of U.S. properties by domestic investors, creating opportunities for foreign investors.

In the late 1980s (1985–88), the Japanese made a major move into U.S. commercial real estate. In this four-year period, Japanese institutions acquired approximately $20 billion of prime U.S. commercial properties. Acquisitions were mostly CBD office buildings and hotels in selected cities such as Los Angeles, San Francisco, Chicago, New York, and Washington D.C. Japanese investors outbid U.S. and other foreign investors for two reasons: the yen/dollar exchange rate clearly favored the Japanese; and their time horizons for ownership are much longer than that of U.S. investors. For these reasons, Japanese investors evidenced little interest in current yields. Instead, they focused on the intrinsics of asset quality and location. Location, more than any other factor, influenced asset selection and pricing.

At the end of the 1980s, foreign investment in equity real estate was estimated at $32 billion. Assuming borrowed funds were employed to acquire investment assets, holdings of U.S. commercial real estate by foreign investors may have reached $70–$80 billion. Whatever the exact amount, during the 1980s, foreign investors provided substantial capital to the real estate market's flow of funds.

Real Estate and Inflation

The five-year period from 1985 through 1989 was, in many respects, a virtual repeat of the first half of the decade in terms of a seemingly endless flow of capital from many different sources seeking additional investment in U.S. commercial real estate.

However, the second half of the decade was quite different from the first half in two significant ways (see Table 1–17). First, the supply side of the market caught up with demands and accelerated to such an extent that commercial real estate overbuilding soon reached an all-time high. Second, inflation rates, which were in the double-digit range at the beginning of the decade, dropped dramatically and unexpectedly. Inflation reached its lowest level of 1.1 percent in 1986, and has averaged, on an annual basis, less than 5 percent since 1982.

Changes in inflation rates resulted in lower overall interest rates. Investor expectations for inflation dramatically changed from high to low rates of inflation. Investor expectations with respect to opportunities in financial assets were positive. The economy expanded; interest rates remained relatively low; and inflation rates remained under control. These events had a material impact on the investment returns of the various asset classes from 1985 through 1989.

During the five years 1985 through 1989, common stocks produced positive inflation-adjusted returns each year. The five-year annualized

TABLE 1–17
Stocks, Bonds, Real Estate, and Inflation, 1985 through 1989 (One-Year Periods Ending December 31)

Year	Nominal Returns			CPI	Real Returns		
	Stocks	Bonds	Real Estate		Stocks	Bonds	Real Estate
1985	31.6%	30.1%	10.0%	3.8%	26.8%	25.3%	6.0%
1986	18.2	19.8	6.5	1.1	16.9	18.5	5.3
1987	5.2	(0.3)	5.4	4.4	0.7	(4.5)	0.9
1988	16.5	10.7	7.2	4.4	11.6	6.0	2.6
1989	31.4	16.3	6.0	4.6	25.6	11.1	1.4
Annualized Returns							
5 yrs. 1989	20.2%	14.9%	7.0%	3.7%	15.9%	10.8%	3.2%

Source: S&P 500, Salomon Brothers, Russell-NCREIF, U.S. Bureau of Labor Statistics.

real rate of return for common stocks of 15.9 percent was the best five-year period since 1958, although the five years ending 1986 was very close at 16.9 percent. The 10.8 percent real rate of return delivered by bonds for the five-year period (annualized) was the third best five-year period since 1936. The were only two five-year annualized periods that were better: 1985 and 1986.

Common stocks produced real rates of return in each of the one-year periods. Bonds failed to produce a real rate of return in only one year—1987.

Alternatively, equity real estate returns began a downward trend in 1985. In 1985 and 1986, equity real estate's real rates of return, while not comparable with stocks and bonds, were historically competitive. This is the only positive note. The annual rate estate returns from 1987 through 1989 were barely above the CPI. The five-year annualized total returns were, for the first time, bordering on acceptable minimums, but only when real estate is viewed as a stand-alone investment.

In almost 20 years of real estate investment performance history, no single five-year period reported lower annualized real rates of return. Clearly, the 1985–89 period was not good for real estate investment.

Table 1–18 provides 10 years of nominal and real rates of return on stocks, bonds, and real estate for the period 1980 through 1989.

Over the 10-year cycle, equity real estate produced consecutive years of real rates of return. However, on an annual basis, these returns started

TABLE 1–18

Stocks, Bonds, Real Estate and Inflation: 1980 through 1989 (One-Year Periods Ending December 31)

Year	Nominal Returns			CPI	Real Returns		
	Stocks	Bonds	Real Estate		Stocks	Bonds	Real Estate
1980	32.4%	(2.8%)	18.1%	12.4%	17.8%	(13.5%)	5.0%
1981	(4.9)	(1.2)	16.9	8.9	(12.7)	(9.3)	7.3
1982	21.6	42.5	9.4	3.9	17.1	37.2	5.4
1983	22.4	6.3	13.3	3.8	17.9	2.4	9.1
1984	6.1	16.9	13.0	4.0	2.1	12.4	8.8
1985	31.6	30.1	10.1	3.8	26.8	25.4	6.0
1986	18.2	19.8	6.5	1.1	16.9	18.5	5.3
1987	5.2	(0.3)	5.4	4.4	0.7	(4.5)	0.9
1988	16.5	10.7	7.0	4.4	11.6	6.0	2.6
1989	31.4	16.2	5.8	4.6	25.6	11.1	1.4
Annualized Returns							
10 yrs. 1989	17.4%	13.0%	10.5%	5.1%	11.7%	7.5%	5.1%

Source: S&P 500, Salomon Brothers, Russell-NCREIF, U.S. Bureau of Labor Statistics.

declining in 1986, and then went into a steep decline. By real standards, it was almost a free-fall.

Common stocks reported only one year (1981) of negative real rates of return, and six years of extremely high real rates of return. Bonds reported three individual years when real rates of return were negative. It is necessary to go back 27 years to find a better 10-year period of annualized real rates of return. In the period ending December 31, 1963, the 10-year annualized real rate of return was 14.2 percent. Clearly, the decade of the 1980s was an exceptional 10-year period for holding common stocks.

The 10-year period annualized real rate of return produced by bonds of 7.5 percent surpassed any 10-year period since 1940. The decade of the 1980s was good for investing in bonds as well. Yet, bonds, which are supposed to be less risky than stocks (at least when standard deviation of returns is the risk measurement standard), displayed a much wider range of annual rates of return: 42.5 percent to −2.8 percent. The range for stocks was 32.4 percent to −4.9 percent.

For the 10-year period ending December 31, 1989, real estate produced annualized rates of return of 5.1 percent. Real estate's benchmark portfolio is the CPI. An investment objective of the asset class is to earn a stable and consistent real rate of return of 300 to 500 basis points above the CPI. Real estate delivered what it was supposed to deliver. However, this occurred in a 10-year period when both stocks and bonds had banner decades. In 12 of the last 25, 10-year periods, common stocks failed to produce 10-year annualized real rates of return in excess of 500 basis points above the CPI. Bonds accomplished that only once—in 1989.

What is disconcerting about equity real estate rates of return is not the 10-year number, or the 15- and 20-year numbers. The returns from the last five years are disturbing (the last three years in particular). The trend line is flat to downward.

Overbuilding, the source of the subpar investment performance, was caused by too much capital from too many sources, combined with too much government support (i.e., the tax system, deregulatory processes, and its role as the final guarantor behind insured deposits). The risk of real estate development shifted from the developer to the suppliers of capital, which in may cases was backed by government intervention.

OUTLOOK FOR THE 1990s

The foregoing provides a historical perspective on institutional involvement in real estate and the factors underlying the performance of that asset class in recent years. For institutional investors to continue to participate in equity real estate, they must believe that portfolios holding investments in equity real estate perform better than those portfolios without this asset class. To accept this premise, an investor must conclude that the commercial property market is, in fact, very cyclical in nature, and therefore has not experienced a structural reorganization, but rather is in the trough of the bear market segment of the cycle.

Tenant demand for additional rental space has historically been the driving force behind new development. However, during the latter half of the 1980s, the rationale for new construction shifted dramatically. Instead of building for pent-up user demand, the real estate development industry built for expected future demand and for investor demand. The bias exhibited by the capital markets that favored real estate investment during the 1980s provided all of the capital requested by the real estate developer community.

For the greater part of the post–World War II era, capital did not flow to the commercial real estate sector until there was evidence that a proposed project would be leased up at occupancy levels and rental rates high enough to justify the capital outlay. As a result, commercial property expansion and retraction cycles moved around a relatively narrow band of vacancy rate measures.

Historically, the market's established "norm" for vacancy has been 5 percent, a level of unoccupied space deemed adequate to accommodate the space-change needs of the existing tenant market. In other words, the market's 5 percent vacancy level represented an inherent structural component required in order to "cover" the existing tenant "float."

For most of the post–World War II era, commercial property mortgage underwriters and income property appraisers automatically assumed rental income losses commensurate with 5 percent vacancy levels. As a result, estimated appraised values, whether determined by capitalizing current income or by discounting expected future cash flows, were based on an assumed normal vacancy level of 5 percent. By monitoring and measuring local market vacancy rates, developers and capital suppliers assessed local commercial real estate supply and demand characteristics. Vacancy rates of 3 percent trigger new development, and 10 percent signified overdevelopment. The market's expansion and retraction cycle generally operated between relatively narrow occupancy ranges of between 90 percent and 97 percent. When vacancy rates were clearly heading for the 10 percent level, capital suppliers began withdrawing from the market, thereby winding down the development process.

Throughout the second half of the 1980s, capital suppliers continued to fund new real estate development, even when vacancy rates shot past 10 percent and headed for 20 percent. Market observers began to ask: Why were the historical vacancy rate indicators that signaled oversupply being ignored? Has there been a structural change in the marketplace? Is the new vacancy rate norm 20 percent? Will the commercial property market of the 1990s be as driven by excess capital?

One can conclude that there was an abnormal bias built into the capital markets during the 1980s that resulted in significant overinvestment in real estate. This capital market real estate bias was, in turn, the product of a confluence of an unusually large number of economic and political events coming together in a very short period of time. These events were:

- High inflation: 1978–82.
- Tax reform: 1981.
- Rapid growth of pension fund assets: 1978–85.

- Globalization of investment markets: 1980–90.
- Financial deregulation: 1982–86.

The combination of these events caused excess capital to be invested in the real estate sector. It is reasonable to assume that, had any of these events not occurred, the overcapacity of today's market would not be as severe. Had any two of these events not occurred, current market would, in all probability, be in relative equilibrium. Commercial real estate should have begun its correction in 1985–86, not in 1989–90.

Today and Beyond

Figures 1–2 and 1–3 reveal the current market conditions with remarkable simplicity and clarity.

There is only a limited volume of new construction because there is only a very small volume of financing available. At long last, the feedback mechanisms inherent in the operation of any marketplace are producing the desired effect. The real estate "supply machine" has been turned off.

Unfortunately for investors there are still some poor returns to be endured.

FIGURE 1–2
U.S. Contract Awards

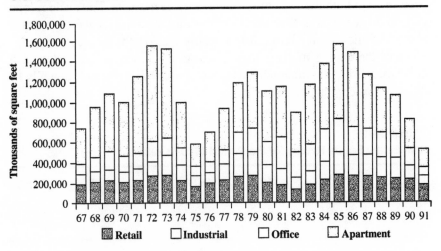

Source: F. W. Dodge Construction Contract Awards.

FIGURE 1–3

The Inflation-Adjusted Flow of Funds into Commercial and Multifamily Mortgages

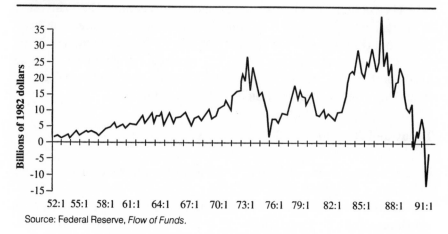

Source: Federal Reserve, *Flow of Funds*.

Table 1–19 presents real estate equity returns for the entire period from 1980 to 1991. The slide is apparent and likely to persist through the early 90s. The recognition of falling values is driving the poor performance. Until real estate values have fallen significantly enough to produce sensible and attractive yields the price and performance corrections will not be completed.

The markets are, in fact, price correcting. The seeds of recovery have been sown in both the investment and the space markets. The cycle is long and, in this case, was lengthened by unfortunate coincidence of political and economic events. While it is possible that, in the future, a reoccurrence of the capital markets bias favoring investment in real estate will develop, it is hard to imagine. Today's real estate markets may actually be described as capital deficient.

TABLE 1–19

Real Estate Equity Return for the Period 1980 to 1991

1980	18.07%	1984	13.04%	1988	6.95%
1981	16.86	1985	10.05	1989	5.81
1982	9.44	1986	6.50	1990	1.39
1983	13.34	1987	5.37	1991	−5.42

Source: Russell-NCREIF Property Index.

Today's investor's are cautious and research oriented. They are focused on current yields and are not tolerant of speculative activities. Replacement costs generally exceed current prices and carrying values. A new source of investor capital is not visible—the only investor group remaining with both the willingness (conservatively) and the ability to invest is the pension fund.

Outlook for Pension Fund Investment In Real Estate

What does all of this mean to U.S. pension funds? Despite the capital surplus nature of the commercial property market from 1985–89, research reaffirms that commercial real estate is a distinct and inherently different asset class. Its unique characteristics of heterogeneity, significant investment unit size, and lack of liquidity, combined with the contractual nature of leases, clearly separates real estate from the investment characteristics inherent to most types of financial assets. Five years of overinvestment, the by-product of a unique combination of economic and political events, should not alter the longer term outlook for this asset class.

The very unique set of investment characteristics that separate real estate from financial assets strongly argue for its inclusion in a multiasset portfolio as a diversification agent. The opportunity to truly diversify within the asset class supports this argument. Thus, the original theoretical and academic arguments for managing portfolio risk through diversification are every bit as valid in the 1990s.

Commercial real estate wealth, as measured against the wealth components of other investable assets, is enormous. It represents a significantly high percentage of total U.S. investable assets. Investors that require portfolios to replicate "the market" may someday want to allocate up to 25 percent to real estate. Institutional investors, including pension funds and insurance companies, in many other countries have much higher allocations to property than their U.S. counterparts. In virtually all cases, their respective property markets are much more closely controlled by supply and demand economics.

During the late 1970s and early 1980s, real estate proved to be a superior hedge against high inflation. The asset class has the inherent ability to pass through inflation costs, providing real rates of return, even when inflation rates are much higher than anticipated. This capability, however, is dependent on the market's supply and demand factors. Over time, real estate returns have been competitive and have demonstrated a low correlation to financial assets. Even the total real returns for the 1980s were acceptable, had it not been for banner 10-year periods for both stocks and bonds. The only period in which real estate did not compare favorably to the other asset classes was 1985 through the early 1990s.

Not only do institutional investors with long-term time horizons have the resources and staying power to successfully invest in this huge market, but they are also uniquely positioned to exploit the market's inherent inefficiencies: pension funds are the only major capital supplier that does not need to borrow in the financial markets in order to invest in real estate.

Nevertheless, real estate investing is not appropriate for investors that:

- Have short-term time horizons.
- Market-time by making periodic changes in asset allocations.
- Are regularly concerned with short-term liquidity.
- Cannot develop a comfort level with the inherent characteristics of the market.
- Are unwilling to deal with the realities of the market during times of difficulty.
- Use an investment decision-making process driven by precise risk and return measures.

The subpar investment returns currently exhibited by real estate are directly attributable to excess supply. The market is currently evidencing all the characteristics of a bear market. Because the expansion cycle was effectively extended for nonmarket reasons, the recovery phase will also be elongated. In the interim, new opportunities will begin to surface.

New speculative real estate development has now come to a virtual standstill. Given the fact that most markets are currently soft and values are close to or below replacement costs, new construction activity has dropped sharply. The only new development will be build-to-suits for creditworthy borrowers.

A lack of new supply will allow overbuilt markets to revert to more traditional supply and demand balances. Additionally, because there is currently a major liquidity crunch (which will probably last for some time), values of existing real estate will now be determined by fundamental investment economics rather than excess liquidity, unrealistic growth expectations, tax incented investing, or international currency arbitrage. In other words, the market is reverting back to investment fundamentals.

In the coming decade real estate's relative attractiveness will be determined in part by the asset's path to recovery and in part by the performance of stocks, bonds, and inflation. How long have the stock and bond bull markets sustained? How long will they sustain? Has inflation been permanently controlled? Can Congress stay away from real estate? Will the demise of the Soviet Union and the rise of the Commonwealth of Independent States (CIS) bring political stability internationally? As usual, economic forces will largely control the performance of real estate in the future, but these economic forces will be abetted and confounded by domestic and international political events and uncertainties.

CHAPTER 2

COMMERCIAL AND MULTIFAMILY REAL ESTATE INVESTMENT VEHICLES

Mark P. Snyderman, CFA
Aldrich, Eastman & Waltch

The author would like to acknowledge the research work of Stacy R. Sandler.

INTRODUCTION

Just as our economic system provides a multitude of ways to invest in private businesses such as stocks, bonds, and commercial paper, it also provides many vehicles for investment in real estate. This chapter will discuss the various ways the market organizes the cash flows derived from the operation of real property for investment purposes. Real estate investment vehicles discussed here include free and clear equity, leveraged equity, options, mortgages, hybrid debt, and senior ground leases. The chapter will also cover the various aggregations of these real estate investments available to the investor (i.e., real estate investment trusts, partnerships, corporations, and government agency paper). The discussion of each organization of cash flows and aggregation vehicles will include a description of the vehicle, the market size, the market participants, cash flow, liquidity, valuation, risks and control/management intensity.

As is so for corporate investment vehicles such as stocks and bonds, real estate investments are claims on the future cash flows of an asset. Like corporations, properties are businesses. Each building is a distinct business with customers (tenants), costs of production (expenses) and profits. One can construct a profit and loss statement and a balance sheet for every real estate asset. Real estate investments are really specialized forms of corporate investments.

Figure 2–1 arrays corporate investments and real estate investments along a risk spectrum. The left side indicates the corporate and real estate assets with the least risk and the right side, the highest risk. The corporate and real estate investments that align with each other vertically are analogous investment types. They are comparable in terms of their risk profile and the priority of their claim on the business' (real estate's) cash flow. A comparison between each real estate investment and its corporate analogue is included in the following descriptions of real estate investment vehicles.

OVERALL MARKET SIZE

Figure 2–2 shows the size of the real estate market compared to corporate and government securities, and state and municipal bonds. The large size of the real estate market may be surprising. It almost equals the corporate market and exceeds the government bond market.

FIGURE 2–1
Corporate Securities Investments and the Real Estate Counterparts

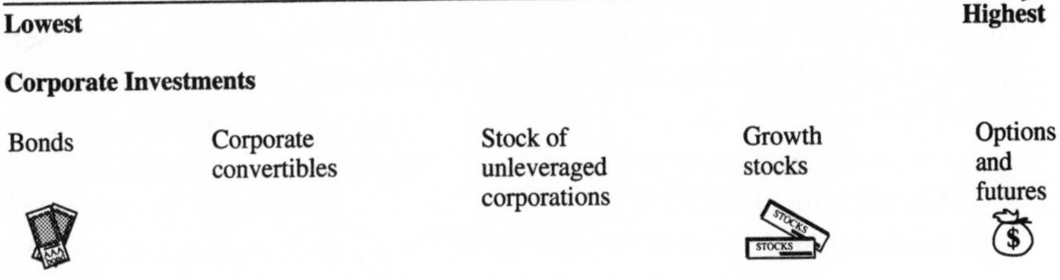

Real Estate Investments

| Senior ground lease | Mortgage | Hybrid debt | Free and clear equity | Leveraged equity | Option |

RELATIVE RISK

Lowest → Highest

Corporate Investments

| Bonds | Corporate convertibles | Stock of unleveraged corporations | Growth stocks | Options and futures |

FIGURE 2–2
Overall Asset Market Size as of September 1990*

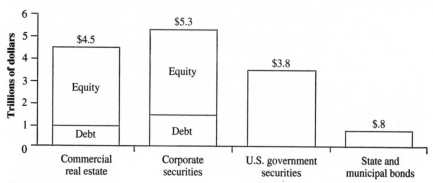

*Real estate market size as of
12/31/89 including multifamily.

Source: Federal Reserve Bank, Boston; The Roulac Group of Deloitte & Touche, "Capital Flows 1990: Real Estate Alternatives for Institutional Investors"; 1980 Census of Housing Residential Finance (figures grossed up to 1989 values using historical housing rent growth).

Although the real estate market is huge, it receives less attention from the investment community than corporate securities. There are two major reasons for the discrepancy. First, much of real estate is owned by corporations, where it is incidental to the corporation's main business and is generally not traded. Corporate real estate includes properties from mundane warehouses and production facilities to grand office buildings. For example, until 1990, the world's tallest building (the Sears Tower in Chicago) was fully owned by Sears, Roebuck and Co. and thus was not available to investors. Figure 2–3 shows that nearly two-thirds of commercial real estate assets are owned by corporations.

Second, the majority of real estate transactions are private and not reported on an exchange or in the newspaper. The transactions are hidden from the normal investment information flow. Private transactions present the investor with information and expertise barriers. Thus many investment professionals ignore real estate in favor of the more readily observed and transacted corporate and government securities.

Throughout the following discussion, the differences between private market transactions (most real estate) and public market transactions

FIGURE 2–3
Real Estate Asset Owners, 1989

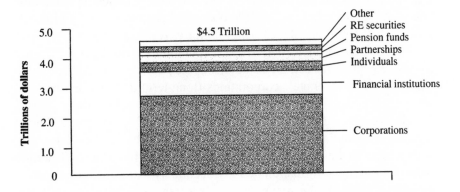

Source: The Roulac Group of Deloitte & Touche, "Capital Flows 1990: Real Estate Alternatives for Institutional Investors"; 1980 Census of Housing Residential Finance (figures grossed up to 1989 values using historical housing rent growth; Federal Reserve Flow of Funds Accounts, "Financial Assets and Liabilities," 1989.

will be highlighted. Private market investments offer the investor advantages and disadvantages. In general the investor must spend more time (or money) per transaction, give up liquidity and ease of valuation in exchange for a higher risk-adjusted return (arguably) and greater control over the operation of the asset. The return arguments are visited in the discussion of the various vehicles.

FREE AND CLEAR EQUITY

One of the most common forms of real estate investment is to own property free and clear. Free and clear or, fee simple, means ownership without encumbering the property with debt. Many institutional investors favor fee simple ownership.

Free and clear real estate ownership is most comparable to owning equity in a corporation that has little or no debt (other than payables). In both cases, the equity owners have no interest expense. All net operating income becomes profit before tax.

Market Size

The value of investment holdings of free and clear commercial and multi-family real estate equity as of December 1989 is approximately $195 billion.[1] That figure excludes single-family residences and corporate holdings which are incidental to the corporation's business (i.e., are not for investment purposes). By comparison, the publicly available corporate equity of "low-leverage" corporations (long-term debt divided by total capital is less than 7 percent) totaled $494 billion as of December 1989.[2]

Historically, the free and clear real estate equity market tended to be regional in nature; it became more national during the 1980s—especially with respect to the larger properties (greater than $10 million). The high costs of gathering information (to most accurately assess the prospects of a property) is one of the major factors favoring local investors in a real estate market. Such investors have a huge advantage in gathering information on rents, occupancy and the nuance of location. The economies of scale for larger properties are sufficient to make it worthwhile for nationally oriented investors to incur the costs of gathering the necessary information. National brokerage agencies (including banks) often are hired to sell larger properties. The creation of real estate investment portfolios by pension funds and foreign institutions during the 1980s had the effect of transforming the market for large properties into a national market, because pensions and others sought geographical diversification in making their investments.

Cash Flow

Unlike corporate stocks where dividends are paid quarterly, fee simple property ownership provides the investor with monthly cash flow. Monthly rental payments lead to monthly investor payments. In free and

---

[1]Based on an estimate of free and clear ownership as a percent of real estate equity owned by various holders (excluding corporations) of commercial property as reported by the Roulac Group of Deloitte and Touche ("Capital Flows; 1990: Real Estate Alternatives for Institutional Investors,") added with the market value of equity REITs as reported by the National Association of Real Estate Investment Trusts ("REIT WATCH, Winter 1991) and limited partnerships as reported by Robert A. Stanger & Company and nonmortgaged multifamily properties with five or more units as reported by the 1980 Census of Housing (*Residential Finance*, vol. 5) grossed up to 1989 values using rental growth.

[2]Standard and Poor's Compustat PC Plus Database; Market Value, Long-Term Debt and Total Assets.

clear property investing, the cash flow is the difference between rental receipts (including utility and tax reimbursements, if required by the leases) and the expenses of operating the property plus capital expenditures. Expenses typically include taxes, utilities, maintenance, leasing commissions, and management. Capital expenditures would include improvements provided for tenants such as carpet and demising walls, as well as overall building improvements such as landscaping or new elevators. The operating margins of properties vary, but on average, well-run, multitenant properties achieve a 60 percent gross revenue margin.

The cash flow of fee simple real estate ownership tends to be less volatile than that of the unleveraged corporation. Figure 2–4 illustrates the point. One can see that cash flow from property as reported by the Frank Russell Company is significantly less volatile than the average operating profit (before depreciation and interest expense) of the S&P 500 low-leverage corporations.

Three reasons might be offered for the difference between real estate and corporate cash flows. First, a corporation's cash flow depends on product sales which, in turn, depend on the daily (and, hence, volatile) decisions of customers. Property cash flows are more stable because they are based on leases which tend to be 3–15 years long. Second, the uses of a corporation's cash flow can change dramatically over time, whereas uses for a property's cash flow are more predictable, being constrained by the fact that buildings are immovable, fixed assets. A corporation is much more dynamic. It can buy and sell businesses; it can enter and exit businesses; it can change its balance sheet; it can expand or downsize.

Finally, corporate operating margins are generally less than those of property. The S&P 500 shows average operating margins of 15 percent for 1989 compared to our estimate of 60 percent for multitenant property.[3] This is logical because of the asset intensive nature of the real estate business compared to most businesses. The higher margin is required by property owners to compensate for the fixed capital invested in the property. A normal return on that capital is a large sum compared to the other expenses of operating the property. In a corporation, salaries, raw materials, rent, and so on are usually quite large compared to the required return on assets.

---

[3]Standard and Poor's Compustat PC Plus Database; Gross Profits, Selling General and Administrative Expenses, and Net Sales.

FIGURE 2–4
Annual Changes in Property and Corporate Cash Flows (1981–1990)

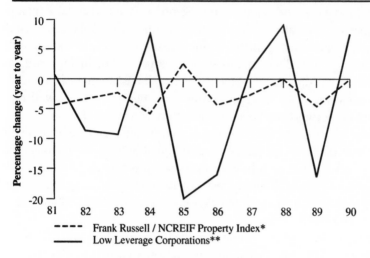

    ---- Frank Russell / NCREIF Property Index*
    ——— Low Leverage Corporations**

* Property Income component only.
** S&P 500 corporations with less than 7% debt to equity. Operating income
  (before depreciation and interest expense) divided by market value.

Source: Standard and Poor's Compustat PC Plus for low-leverage corporations, Frank Russell-NCREIF
Property income index.

Liquidity

Of all the types of real estate investments shown in Figure 2–1, free and
clear equity is probably the most liquid. A simple property sale usually
takes 90–120 days to complete. Marketing the property to potential buyers
and negotiating a purchase and sale agreement would absorb 30–60 days.
Subsequent to the signing of a purchase and sale agreement, the buyer is
traditionally allowed another 60–90 days to complete the due diligence
and obtain financing.

However, if the seller misjudges the appropriate sale price or owns
less than the entire property, the liquidity of his or her position is greatly
reduced. Unlike a stock market trade, where the price is readily discernible, the appropriate price for a building is unclear because there usually
have not been recent sales of the particular building. Buildings that might
have recently sold are usually significantly different. Thus, if the seller
asks too high a price, the marketing time period would be greatly
extended.

There are also significant transaction costs associated with a sale. The seller of commercial property should expect to pay a broker approximately 1 percent of the sale price (more for small properties). Other costs shared between the buyer and seller might include legal costs, engineering reviews, environmental assessments, market research, and adviser costs.

From time to time, the real estate markets become even more illiquid than normal. Both in the mid-1970s and the early 1990s, real estate property liquidity diminished considerably. In the case of the mid-1970s, financing sources for purchasers became unavailable as credit availability was tightened nationally in an effort to reduce inflation. In the early 1990s, a drop in property values left substantial gaps between the bid and asked prices causing many fewer sales of property to be consummated than during normal periods. The early 1990s' lack of liquidity was also fueled by the withdrawal of depository institutions from real estate lending.

If the seller owns less than the entire building, then his or her liquidity is also greatly reduced. A portion of a property is tougher to sell, because the owner of a portion of a property usually has less control over the operation of the property than the owner of an entire property. Partial owners often cannot unilaterally make financing and sale decisions. Thus, the market for portions of properties is different than for whole properties. Usually portions of ownership are most liquid if organized into a real estate investment trust (REIT) or limited partnership form and offered publicly, as described later in the chapter.

Public corporate equities, on the other hand, are generally most liquid and tradable in a matter of hours on an exchange. Clearly, the difference in liquidity between free and clear commercial real estate equity and corporate equities is a major obstacle to commercial real estate investing.

Private corporate equities probably have similar or less liquidity than free and clear commercial property equity. Private corporate equities, lacking public information and recent trades, have marketing, due diligence, and settlement processes that look similar to the process for whole properties.

Having observed that private corporate equities are no more liquid than properties, we can say that the major difference between real estate equity and corporate equity liquidity hinges on whether or not the investment is public or private. Since real estate is transacted privately, it is largely illiquid; corporate equities are more often traded publicly and are more liquid. Vehicles to invest in free and clear property equity that provide public stock market-type liquidity, such as REITs and public limited partnerships, represent a small portion of the real estate investment market (7 percent)[4] compared to public corporate equities' share of all corporate equities (74 percent).[5]

Valuation

Because most commercial real estate equity investments are private market transactions, investors lack the reference point of daily trades to value their positions. Instead, real estate investors analyze several fundamental character-istics of the property to value their equity. The analysis is similar to what is often done to evaluate the reasonableness of the market price for a corporate equity. A full discussion of real estate appraisal is presented in Chapter 5. Here we will compare real estate valuation to public market vehicles valuation.

Free and clear real estate equity and corporate equity offer the owner the same thing—all future net cash flows. Therefore, the value of each is often analyzed by calculating the net present value of the anticipated future cash flows. For free and clear property, one would analyze the net operating income after all capital expenditures; for corporate equities, dividends would be used. The difficult part of the analysis for corporate or real estate equities is choosing the discount rate and an appropriate cash flow growth assumption. Real estate cash flows are grown at some rate for 10 years. The 10th-year cash flow is then valued and is included in the discounting analy-sis. This is different from a stock where the cash flows are regarded as a perpetuity. The cash flow growth rates are similarly difficult to select in both markets. The public markets have a more rigorous approach to the selection of a discount rate than does the real estate market. The discount rate should be "built up" from the risk-free rate, an inflation consideration and the relative volatility of the investments cash flows. In practice the real

---

[4]Based on the total of publicly traded REITs as reported by the National Association of Real Estate Investment Trusts (*REIT Watch*, Winter 1991) and public limited partnerships as reported by the Robert A. Stanger & Company divided by total real estate equity excluding corporations. Total real estate equity is the total equity of 5 + unit multifamily properties (nonmortgaged properties and equity portion of mortgaged properties) as reported by the 1980 Census of Housing (*Residential Finance*, vol. 5, 19) grossed up to 1989 values using rental growth and the equity portion of total commercial properties as reported by the Roulac Group of Deloitte and Touche (*Capital Flows 1990: Real Estate Alternatives for Institutional Investors*).

[5]Wilshire Associates market capitalization, top 2,500 companies as of December 1990; and the Federal Reserve Bank of Boston Library Total Corporate Equities as of September 1990.

estate industry is extremely casual and intuitive in its selection of a discount rate for each asset. A "herd mentality" prevails that produces highly consistent discount rates across individual properties.

The discounted future cash flow analysis for both real estate and corporate equities is often abbreviated. The real estate shortcut is expressed as a capitalization rate (cap rate) and for corporate equities it is the price-earning (P/E) multiple. The cap rate is defined as the earnings of a property (net operating income less "normal" capital expenditures) divided by the price of the property. Thus it is the inverse of a P/E multiple. To determine equity value of property one would divide earnings by the cap rate. Free and clear real estate cap rates ranged between 7 percent and 11 percent, with an average around 9 percent in the late 1980s. The earnings-price multiple of the S&P 500 was 7.1 percent as of September 1990; if we were to look at a sample of low-leveraged companies, the earnings-price multiple would be 7.4 percent.[6] This difference would imply that investors expect corporate dividends to grow faster than property cash flows by a factor of nearly 2 percent, on average.

One might ask, "Is it reasonable that the cap rates on commercial property and average corporate earnings-price ratios were roughly 2 percentage points apart?" What can one expect in terms of cash flow growth from a fixed building compared to a dynamic corporation? Presumably, the building owner can charge higher rents, proportional to inflation (subject to fundamental market conditions), because replacement cost (i.e., competitor costs) will grow with inflation over the long run. However, the building owner is very limited in his or her ability to add more space. The corporation is free to add product lines, create new divisions, and so forth. In general, it seems that one should expect a higher cap rate, reflecting lower cash flow growth assumptions, in real estate equities than for earnings-price in equities of unleveraged corporations. When this relationship has been violated in the past, a correction has eventually occurred.

Risks

The risks to free and clear commercial real estate ownership can be thought of in three different ways: (1) the sources of risk, (2) the riskiness

---

[6]Standard and Poor's Compustat PC Plus Database; Market Value and Income before Extraordinary Items.

relative to other real estate investments, and (3) the riskiness relative to corporate equities of unleveraged companies.

First, the sources of risk can be listed:

Property-type risk (supply and demand).

Location risk (local supply and demand).

Tenant credit risk.

Physical obsolescence and deterioration risk.

Regulatory and tax risk.

Inflation risk.

Reinvestment risk.

Some of these types of risk are obvious and others less so. Property-type risk refers to the condition of supply and demand for a given property type, irrespective of location. For example, there is a nationwide oversupply of office buildings that has profoundly affected investor interest in the product and has caused real and nominal rental rates to plummet. Location risk adds consideration of the condition of the local market in which a property resides as well as the possibility that the property's specific location within a local market might become relatively less attractive. Tenant credit risk is the risk that a tenant fails to pay all of the contractually owed rent. A tenant credit loss costs the owner because time is required to evict a tenant and refinish the space for a new tenant. This type of risk is most pronounced in a single-tenant property.

Physical obsolescence and deterioration could also reduce the total revenue of a property. Owners often choose to make substantial capital expenditures to bring their buildings up to date. It is difficult to assess the rate of physical obsolescence of a property because it depends, in part, on the development of new technologies. As new technologies, such as elevators, climate control, and security, are incorporated in new competing buildings, an older building loses its tenant appeal and must either charge relatively lower rents, spend money to make improvements, or suffer lower occupancy.

Regulatory and tax risk is the risk that the authorities will require unforeseen expenditures or increase property taxes. For example, in the past, various municipalities have required owners to make expenditures to adhere to new fire, life, and safety codes. Either regulatory or tax changes, if unforeseen, will change the building's cash flow from what was anticipated.

Inflation and reinvestment risks are smaller risks for free and clear property investments than they are for other types of real estate investing. Inflation risk is the risk that the contractual cash flows from tenant leases could be worth less than anticipated due to inflation. The longer the lease term, the greater the inflation risk. In the extreme, sale-leaseback property investments contain the most inflation risk of all types of free and clear equity investments due to their long lease terms (15–25 years). Reinvestment risk is the converse of inflation risk. It is the risk that the cash flow received cannot be reinvested to earn the same rate of return as that of the original investment. This risk, too, is less for free and clear real estate equities than other real estate investments because the growth in future cash flows is an important component of return and the owner can choose to reinvest in the property.

The riskiness of free and clear real estate equity ownership falls in the middle of the real estate investment risk spectrum. It is easy to see why leveraged equity and options are riskier. Leveraged equity has all the risks of free and clear equity plus the risk of loan default and of loan refinancing. Options are riskiest because they are generally only valuable if the value of the property grows. On the other side of the spectrum, mortgages and senior ground leases are less risky because mortgage and senior ground leaseholders do not absorb the first dollar lost when a property declines in value or when cash flow is less than projected.

Finally, we might ask, "How does free and clear commercial real estate equity risk compare to the risk of owning equities of unleveraged corporations?" Since both investment types face a similar battery of risks, the best way to analyze comparative risk is to look at the variance of each investment's return over time. Figure 2–5 shows the quarterly total returns of free and clear real estate equities and the S&P 500 Index (adjusted to include only low-leverage companies). One can see that real estate returns are significantly less volatile than corporate equities. Annual real estate returns show a standard deviation of 1.3 percent[7] and low-leverage corporate equities, 7.5 percent.[8] Some argue that the lower volatility is due to the use of artificially slow-moving appraisals to determine property appreciation or depreciation. Others believe that the lower volatility is real because property cash flows are fundamentally more stable than corporate flows.

---

[7]Frank Russell Company-NCREIF Property Index.
[8]Standard and Poor's Compustat PC Plus Database; Market Return.

Return

The return achieved by free and clear real estate equity investors can be estimated using the Russell/NCREIF Property Index. It shows that quarterly returns from 1980 to 1990 averaged 2.5 percent.[9] One can compare this return to that of the S&P 500 adjusted to include only low-leverage corporations, which is 4.7 percent per quarter.[10] One would expect the S&P 500 to have higher returns to compensate the investor for higher volatility or risk.

Control

Free and clear real estate equity ownership offers a strikingly different amount of control compared to corporate equity. The control difference stems primarily from the difference in the units of trade. Free and clear property is traded mostly in whole building units. Decision making occurs on a whole building basis. Thus the free and clear property investor is often in the position of controlling all property level decisions. (See box.)

Corporate equities are most frequently traded in shares—small fractions of the ownership of the company. Since decisions are made on a whole company basis, the owner of shares must cede control to centralized management. Thus the corporate equity investor usually has little control.

For small segments of each market the tables turn. Corporate equity investors can have complete control by buying whole companies. Some investors pursue this strategy (leverged buyout funds and venture capitalists). Similarly, in the case where real estate equity has been broken into shares and sold to many investors, control is no greater than for the owner of a share of corporate stock.

Control can be worth a great deal to some real estate equity investors and virtually nothing to others. Investors that have superior property management techniques or can achieve market power by controlling a number of buildings in a market can derive significant value from control. Some investors want to control future financings and sale decisions. Others find active property management responsibilities burdensome and are not investors of sufficient scale to hire third parties at a reasonable cost. On balance,

---

[9]Russell-NCREIF Property Index.
[10]Standard & Poor's Compustat PC Plus Database; Market Return.

FIGURE 2–5
FRC Total Return versus Low Leverage Corporations (1980–1990)

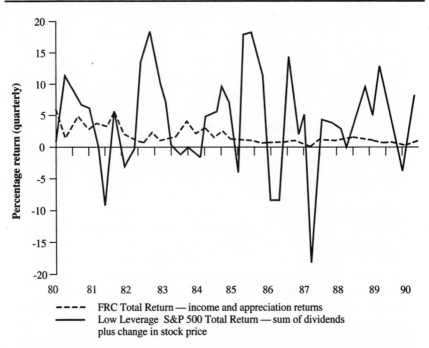

FRC Total Return — income and appreciation returns
Low Leverage S&P 500 Total Return — sum of dividends
plus change in stock price

Source: Standard and Poor's Compustat PC Plus for Low-Leverage S&P 500, Frank Russell Company-NCREIF Property Index.

the dominant size of the whole building private market as compared with the securitized real estate equity market such as REITS and public partnerships is evidence that control is valued by real estate equity investors.

LEVERAGED EQUITY

Leveraged real estate equities are investments in property ownership utilizing mortgage debt financing. The mortgage debt allows an investor to acquire a property for less capital than would be required for a free and clear purchase. Debt financing is normally available for up to 75 percent of a property's value. In other words, leveraged real estate equity investors can lever their equity using a 3:1 ratio. (A full discussion of mortgages can be found later in this chapter.)

Public versus Private Markets: An Issue of Control

One could say that control over the asset is one of the major differences between private markets and public markets. This is evidenced by their respective units of trade. Private markets tend to deal in very large units—often whole businesses. Public markets tend to trade in shares, with individual units often priced at less than $100. While whole business units come with control, shares do not.

In real estate, for example, the unit of trade is most often the entire property. Real estate sellers face a choice between securitizing the ownership in their property and issuing public or private shares or selling the whole property privately. Presumably, real estate sellers generally choose to sell the whole property privately because the price is better. The whole property buyers must be willing to pay a better price because they value control. Otherwise, they could, in theory, buy shares of the same asset in the public market and more easily diversify their holdings. Publicly traded real estate shares would also have the advantage of liquidity, which investors should value.

If the real estate investment community changed and most players preferred to hold shares, real estate would trade in shares on the public markets. It is worthwhile to ask whether or not any real estate buyers will continue to be willing to pay more for control than liquidity. It is the control versus liquidity decision that ultimately determines the balance between the amount of publicly offered shares of property ownership and private, whole property ownership.

Like free and clear real estate equity, leveraged real estate equity investments are usually made in whole building units by single investors. Less frequently, shares of leveraged equity investments (in one or many properties) are offered to multiple investors in REIT or partnership form.

Some investors view leveraged equity as free and clear equity less a bond sold to a third party. The bond sold to the mortgage lender represents the bulk of the stable cash flow, the equity is the remainder. Thus, one would expect leveraged real estate equity returns to be significantly more volatile than free and clear investments.

Modern portfolio theorists find that leveraged equity is more useful to a portfolio than free and clear real estate because it is more responsive to the cycles of the real estate market—thus offering more diversification value when combined with stocks and bonds. Free and clear equity, on the other hand, is more correlated to bonds than leveraged equity because a large amount of the return (more than 50 percent) can be characterized as a bond. The bond portion of real estate behaves in much the same way as corporate bonds. When the bond portion is sold, the diversification value of leveraged real estate equity is maximized.

Although it is difficult to precisely compare leverage properties and corporations, stock ownership in leveraged corporations can be compared to leveraged real estate investing. The relative riskiness of each is very much affected by the stability of the cash flow, which will vary by business and property type. However, it is clear that some properties are leveraged to a degree that their equity is as risky as the equity in a leveraged buyout (LBO) corporation; others are more modestly leveraged as are investment-grade corporations.

Market Size

While some institutional investors utilize a leveraged equity approach to real estate investing, almost all real estate developers and individual owners find it necessary to employ mortgage debt. They do not have the capital necessary for free and clear property ownership or wish to spread the capital they do have over multiple properties. Sometimes corporations also employ real estate debt if it offers a lower cost of funds than their other sources.

Approximately $365 billion or 23 percent of the total real estate investment market is in the form of leveraged equity, estimated on the basis of net equity value. This would be almost double the size of investments in free and clear equity.[11]

Cash Flow

The cash flow of leveraged real estate equity are appreciably different from that of free and clear equity, even though both investment types are based on the same property fundamentals. As shown in Figure 2–6, the

---

[11]Based on an estimate of leveraged equity owned by various holders of commercial property (excluding corporations) as reported by the Roulac Group of Deloitte and Touche, (*Capital Flows* (1990) and *Real Estate Alternatives for Institutional Investors*), added with equity REITs as reported by the National Association of Real Estate Investment Trusts, (*REIT Watch*, Winter 1991) and limited partnerships as reported by Robert A. Stanger & Company and the equity portion of mortgaged 5 + unit multifamily properties as reported by the 1980 Census of Housing (*Residential Finance*, vol. 5) grossed up to 1989 values using rental growth.

peaks and valleys of the cash flow are greatly magnified when investing in leveraged equity because a stable smooth payment is due the mortgage holder. Thus, all of the cash flow volatility falls to the equity owner and is magnified because it is large relative to the dollars invested. The second chart in Figure 2–6 shows how the volatility gets magnified when viewed on a per dollar invested basis.

A leveraged corporation's cash flow dynamics are similarly affected. The debt provider demands a level set of payments due on a prior claim basis. The subtraction of this stable core of cash flow from a corporation leaves the equity holder with a much more volatile remainder.

Liquidity

Leveraged real estate equity investments are less liquid than free and clear property investments. Most property trades in free and clear form. Property trades in fee simple form because mortgages are not usually transferable and, when the mortgages are transferable, the new owner often prefers to obtain a new mortgage loan or none at all.

Furthermore, mortgage debt often has prepayment prohibitions or penalties which inhibit the conversion of a leveraged property to a free and clear property. Thus, the presence of mortgage debt adds an extra step and costs to the process of liquidating a leveraged equity position. Once the step of removing the mortgage is taken, the sale of the property is identical to the sale of a free and clear investment. The new investor might choose to own free and clear or to hold the property in leveraged form.

Because a significant number of buyers want to own in leveraged form, the availability of real estate debt also affects the liquidity of real estate investments (leveraged as well as free and clear). When debt is readily available, the property markets are more liquid because there are more buyers. When debt is scarce, fewer buyers exist causing the transaction volume and rate to slow down appreciably. Therefore property prices often decline.

Valuation

Leveraged real estate equity investments can be valued two ways. First, one can value the underlying property as if it is owned free and clear, then subtract the present value of the outstanding payments due under the mortgage debt. An adjustment should probably also be made for unusually favorable or unfavorable mortgage terms.

FIGURE 2–6
Hypothetical Property Cash Flow

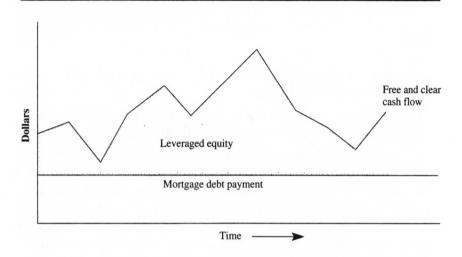

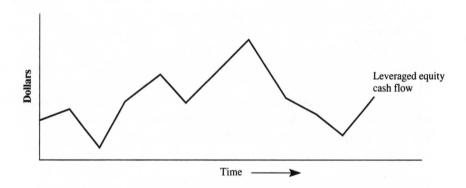

One could also value leveraged real estate equity investments by calculating the present value of all future cash flows. Such an analysis, while technically correct, is subject to a high degree of error because the volatility of the cash flows makes it extremely difficult to reasonably estimate their growth.

Since most corporations are public, the equities of leveraged corporations are generally valued by the public markets. In cases where corporations are not public, the preferred technique for valuation depends on the quantity of leverage. If the leverage is relatively low, the present value of future cash flows (i.e., net of interest charges) would be analyzed. If the leverage is higher, one might value the company as if unleveraged and then subtract the present value of the debt payments—similar to the technique one would employ for leveraged real estate.

Risks

Leveraged real estate equities have all the same risks as free and clear real estate equity plus two more.

Leveraged real estate equity risks = Free and clear real estate risks + Debt service shortfall risk + Balloon refinancing risk

The two additional risks are most significant; they tend to add to the impact of market, location, and tenant risks. Debt service shortfall risk is the risk that the equity owner might fail to meet the required debt service payments on a timely basis. If debt service payments are not made, the property will most likely be forfeited to the lender. Thus, a downturn in the market or location, even if temporary, could result in the loss of a leveraged real estate equity position.

Similarly, the risk of not being able to refinance a mortgage debt balloon payment could result in the loss of the property. The refinancing risk includes exposure to both the cash flow of the property and the state of the real estate capital markets. Even if the property has done well, high interest rates or low availability of debt funds could cause the leveraged equity investor a grave problem.

The equity owners of leveraged corporations face the same two additional risks. In fact, many leveraged buyouts have failed due to not meeting debt service payments and/or failing to refinance balloon principal payments.

Return

Although there are no publicly available data on leveraged real estate returns, we can impute the return by subtracting mortgage returns from free and clear real estate returns. If we assume a leveraged property has 3:1 debt to equity, we can calculate the annual returns to a hypothetical average leveraged real estate position. The analysis is shown in Figure 2–7. One can see that from 1978 to 1989 leveraged equity returns averaged 10.9 percent and peaked in 1979. It is worth noting that leveraged real estate equity returns only slightly outperformed free and clear real estate

FIGURE 2–7
Derived Leveraged Real Estate Returns

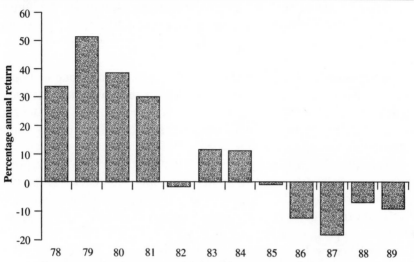

Note: Assumes 75% leverage. Equal amount invested each year for 7 years.
Debt cost equals average annual 7 year Treasury for that year plus
a 175 basis point spread. Cash flow from Frank Russell-NCREIF
total return each year. Annual cash flow less debt service
divided by equity invested equals annual return.

Source: 7 Year Treasury from Federal Reserve Bulletin: "Interest Rates in Money and Capital Markets."

equities during the decade of the 1980s. This should be viewed as poor
performance for leveraged real estate equities due to their higher degree of
riskiness.

Control

The control of the leveraged real estate equity investor is similar to that of
the free and clear investor (strong control) with several important limitations. The limitations occur because the leveraged real estate equity investor yields some control rights to the mortgage lender. Mortgage lenders
often have a veto right over major new leases or major capital improvement programs. Mortgage lenders also almost always constrain the equity
owner's ability to obtain additional mortgage debt and restrict the owner's
rights to pay off the debt. These restrictions can significantly impact a
property owner.

OPTIONS

The riskiest type of real estate investments are options on the future increase in value of property. Options are shown on the far right of the risk scale of Figure 2–1, roughly equivalent in risk to corporate equity options and futures.

Options are usually written on a single building or group of buildings. It is usually a private transaction between a single option buyer and a single owner. The owner offers the option to raise additional capital or to induce the option buyer to provide other types of financing, such as a high loan to value mortgage. (See the discussion on hybrid debt.)

The option buyer usually pays a sum that is small relative to the property's value for the right to some or all of the appreciation in the property's value beyond an agreed-upon strike price. The option is usually exercisable after a certain number of years and before the agreed-upon expiration. It is common for options to run 5 to 30 years in length and be exercisable after 3 to 10 years. If the property's value does not exceed the strike price before the option expires, the option would be worthless. If the property's value exceeds the strike price when the option is exercisable, the option is worth whatever share of the appreciation its terms specify.

The cash value of an in-the-money real estate option can be realized three different ways. First, the property could be sold to a third party and the sale proceeds shared by the former property owner and the option holder. The property sale method of settling an in-the-money option is the most common technique. It has the advantage of providing cash and minimizing disputes over the calculation of the value of the option. Second, the property owner could settle with the option owner without selling the building. The cash could come from property cash flow or other sources available to the owner, and the value of the option would be calculated based on one or multiple appraisals (using the two closest of three is common). Third, the building could be financed or refinanced to raise the cash to pay off the option holder. This method also depends upon a property appraisal to determine the value of the option. These last two techniques for settling options would be more likely to be used when the option is for less than half of the appreciation above a strike price. When the option holder has a claim for less than half of the appreciation, it is easier for the property owner to produce the cash necessary for settlement without selling the property.

Real estate equity options are comparable to corporate equity options. Corporate options give the holder the chance to buy a corporate equity at a given strike price for a certain period of time. Like real estate options, if the value of the stock appreciates beyond the strike price, the option is said to be in-the-money and has cash settlement value. Corporate equity options, however, are more liquid than real estate options since they are generally traded daily on an exchange. The holder does not have to wait until the option's settlement period to realize the gain. However, corporate equity tends to have significantly shorter maturities than real estate options: corporate options tend to run from 1 to 24 months whereas real estate options are usually measured in years.

Market Size

The dollar value of stand-alone real estate options in existence is small compared to the other types of real estate investment vehicles. Property owners rarely find it worthwhile to sell a separate option on the future appreciation of their property. More commonly, options are sold as an inducement for a lender to provide a high loan-to-value or low-coupon mortgage loan. Senior ground lease investments (discussed separately) which contain an implicit option on the value of the property, might be the largest segment of the market.

Cash Flow

Options usually provide their holder no cash flow until settlement. The investor usually pays a single payment for the option, then neither pays nor receives any cash until settlement. The same is true of corporate equity options.

Liquidity

Stand-alone real estate equity options are highly illiquid; more so than other forms of real estate investing. The illiquidity stems from three factors. First, like most real estate investments, options are bought and sold privately, in whole building units. Second, real estate option holders have limited control over the property's operations. Third, most real estate options are linked to other forms of property financing, such as debt. The passive nature of options, particularly in the context of a private market that generally values control) and the linkage to other financing on the property severely limits the number of potential buyers.

Corporate equity options, on the other hand, are highly liquid, public market instruments. They are traded regularly on various public exchanges. The investor need not wait until the option's maturity to realize profits from the appreciation of the underlying stock. The market price for the option will quickly reflect an increase in the underlying stock price.

Valuation

Valuing real estate options is difficult. No single technique has emerged as an accepted standard. Two approaches are common.

First, some investors value options based on how much cash could be currently realized if the building were sold today and the option were exercisable. The investor obtains a current appraisal and calculates the value, if any, of the option holder's share of the incremental value above the strike price. If the property's value is not above the strike price, the option is valued at zero. This approach is conservative because it does not recognize any future appreciation of the property. Clearly, a long-term option where the property's current value is close to the strike price has value.

The second method involves calculating the "expected value" of the option. One would project various scenarios of property value over the life of the option. The investor then calculates the present value of the option under each scenario and estimates the likelihood of each scenario occurring. The sum of the multiplications of the value of the option in each scenario by the probability of that scenario occurring would lead to the expected value of the option. The drawback of this method is that the valuation is highly sensitive to the estimate of the probability of occurrence.

Risks

An option is the riskiest form of real estate investment. It is risky because its return is dependent on the most uncertain aspect of a property's performance—its appreciation. If the property appreciates too little, or too slowly, the option could expire worthless. Alternatively, higher than expected appreciation could produce very high returns relative to the capital invested. Thus, the volatility of the return is exceptionally high.

Real estate equity options, however, should be considered less risky than corporate equity options. Two rationales can be offered. First, as option values are directly dependent on the value of the underlying asset, less volatility in the asset compared to stocks should translate into less volatility in the real estate options.

More importantly, real estate options have long maturities compared to corporate equity options. Options with longer maturities are less volatile than ones with short maturities. Long maturities make the option's value less sensitive to short-term asset value changes because there is more time remaining to catch up. In other words, the option's value is determined by the anticipated long-term asset value growth, which changes more slowly than short-term value. Short options are more sensitive to short-term asset value movements because there is no benefit available from long-term growth.

Control

Options are generally passive instruments. As discussed in the "Liquidity" subsection above, the real estate equity option holder has very little control over property level decisions. Sometimes, options holders (especially those who are also lenders or partners) have rights of approval over major capital improvement or financing decisions, based on the theory that these decisions will affect future property value.

Of course, the option holder can force a sale, financing, or refinancing of the property when the option is exercisable if it is in-the-money.

MORTGAGES

The mortgage investor buys the senior, most stable portion of a property's cash flow for a specified period of time after which the loan is due. The borrower's payment terms are specified in the terms of the mortgage loan and the payments to the loan provider take priority over all payments except for taxes. If the borrower fails to make all specified payments the lender is entitled to foreclose and take possession of the property. Returning to Figure 2–6, the mortgage holder's portion of the cash flow from a property is shown in the unshaded area.

Investors lend money to property owners, secured by mortgages as a substitute for (or complement to) corporate bond investing. Both are fixed-income investments. In general, the mortgage investor sacrifices liquidity in exchange for a higher yield and better control.

Market Size and Participants

A large portion of the capital invested in commercial and multifamily property is in the form of mortgages. The mortgage market represents 65 percent of the entire property investment market (excluding single-family residences).[12] By comparison, corporate debt only represents 22 percent of the outstanding capital invested in corporations.[13] The real estate mortgage markets are relatively larger because property is more capital intensive than corporations and property generates a stable, mortgageable flow of cash.

As of December 1989, the total value of commercial and multifamily mortgages outstanding exceeded $1 trillion, having grown by approximately 12.2 percent per year from 1981 to 1989.[14] The year-by-year size of the market is shown in Figure 2–8. By comparison, the corporate bond market totaled $1.4 trillion and had grown by 14.6 percent per year over the same time period.[15]

The mortgage and corporate bond markets are shown by holder in Figure 2–9. Both markets are dominated by financial intermediaries, with very little individual investor participation. For example, Prudential Insurance Company and Metropolitan Life are probably the largest providers of commercial mortgage capital. During the late 1980s, each invested several billions per year in new commercial mortgage originations. Pension funds make up only a tiny portion of the mortgage market (Figure 2–9)—evidence that though pension funds invest substantial amounts in corporate bonds they invest very little in commercial mortgages. Life insurance companies, on the other hand, are more balanced in their participation in the two markets. One should also note that depository institutions hold a large share of the commercial mortgage market. With the passage in 1989 of Financial Institution Reform Recovery and

---

[12]Total 1989 commercial and multifamily mortgage market from "Credit Market Debt Outstanding," *Federal Reserve Bulletin*. Total property investment market is total commercial real estate value less corporate holdings as reported by the Roulac Group of Deloitte and Touche, "Capital Flows 1990: Real Estate Alternatives for Insitutional Investors" and total value of 5 + unit multifamily properties as reported by the 1980 Census of Housing, *Residential Finance*, Vol. 5 grossed up to 1989 using rental growth.

[13]"Long-Term Debt and Total Assets," (December 1989), *Standard and Poor's Analyst Handbook* (S&P Industrials).

[14]"Credit Market Debt Outstanding, Year-End 1981–89." *Federal Reserve Bulletin*.

[15]Federal Reserve Flow of Funds Accounts, "Financial Assets and Liabilities Year-End 1966–1989," Summary of Credit Market Debt Outstanding.

FIGURE 2–8
Commercial and Multifamily Mortgage Market

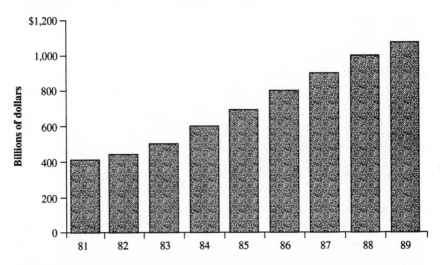

Source: Federal Reserve Flow of Funds Accounts, "Financial Assets and Liabilities, Year-end 1966-1989."

Enforcement Act (FIRREA) and the advent of risk-based capital rules for thrifts and banks, one might expect their participation in this market to decline because the new rules penalize depository institutions for holding mortgages compared to other assets.

Commercial and multifamily mortgage investing has almost exclusively been done by making new originations and holding the resulting portfolios to maturity. Only $1–3 billion (or 0.1 percent–0.3 percent, of the outstanding inventory of commercial and multifamily indebtedness) traded each year from 1981 to 1989.[16] One should expect the secondary market to grow as depository institutions consolidate and scale back due to risk-based capital rules and as market participation broadens.

Cash Flow

Real estate mortgage holders generally enjoy a stable, predictable cash flow pattern because they have a senior contractual claim to a defined dol-

---

[16]Mortgage Bankers Association.

FIGURE 2–9
Bond and Mortgage Market Size June 1990

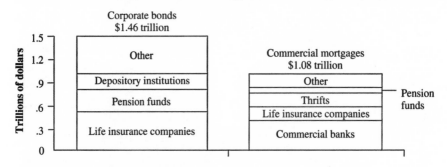

Source: Federal Reserve Bulletin, January 1991, A38, A44

lar amount of a property's cash flow. Most mortgages are designed so that the property's cash flow exceeds the required debt service payments by a 15 percent to 25 percent margin. The payments are generally made monthly throughout the term of the financing (usually 5–15 years) and a balloon principal payment is due at the maturity.

Although commercial mortgages pay interest on a monthly basis and bondholders are paid semiannually, the two types of assets are largely similar in their cash flow patterns. In the case of mortgages, some principal is generally amortized each month, starting with the first payment. For example a 30-year amortization schedule might be employed on a 10-year "bullet" loan. Bond issuers often pay amortization of principal in the form of sinking fund payments in the later years of a bond's life. In both cases, it is usual for there to be substantial balloon payments at maturity. When comparing mortgage and bond returns, one usually accounts for monthly mortgage payments by quoting mortgages on a "bond-equivalent" basis, where reinvestment at the yield of the mortgage is assumed. The conversion formula is:

$$((\text{Mortgage coupon}/12 + 1)^6 - 1) \times 2$$

Liquidity

Commercial mortgages, unless held in REITs or public partnership form, are moderately illiquid. Free and clear equity investments are probably more liquid.

Commercial mortgages can be sold on the secondary market; however, most are held to maturity by the originating institution. Figure 2–10 shows the volume of secondary market trading in mortgages from 1981 to 1989. One can see that only 0.1 percent–0.3 percent of the outstanding mortgage debt has traded each year excluding interbank participations. One might expect the volume to increase as a result of the 1989 legislation and regulatory changes for depository institutions. The barriers to increased mortgage trading are the lack of standardization of debt instruments and the labor required to analyze the credit risk of each individual mortgage.

Commercial mortgage trades are generally expensive and time consuming. The commercial mortgage seller incurs fees for brokerage, appraisal, environmental review, engineering, and legal work. The seller's transaction costs can easily exceed 1 percent of the value of the

FIGURE 2–10

Securitized Commercial and Multifamily Mortgage Transactions (Institutional Portfolios) 1981–1989

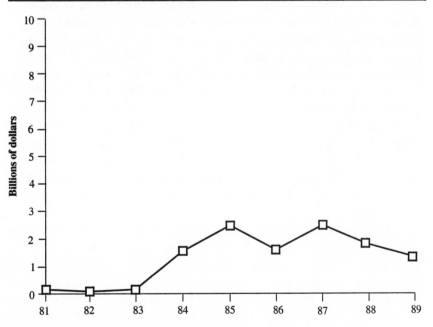

Source: Mortgage Bankers Association, Washington, D.C.

mortgage being sold. A mortgage sale takes at least three months. This length of time is required to prepare for the offering, locate a buyer, and allow the buyer to perform adequate due diligence.

The difficulties of selling individual commercial mortgages can be partially overcome by grouping mortgages into large pools and issuing rated securities backed by the pools of mortgages. The securities could be mortgage-backed bonds, mortgage pass-throughs, or collateralized mortgage obligations. These securitization techniques have the advantage of creating a more accepted, larger debt issue. The investor may then analyze aggregate statistics and depend on the rating agencies' review.

However, groups of ordinary commercial and multifamily mortgages will not usually earn a high enough rating to create a marketable security. A successful program of pooling commercial mortgages into marketable securities usually involves credit enhancement. The most common kinds of credit enhancement are third-party guarantees and the issuance of a junior class of securities. In the case of credit enhancement, a third party with an AA or AAA credit rating guarantees investor payments of all or a portion of the investment. The issuance of a junior class enhances the creditworthiness of senior bonds backed by the mortgages because the dollar amount of the mortgages is greater than the amount of the senior bonds. A usual structure might be $80 million of senior bonds backed by $100 million of mortgages. In this scenario, a $20 million loss can be incurred on the entire pool before the senior bondholders incur a loss. This kind of protection can enable the senior bonds to earn a high credit rating.

For example, in 1988, the Empire Savings Bank sold $52 million of senior mortgage-backed bonds backed by $62 million of commercial mortgages. The senior bonds were rated Aa2 by Moody's on the strength of the $10 million of extra mortgages. The senior bonds sold at roughly 125 basis points (BP) over comparable Treasury securities. There were 145 loans in the pool with an average remaining life of 7 years and an average seasoning of 11 years. In this case the seller (Empire) kept the junior bonds.

The credit enhancer (be it the junior securities holder or a third party) will still need to perform all the due diligence involved in a single mortgage trade. However, pooled mortgage-backed securities transactions have a large enough quantity of mortgages to make the due diligence process economically feasible. The smaller the average size of the mortgages, the more necessary it is to pool the mortgages to sell them in the secondary market.

Liquidating most corporate bonds is totally different from commercial mortgages. Sales costs are closer to 1/8 percent, rather than 1 percent plus. Buyers of public corporate bonds do not require the same due diligence process as with mortgages, since most of the necessary information is regularly reported to the public by the issuing corporation. The corporate bond time to settlement is approximately one to two weeks. Investment grade corporate bonds are rarely pooled for resale—the costs of such pooling would outweigh the benefits.

Valuation

As shown in Figure 2–11, the fundamentals of corporate bond and commercial mortgage valuation are comparable because both asset types are fixed-income investments. As such, the general model for valuation involves calculating the present value of all future scheduled cash flows using an appropriate discount rate. The discount rate is a function of the risk-free rate of return (Treasury yields) and a risk or credit spread.

Thus, both corporate bond and commercial mortgage valuations are driven largely by Treasury yield movements. When Treasury yields rise, bond and mortgage values fall; when Treasury yields fall, bond and mortgage values rise.

Credit spread movements are less in magnitude, and therefore have less valuation impact than Treasury movements. Credit spreads of bonds and mortgages are driven by overall market forces and by the improvement or deterioration in the bond issuer's credit or the mortgage collateral. With respect to bonds, for example, changes in a corporation's creditwor-

FIGURE 2–11
Valuation

Corporate Bonds	*Commercial Mortgages*

• Market interest rate movements:
  —Treasury
  —Credit spread
• Corporate creditworthiness
• Capital structure event risk
• Default
• Call protection
	• Market interest rate movements:
	  —Treasury
	  —Mortgage spread
	• Property value
	• Default
	• Call protection

thiness (and a subsequent change in the credit spread applied to its bonds) can be caused by the relative success of the corporation's products, changes in its relative cost structure, or changes in its capital structure. By the same logic, changes in the value of the property underlying a commercial mortgage affect the appropriate risk spread for the mortgage loan's valuation.

As with all fixed-income instruments, call protection will also affect value. Less than perfect call protection gives the borrower an option to prepay and, hence, decreases the value of the asset to the holder. The impact of call protection on the value of the asset (i.e., bonds or mortgages) will depend on the level of interest rates relative to the asset's coupon rate. The higher the coupon relative to prevailing interest rates, the more important call protection will become for valuation because the borrower is more likely to prepay expensive debt when cheaper debt is available. Conversely, for lower coupon debt, call protection becomes less critical to valuation.

Although the fundamentals of valuing corporate bonds and commercial mortgages are similar, the mechanics of valuation are different. Mechanically, corporate bonds are usually valued by obtaining a market quote for their sale. Commercial mortgages, however, are not liquid enough to obtain a dependable market quote when there is no intention to sell. Instead, commercial mortgages may be valued by looking at new originations of comparable risk and term. The new origination coupon may be used to discount the future cash flows to their present value.

Risks

Commercial and multifamily mortgages are generally less risky than real estate equity investments. Since mortgages are generally made for a principal amount that represents only 75 percent of the property's value, the mortgage holder's ultimate returns do not suffer if the property's value declines moderately (remaining above the mortgage balance). The equity owner's return, on the other hand, deteriorates with the first dollar of value decline. Thus, mortgage holders are less exposed than equity owners to the property-related risks of real estate equity ownership.

One way to measure the risk of commercial mortgage investing is to analyze losses from defaults. A study by this author on commercial mortgage default rates and costs from 1972–89 calculates a cost of defaults (including the time value of money) to be 31–52 BP per year in terms of reduced return. The study was based on tracking 7,204 individual loans from their origination (1972–84) through their default and liquidation, payoff, or the end of the study.[17]

Mortgage holders are also exposed to the risks of holding a fixed-income investment: namely, inflation risk and reinvestment risk. Inflation risk is the risk that the contractual flow of dollars will be worth less than anticipated because of inflation. Inflation risk also includes the risk that interest rates rise during the term of the mortgage which cause the value of the mortgage to decline because other, potentially more attractive fixed-income investments might be available. Reinvestment risk is the converse of inflation risk. It is the risk that the investor will not be able to reinvest the cash flows in investments with as high a yield as the mortgage. This problem occurs when interest rates decline. Accrual and zero coupon mortgages have less reinvestment risk than normal, current pay mortgages.

As with all fixed-income investments, mortgages also have varying degrees of prepayment risk. Most mortgages contain protections for the lender against being prepaid. Lender protection can be in the form of penalty fees or prepayment prohibitions for a period of time.

Mortgages, like corporate bonds, are available across a wide range of risk. Some mortgages with exceptionally low loan to value ratios and high coverage ratios could be considered equivalent to AA or AAA corporate bonds. Others, where the ratios are weak and the property has little tenant diversification (and few investment-grade tenants) the riskiness might be more akin to high-yield or junk bonds.

When making comparisons between mortgages and corporate bonds, rating agencies demand that a corporation's cash flow to debt service ratio must be about twice as high as that of a property to be considered of equivalent risk because a property's cash flow is more stable than that of a corporation. A property's cash flow usually comes from a diverse group of tenants with long-term leases. In theory, if an individual tenant has financial difficulty, that tenant can be replaced. Also, the lower coverage ratios are required for commercial mortgages because the debtholder is secured by a tangible asset (the real estate) whereas most corporate bonds are unsecured.

---

[17]Mark P. Snyderman, "Commercial Mortgages: Default Occurrence and Estimated Yield Impact," *Journal of Portfolio Management*, (Fall 1991).

Return

Most commercial mortgage investors think about their return in terms of the coupon interest rate. Mortgage lenders usually want a 25–50 basis point premium over comparable risk alternative fixed-income instruments. The coupon interest rates generally required tend to range between 125 and 300 basis points over comparable maturity Treasury securities. Of course, the coupon interest rate represents the return only in the "hold to maturity" scenario with no defaults.

A more sophisticated way to view returns would regularly adjust the value of the investments and consider the default costs. A total return methodology is used to calculate the mortgage returns achieved by life insurance companies shown in Figure 2–12. Between 1979 and 1989, life insurance companies achieved an 11.1 percent average annual return on their commercial mortgage investments.[18] This return is 0.3 percent less than the average return on free and clear equity.[19] However, in 1982, 1983, 1985, 1986, 1988, and 1989, the mortgage returns exceeded the free and clear equity returns. This performance is surprisingly close to that of real estate equities and, again, indicates that the 80s were a disappointing decade for real estate equities.

Control

Commercial mortgage holders have less control over property level decisions than real estate equity owners. In general, debt providers get veto power over decisions that could have a material adverse affect on the value of the security, but have little or no day-to-day management authority.

However, commercial mortgage investors have vastly superior control compared to that of corporate bondholders. As outlined in Figure 2–13, corporations give the bondholder very little control over the corporation's capital structure or over any of its activities. Commercial mortgage lenders, on the other hand, get absolute control over capital structure, reasonable control over ownership and limited control over tenant selection

---

[18]Mark P. Snyderman, "A Commercial Mortgage Performance Index," *Journal of Portfolio Management* (Spring 1990). (Used a mark-to-market methodology based on current market rates.)

[19]Russell-NCREIF Property Index.

FIGURE 2–12
Mortgage Returns

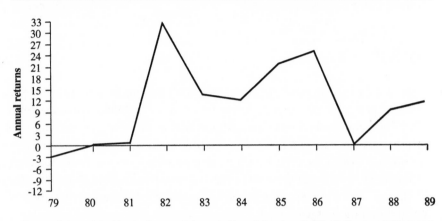

Source: Returns determined using a mark-to-market formulation described in "A Commercial Mortgage Performance Index" by Mark P. Snyderman, *The Journal of Portfolio Management*, Spring 1990.

and capital improvements. Commercial mortgage controls over the property's capital structure are traditionally quite strong. Additional senior debt and pari passu debt is prohibited. Subordinated debt is usually prohibited or controlled.

The problem of the lack of capital structure controls in corporate bonds came to a climax during the barrage of leveraged buyout activity in the late 1980s. Investment-grade bonds were regularly turned into speculative-grade bonds (causing large losses of value) because the balance sheets of issuer-corporations were becoming much more leveraged. Some corporations responded to investor complaints by providing some "event risk" protection in their new issues. However, corporate bond protections

FIGURE 2–13
Control

Corporate Bonds	*Commercial Mortgages*
Little capital structure control Some limited event risk protection	Absolute capital structure control Ownership controls Some limited tenant and capital improvement controls

against changes in a corporation's capital structure are still weak, even in private placement bond issues, compared to the protections afforded the commercial mortgage investor.

HYBRID DEBT

Hybrid debt is a mixture of a mortgage loan and an option. Usually the investor provides the property owner with first-mortgage financing on a more favorable basis than is generally available and receives an option on future appreciation. The first mortgage provided by the hybrid debt investor often provides the owner with more cash than a normal first mortgage (85 percent of value rather than 75 percent) and has lower required interest payments. The hybrid debt coupon is usually 50–100 basis points below normal first mortgages.

The terms of the option (on future appreciation) vary considerably. The option owner usually shares in 20 percent to 50 percent of the appreciation and, sometimes, cash flow after debt service. Options are usually exercisable after 2–5 years and before 7–15 years.

From the property owner's point of view there are two reasons to seek hybrid debt. First, a hybrid debt issuance is often a good substitute for a sale of the property. On an after-tax basis, the all-in proceeds could actually be higher than from a free and clear sale of the property if the property owner has a relatively low tax basis in the property. A sale where the basis is low triggers a significant tax bill whereas a financing is not a taxable event. Hybrid debt could also be an attractive alternative to conventional mortgage financing when the borrower lacks equity funds. By using hybrid debt, the property owner can retain a portion of the property's future appreciation that would be lost in a free and clear sale. These advantages are usually weighed against the negatives (from the owner's point of view) of high transactions costs and the difficulties of managing the property's future operation in partnership with the hybrid debt provider.

The largest single-property hybrid debt investment was made in 1990 on the Sears Tower in Chicago. A group of pension funds organized by Aldrich, Eastman & Waltch provided a hybrid debt financing to Sears, Roebuck. The coupon payments started below Treasury rates and move upward over time. The pension funds share 50 percent in the appreciation of the building and have 15 years to exercise their option.

Real estate hybrid debt could be considered analogous to corporate convertible debentures. Like hybrid debt, convertible debentures offer the investor a lower current coupon payment than would straight debt. In exchange, the investor has a right to convert the debentures into common stock after a certain date and before the conversion right expires.

Market Size and Participants

The hybrid debt market emerged as a major form of real property investing in the 1980s. Its growth was fueled by the pension funds entering the property markets. Pensions felt that hybrid debt offered a good alternative to free and clear investing because unlike free and clear real estate equity, hybrid debt creates an incentivised owner/manager. Perhaps as much as $30 billion of the $100 billion that pensions have invested in property is in the form of hybrid debt. One might estimate that the entire hybrid debt market is $50–75 billion. Other participants include the life insurance companies and, before the regulations changed in 1989, banks and thrifts.

Cash Flow

The cash flow from hybrid debt looks much like that of a mortgage, except the coupon interest rate is usually lower. Upon maturity or exercise of the appreciation option, there is an additional lump sum settlement. By comparison, convertible corporate debt would pay semiannually as do corporate bonds and upon conversion, one could hold the stock or sell to create a lump sum settlement. The real estate hybrid debt owner does not usually have the choice of remaining a property owner after the option is exercised.

Liquidity

Hybrid debt is very illiquid. It is more illiquid than most other types of real estate investing because it is a customized arrangement with multiple contingencies between two parties. Further, hybrid debt transactions are the least standardized of all property transactions because the instrument is fairly new and the market is small. The usual method to make a hybrid debt investment liquid is to unwind the transaction. If the transaction has matured to the point where the lender can trigger an unwind, this technique will produce liquidity—but it could take six months or more.

Alternatively, some hybrid debt investors preserve a right to leverage their position. The investor can leverage its position to create liquidity or to take more risk in hopes of greater return.

Valuation

Hybrid debt should be valued as a mixture of a straight mortgage and an option on property equity. As such, the mortgage should be appraised as described in the "Mortgages" section (the present value of future cash flows appropriately discounted vis-à-vis risk). The option could be analyzed as its current value if exercised (conservative) or its expected value. As described in the "Option" subsection of this chapter, an option's expected value is calculated by adding the option's value in several different scenarios multiplied by each scenario's probability. Obviously, free and clear property value is an important component of valuing both the mortgage (discount rate) and the option.

Risks

One of the major arguments for utilizing hybrid debt investing is that it is less risky than free and clear property equity investing. Declines in the property's cash flow come first out of the borrower's return. Regardless of the property's performance, the borrower owes the lender a minimum coupon payment. If the lender forecloses on the property due to the borrower's inability to pay the coupon, the lender's basis in the property is less than if he had chosen to buy the property free and clear—say, 15 percent less.

Return

While no accepted historical return series exists for hybrid debt, the theoretical risk advantage of hybrid debt over free and clear equity can be shown through an example. Say we invest $10 million in a free and clear purchase of a property compared to providing an $8.5 million hybrid debt mortgage. Let's assume the property is generating a cash flow of $.8 million a year and that the hybrid debt carries a 9 percent coupon and shares in 50 percent of the excess cash flow and appreciation. Let's look at the cash flow and return in two cases: first, the property gains 30 percent in value and, second, the property declines 30 percent in value.

Comparative Cash Flows

Years	0	1	2	3	4	5	Internal Rate of Return
30% gain							
Free and clear	−10	0.8	0.8	0.8	0.8	13.8	12.7%
Hybrid debt	−8.5	0.78	0.78	0.78	0.78	10.78	12.0
30% decline							
Free and clear	−10	0.8	0.8	0.8	0.8	7.8	2.3
Hybrid debt	−8.5	0.78	0.78	0.78	0.78	7.78	6.1

If each of the above cases has a 50 percent probability, then the "expected value" is superior for the hybrid debt compared to free and clear equity. However, in the late 1980s many hybrid debt transactions had very little of the risk advantages mentioned above because they were underwritten such that there was no extra cash flow available from the borrower to cushion downturns and the proceeds reflected almost all of the value. In the case where the borrower fails to pay the minimum coupon, one should also consider the costs incidental to default and foreclosure such as legal fees, transfer taxes, foregone interest, and the potential loss of tenants to other buildings owned by the borrower.

On the other hand, hybrid debt investing is significantly riskier than straight mortgage debt investing. Since hybrid debt usually represents a higher portion of the property's value (80–90 percent) than straight mortgages (75 percent) a decline in property value is more likely to cause a loss in the hybrid debt investment than in straight debt. Also, the quantity of the loss will be higher. The corollary is that there is usually less cash flow cushion between the required hybrid debt payments and the property's cash flow. Thus a downturn in the property's cash flow is less easily absorbed by the borrower than in the straight mortgage situation. A study by Vandell, Barnes et al. supports this assumption by showing that 72 percent loan-to-value mortgages have an 8 percent probability of defaulting through the 150th month, while 90 percent loan-to-value mortgages have a 38 percent probability of defaulting.[20] This study would imply that default is four times more likely for hybrid debt than for normal mortgage debt.

---

[20]Vandell; Barnes; Hartzell; Kraft; Wendt; "Commercial Mortgage Defaults: Proportional Hazards Estimation Using Disaggregate Pooled Data" (December 1989). Presented at the American Real Estate and Urban Economics Association (AREUEA) Annual Meeting, December 1989.

Control

The hybrid debt investor's control over property operations is more than that afforded the straight mortgage investor but less than that of the free and clear owner. In addition to strict controls over indebtedness and ownership, most hybrid real estate debt investors also get approval rights over annual budgets, capital programs, new leases, and the property management company.

On the other hand, hybrid debt lenders cannot take all the controls that they might like for fear of "lender liability" lawsuits. That is, if a lender exerts excessive control, the borrower can accuse the lender of interfering with his or her ability to meet the terms of the debt. Thus, the lender must satisfy itself with approval and disapproval rights over major decisions rather than with direct rights to manage the property.

SENIOR GROUND LEASES

A senior ground lease is created when a property's ownership has been divided into two pieces: a finite leasehold on a building (i.e., the right to be a tenant and to sublet) and permanent ownership of the land and improvements on the land. Leaseholds tend to range from 10 to 99 years. During the term of the leasehold, the leasehold owner usually has the freedom and responsibility to operate and utilize the property as if he or she were a fee simple owner. At the end of the term of the leasehold the ground owner takes possession of the building as well as the land. The leasehold owner pays a regular rent to the ground owner. If the rent is not paid the ground owner can take possession of the entire property. Thus the ground lease is "senior." Occasionally, the ground owner subordinates to leasehold financing. In that case the ground lease is known as a *subordinate ground lease*.

The largest and most famous senior ground lease/leasehold transaction was the 99-year lease of Hong Kong to the British by the Chinese in 1898. In exchange for the rent-free lease, the British agreed not to further expand their Chinese colony. Like a senior ground lease owner, when the lease ends, the Chinese have a right to reclaim "ownership" of Hong Kong and all of the improvements.

Since ground lease payments are the most senior claim (other than taxes) on a property's cash flow, it is less risky than most other kinds of property investments. In many ground lease investments the property's cash flow is many multiples of the ground lease payments. A ground lease in a good location, with a multitenant property that covers the lease payments many times over can be considered to be equivalent in risk to a corporate bond with a AAA rating. Just as the IBM corporation's cash flow covered their long-term debt by 11.9 times in 1990,[21] many New York city office buildings cover their ground lease payments by a similar ratio.

Sale-leasebacks are a specialized form of senior ground lease investing that tends to have a shorter term. In a sale-leaseback, the tenant gets all the rights to the building for 10 to 30 years (plus options to extend) and pays the owner a net (after expenses) rent. As with the traditional ground lease, the owner of the sale-leaseback receives the entire property at the end of the lease. Sale-leasebacks tend to have single corporate tenants. The price paid by the investor usually equals the present value of the lease stream plus tax benefits (if any) and, sometimes, a small residual real estate value.

Sale-leasebacks are significantly riskier than normal senior ground lease investments. The lease payments do not offer any margin to the property owner. And, often the price paid for the property represents the entire value of the property as opposed to a normal senior ground lease where the buyers' price would be a fraction of the entire property's value.

The return on a senior ground lease investment has two components: the lease payments and the residual value of the property. The same is true of the returns to the property owner in a sale-leaseback. Often the senior ground lease payment is a few hundred basis points below Treasury securities (relative to the ground lease's purchase price) and increases over time. Sale-leasebacks, on the other hand, usually have higher current cash flows as a percentage of the investment amount. Sale-leaseback cash flow rates range from 100–400 basis points over comparable maturity Treasury rates depending upon the creditworthiness of the tenant.

AGGREGATION VEHICLES

Some investors prefer to invest in real estate through various aggregate vehicles as opposed to investing in individual properties. Multiple-property real estate investment vehicles include REITs, partnerships, corpora-

---

[21]IBM, Annual Report, 1990.

tions, and commingled funds. Like stock market investors, REIT, partnership, corporation, and commingled fund investors trade away control over individual asset decisions in favor of diversification, passivity and, in many cases, liquidity.

REITS

The REIT or real estate investment trust is a specialized form of business trust that owns property or investments in property. The REITs are owned by multiple shareholders and have special taxation status. A REIT can buy, sell, leverage, and manage property as a corporation without paying any corporate taxes.

To be entitled to this special status, a REIT must follow a few basic rules. First, 95 percent of the REIT's ordinary income must be distributed to beneficiaries. REITs must also have more than 100 investors for most of each year. Furthermore, no five combined investors can comprise more than 50 percent of the REIT's ownership. These restrictions limit the REIT vehicle's utility for large investors. Thus, REIT investing tends to be utilized by individuals and smaller institutions.

Real estate investment trusts are classified into three categories: "equity" REITs, those that actually own property; "mortgage" REITs, those that lend money for real estate purchase or development; and "hybrid" REITs, those that do both. Individual REITs may focus on one type of property ownership or on a mixture, or they might be regionally oriented.

Market Size

As shown in Figure 2–14, in 1990, there were 183 tax-qualified REITs with total assets of $43 billion, according to the National Association of Real Estate Investment Trusts. Of the 183 REITs, 110 are equity trusts, 41 are mortgage trusts, and 32 are hybrid trusts. One hundred seventeen of the REITs trade on a major stock exchange. As of year-end 1990, the market value of all publically traded REITs was $8.7 billion.[22]

---

[22]National Association of Real Estate Investment Trusts, *REIT Line* (February 1991), p. 5 and (March 1991), p. 3; *REIT Watch* (Winter 1991), p. 6.

FIGURE 2–14
1990 REIT Market

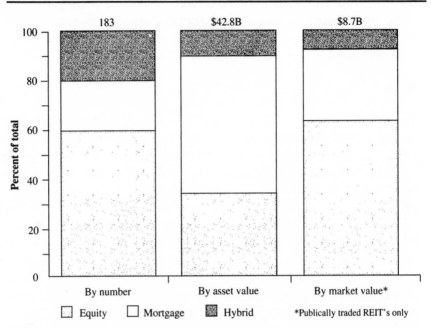

Source: National Association of Real Estate Investment Trusts, *REIT Line*, (February 1991; March 1991).

Liquidity

For public REITs (64 percent of the REIT market by number), the sale of one's interests in a REIT is no more difficult than the sale of shares of publicly listed corporate stock. However, for large institutions, REIT liquidity is uniquely handicapped by the ''no five entities can own more than 50 percent rule.'' This rule often takes the form of blocking any institution from owning over 10 percent. Thus, participation in the REIT market by large institutions who value the ability to garner control is limited.

For private REITs, sale is somewhat more difficult. Private REIT share sales would be akin to selling corporate equity in a private placement.

Valuation

Since most public REIT shares are traded, valuation of REIT ownership becomes merely a question of getting a price quote. Many argue that the smallness of the REIT market (and, hence, the scarcity of research) creates many situations where REIT values are significantly different from the value of the underlying property investments. Of course, the major difficulty in taking advantage of such opportunities is obtaining and analyzing the information; REITs are not required to report on properties in sufficient detail to facilitate detailed valuation analysis.

Risks

The risks of REIT share ownership are dependent on the type of real estate investments being made by the REIT. REITs got a reputation for riskiness in the mid-1970s because many REITs went bankrupt due to risky construction lending and overleverage. On the other hand, REITs that have been more conservative and invested in free and clear equities and permanent mortgages have delivered more stable performance.

The risk of a REIT is also dependent on the quality and incentives of the management. The REIT format (permanently dispersed ownership) often gives management great discretion. If the discretion is misused, the REIT could be riskier than originally envisioned. Also, there is a history of REIT sponsors charging the REIT excessive front-end fees, which gives the REIT a performance disadvantage.

Return

Between 1978 and 1990, REITs achieved a 10.3 percent average annual return. Equity REITs achieved a 13.6 percent annual return and mortgage REITs achieved a 5.3 percent annual return.[23] By comparison, the S&P 500 achieved an annual return of 15.3 percent and the Russell-NCREIF Property Index achieved a return of 11.0 percent during the same period.[24]

Control

The REIT investor has no real control over investment decisions. The control of the REIT investor is about the same as that of the common stock investor.

---

[23]National Association of Real Estate Investments Trusts, "REIT Sourcebook," 1991, p. 21–23.

[24]National Council of Real Estate Investment Fiduciaries and Frank Russell Company, "Annual Data Supplement to the NCREIF Real Estate Performance Report," p. 19.

PARTNERSHIPS

Partnerships are also a very common vehicle used in real estate investing. Like REITs, partnerships have the advantage of not being taxed at the aggregation level. Two major reasons to use partnerships instead of REITs are: (1) when earnings and losses need to be disproportionately distributed, and (2) when there are not enough investors to satisfy REIT rules. Limited partnerships are utilized more frequently than general partnerships because the limited partnership protects the investors (the limited partners) from liability.

Partnerships can be private or publicly registered. Private partnerships tend to have fewer participants and the partnership interests are not liquid. Public partnerships are registered with the SEC, tend to have many participants, and are moderately liquid.

Partnerships can own multiple properties or a single property. Many partnerships own a collection of property investments which provides diversification for the investors. For example, JMB (a major real estate firm located in Chicago) organized a series of partnerships in the 1980s. Each JMB partnership raised $100–400 million and invested in multiple properties.[25]

The partnership vehicle was very popular in the 1980s (through 1986) due to the tax advantages available to limited partners. The tax laws were so favorable that investors often got a good return on their money from tax deductions without any need for income from the property. Many think those tax laws and the subsequent enormous growth of tax-driven partnerships caused much of the overbuilding that occurred in the 1980s. The tax reform legislation of 1986 significantly curtailed the tax advantages and the partnership market growth halted.

Market Size

In the 1970s and 1980s approximately $28 billion has been raised for public real estate partnership investments. In the private market approximately $32 billion was raised.[26] The current value of these partnerships is probably significantly less because many partnerships were tax motivated

---

[25]JMB Realty Corporation/Carlyle Funds Investor Services.
[26]Robert A. Stanger & Company.

and the net value of the partnerships' property investments is probably less than the capital raised. Also, some partnerships have been liquidated through property sales.

Cash flow, risk, and return are all dependent on the choice of underlying real estate investments of the partnership. In these respects, a partnership is no different from a REIT. In theory, the risk of a multiple-property partnership should be less than a single-property investment due to the benefits of diversification.

Liquidity is dependent on the size of the partnership and whether or not it is registered and publicly traded. Smaller and private partnerships are highly illiquid. Publicly traded partnerships are nearly as liquid as corporate stocks and REITs.

As with most aggregation vehicles the investor has virtually no control over the assets. The partnership documents often restrict what the general partner can and cannot do, but the limited partners cannot control specific courses of action.

CORPORATIONS

Real estate investments can also be made through corporations. This format is used less frequently because a tax is paid by the corporation before distributions are made to the shareholders. One might expect the corporate form to be used when real estate investing is only a portion of the business of the enterprise.

Investments in corporations whose major assets are real estate should also be considered a form of real estate investing. For example, many railroad companies have little net worth in their transportation operations— instead, their value is in the land they own and control. Also, much of the value of some hotel companies, home builders, and retailers is in the value of the property they own. Often the markets do not recognize the value of the real estate owned by corporations. As a result, many railroad companies spun off their real estate businesses to enhance their shareholder's wealth. For example, in November 1990, Santa Fe Pacific Corporation spun off its real estate subsidiary into a separate entity called *Catellus Development.*[27]

---

[27]"Corporate Profile for Catellus Development Corporation," *Business Wire* (August 9, 1991).

Since corporations own $2.9 trillion dollars[28] of property and their debt and equity capitalization totals $6.7 trillion dollars,[29] then on average, 43 percent of corporate assets are real estate. Assuming that real estate is not evenly distributed among corporations it is not surprising to find that many corporations have most of their assets in property. Clearly, an investment in these types of companies is a real estate investment with all the risks of property investing. Real estate investing through public corporations has the advantage of being liquid. Since the stock is traded daily, one can sell (or buy) at any time with very low transaction costs.

Property investing through public corporations suffers major disadvantages in investor control and information. The investor has no control over the operations of the corporation and even lacks basic investment and disposition guidelines which are common in REITs and partnerships. The investor is totally dependent on the corporation's management. Also, most investors will find it difficult to obtain information on the properties owned by the corporation. The information problem is further compounded by the accounting rule that property be carried at the lower of cost (less depreciation) or market value. In an appreciating market the property values shown on the balance sheet will be too low. In a volatile market, it is exceedingly difficult to value the property without detailed knowledge of each parcel.

GOVERNMENT AGENCIES

The government agencies, Federal National Mortgage Association (FNMA), Government National Mortgage Association (GNMA), and Federal Home Loan Mortgage Association (FHLMC), serve as aggregators of real estate mortgages. The charters of these entities limit their activity to residential mortgage loans. They typically buy residential mortgages from originators and issue securities backed by the mortgages. These entities usually provide a guarantee of payment of principal and interest. As of December 1990, there were approximately $1.1 trillion

---

[28]The Roulac Group of Deloitte and Touche, "Capital Flows 1990: Real Estate Alternatives for Institutional Investors."

[29]Federal Reserve, *Flow of Funds, Balance Sheets for the U.S. Economy 1945–1989, Non-Financial Corporate Business Total Assets* (1989).

dollars of government agency mortgage-backed debt outstanding.[30] These securities tend to pay monthly, are very liquid, and have little credit risk. The trade-off is that the investor must accept a lower return than for non-government agency mortgage debt. Also, since single-family lenders cannot legally restrict prepayment (unlike commercial or multifamily mortgage lenders) the investor must accept prepayment uncertainty.. The disadvantage is that prepayments tend to occur more frequently when interest rates decline and reinvestment opportunities are not as attractive as the original mortgage. The agencies address this risk by using Collateralized Mortgage Obligation (CMO) and Real Estate Mortgage Investment Conduit (REMIC) vehicles that allow the issuer to focus the prepayments by tranche and so offer less prepayment uncertainty. Investing in these types of securities is often done as a complement to government and corporate bond investment programs.

CONCLUDING THOUGHTS

In many ways the U.S. real estate capital market is like a developing country's corporate equity market. Most major transactions are private, information flows are spotty, and the markets are prone to extreme boom and bust cycles. So it is with U.S. real estate; most major transactions are private, capital flows have been sticky by geographical region, the information flows are poor, and there are astounding boom and bust cycles.

Over time many non-U.S. corporate equity markets have moved toward a more public, U.S.-like equity market. This pattern of development occurs because the users of capital ultimately find it in their best interest to raise capital from a broader base and hence, in a more public format. Issuers find that public capital is cheaper than private, once the public markets are deep and broad enough.

One might expect the U.S. real estate capital markets to follow this trend. Property owners, sometime in the future, will find that a sale by issuing public shares (through a REIT, maybe) will offer the best price. The same conclusion holds for real estate debt. We will see less sales of property from developer to pension fund or from wealthy family to foreign institution. Sales of large buildings will begin to look more like new company stock offerings (although the P/Es should be lower).

---

[30]"Total Mortgage Pools or Trusts," *Federal Reserve Bulletin* (August 1991), p. A37.

Why do the public markets pay more for ownership or debt than private markets? Two reasons are commonly cited. First, most investors value liquidity. Publicly issued securities offer investors the ability to trade their shares easily. Investors pay up for this privilege. Second, by publicly issuing shares or debt, the issuer puts many investors into competition with each other. A "bidding" war is created. In private transactions, the ability of the issuer to create investor competition is much more limited.

The securitization of the U.S. real estate market will not render obsolete the basic forms of property investing discussed in this chapter. Free and clear real estate, leveraged equity, mortgages—these are all common ways to invest in any wealth-generating asset. We showed that corporate equities and debt are similar. The only major difference will be how broadly these real estate assets are owned and how easily they can be traded.

Will current real estate investors earn extraordinary returns as real estate markets become more public? Not necessarily. Private markets imply imperfect information and, hence, less efficiency. One would expect that the variation in real estate trading prices has been high relative to what they would have been in a more efficient market. Thus, as markets become more public some private market investors should find that they overpaid and others, that they underpaid. The variance of current investor returns will be high but not consistently superior.

Although individual investors might not necessarily benefit, an overall economy benefits greatly when capital markets become more public. Capital can be raised more easily and distributed more broadly. The market becomes less subject to extreme booms and busts. Pricing becomes more efficient. In general it seems that more efficient capital markets are associated with more vibrant and diversified economies. Most of us will benefit, albeit indirectly, as the U.S. real estate capital markets gradually evolve toward their next stage of development and create broadly traded public instruments of ownership.

CHAPTER 3

REAL ESTATE IN THE MULTIASSET PORTFOLIO

Mark Coleman
F.W. Dodge McGraw-Hill Construction Statistics and Forecasts
Susan Hudson-Wilson, CFA
Aldrich, Eastman & Waltch
James R. Webb
James J. Nance College of Business Cleveland State University

INTRODUCTION

The term *multiasset portfolio* simply means that more than one class of assets may be considered for inclusion in a portfolio. In other words, not just different types of stocks or different types of bonds could be included, but stocks and bonds and other asset classes (real estate is the most notable) could be combined in various proportions.

Some studies refer to "restricted" multiasset portfolios, since not all asset classes would be considered. The most notable exclusions (after real estate) are human capital and collectibles (e.g., antiques, coins, stamps, and so on). Including human capital and collectibles would be more appropriate for individual portfolios than for institutional portfolios. However, the discussion in this chapter will be limited to the consideration of commercial and multifamily residential real estate for inclusion in a multiasset portfolio.

It is important to note that currently many institutional portfolios consist of a very restricted set of assets—usually common stocks, bonds, and cash equivalents. Often investment real estate, or real estate of any kind, is entirely omitted from institutional portfolios. Some portfolio managers include various types of mortgage derivative securities and think of them as real estate. Mortgages and mortgage-derivative securities are just special types of fixed-income securities and are, for portfolio purposes, essentially the same as bonds! They are not a substitute for equity real estate. Hybrid mortgages with participation features change this some, but there is virtually no research at present on hybrid mortgages in a multi-asset portfolio context.

For a portfolio manager not to include real estate equity in their multiasset portfolio probably means that the asset mix is suboptimal. That is, the portfolio is riskier than it needs to be for a given level of expected return, or the expected return is lower than it should be at a given level of risk. If the return could be increased by just 1 percent at a given risk level, the effect on the value of the portfolio would be tremendous, due to the compounding effect of returns over the long holding periods of institutional investors.

To further complicate matters, the stock portfolio manager, bond portfolio manager, cash/cash equivalent portfolio manager, and real estate portfolio manager (if they have real estate) for large institutional portfolios do not seem to communicate effectively with one another. In addition, few people in investments seem to have formal education in real estate investment and therefore do not fully understand the subtleties of the asset.

Commercial real estate is becoming an increasingly important component of many institutional and individual investment portfolios. The real estate boom of the mid-1980s, and the rapid growth of pension funds and other institutionally based pools of capital, have resulted in a focusing of investor attention on commercial real estate.[1] Indeed, given the sheer size of this asset class—estimates range from $800 billion to as high as $5 trillion[2]—this increased attention seems warranted. However, commercial real estate remains the least understood of the major asset classes. Much of

---

[1]One measure, compiled by Greenwich Associates, estimated that the 2,100 largest tax-exempt U.S. pension plans had total assets of $1.8 trillion at the end of 1989. Of this, approximately $94 billion, or 5.2 percent of total assets, was invested in real estate.

[2]See Mike Miles, "What Is the Value of U.S. Real Estate?" *Real Estate Review* 20, no. 2 (Summer 1990), pp. 69–77, for a range of estimates and a discussion of the difficulties in measuring the size of the commercial real estate market. To get a sense of how large this asset class really is, some analysts have estimated that fully one-third of the market value of Fortune 500 corporations flows directly from their real estate holdings.

this lack of understanding stems from the institutional features of the market in which commercial real estate trades and the resultant lack of reliable data on cash flow and changes in value. These features—most notably the lack of an organized public exchange from which traders can learn each others' assessments of current and future market values, the nonhomogeneity of traded assets, and the existence of "market power" (i.e., the ability of buyers and/or sellers to influence price)—make it difficult for market observers to reliably infer the relevant economic characteristics of commercial real estate as an asset class. The objective of this chapter is to review the rationale for the inclusion of real estate in a multiasset portfolio. We begin with a perspective on the economic characteristics and data used to examine the return performance of commercial real estate. The major institutional features of the commercial real estate market are discussed.

The central theme of the chapter is presented next: an analysis of the role of commercial real estate as one component of a multiasset portfolio. Though traditional equity and fixed-income instruments have been routinely viewed from this perspective for over 50 years, a portfolio-based focus is still a fairly novel approach to managing commercial real estate investments.[3] In particular, the ability of real estate to preserve the purchasing power of a portfolio (i.e., its effectiveness as an "inflation hedge"), along with its ability to bring important risk management, or diversification, benefits to the portfolio will be discussed. Finally, the impact that a variety of important macroeconomic factors may exert on commercial real estate performance are briefly presented.

THE CHARACTERISTICS AND DATA OF COMMERCIAL REAL ESTATE

Market Characteristics

In order to understand and interpret the behavior of investment returns in the commercial real estate market (or any asset market for that matter), it is imperative to be aware of the way in which the institutional features of

---

[3]See Susan Hudson-Wilson and Katrina Sherrerd, eds., *CFA Readings in Real Estate* (Charlottesville, Va.: 1990).

the market influence the way in which investors value assets and the constraints these characteristics have on their trading activities. Broadly speaking, the commercial real estate market is characterized by a number of important economic features that distinguish it from the markets in which other large asset classes are traded. The most important economic differences between the commercial real estate market and the markets for common stocks and bonds are discussed below.

"Incomplete Markets"

A market is said to be incomplete when certain transactions that rational investors find desirable are prohibitively expensive, or for practical purposes are simply impossible to execute.[4] For instance, real estate cannot be sold short. Since some investors may not be able to execute trades that they otherwise could and would if markets were complete, then second-best transactions must be pursued. This has a number of important effects. First, fewer transactions are undertaken, reducing both market liquidity and the amount of information investors can learn from each others' actions. Second, the time between initiating and completing a transaction increases. This is both costly and risky, since, in the intervening period, the conditions that make a transaction appear optimal may change. This forces the investor either to absorb the costs of hedging the transaction or to run the risk that the deal will become less attractive. Clearly, the longer the time lag, the more likely that market conditions may work against the investor (lags of one year or more are not unusual in commercial real estate). Finally, transactions costs increase—measured in terms of time and money—since additional effort must be expended to search out qualified buyers and/or sellers.

---

[4]This is in contrast to the notion of market (in)efficiency. Financial economists define a market to be efficient in terms of the manner in which investors use information to value assets. A market is said to be efficient if the current price of an asset fully reflects all the relevant information investors use in valuing the asset. Thus equity prices reflect "investors" aggregate expectation of the present discounted value of future earnings, along with their best guesses about future economic policy and so on, in such a way that price changes come about only through the accumulation of new information. Market efficiency implies that profits cannot systematically be earned by trading on the basis of the information implicit in current prices. Note that incomplete markets can be efficient by this definition. As such, real estate markets may be efficient subject to the constraints under which investors are forced to operate (see e.g., George W. Gau, "Efficient Real Estate Markets: Paradox or Paradigm?" *AREUEA Journal* (Summer 1987), pp. 1–12. Whether in reality they are or not is still an important open question.

Multiperiod Contracting

For most types of commercial real estate, a substantial portion of the asset's total return is the income derived through leasing arrangements. Leasing provides a means for risk-averse lessors to guarantee future income while permitting risk-averse lessees to lock in future costs. Since future income streams are effectively "locked-in" it is clear that some of the period-to-period variation in total real estate returns (the sum of income return and price appreciation) will be less than if leases did not exist. Another important consequence of multiperiod contracting is that real estate returns tend to be strongly positively auto-correlated over time—that is, high (low) returns tend to be followed more often than not by high (low) returns. This positive correlation helps account for the strong and predictable effect that changes in inflation have had on real estate returns over the past decade. In some properties (particularly office buildings and net leased industrial facilities) the leases display the performance characteristics of bonds.[5] This makes sense since both bonds and leases comprise contractual agreements to make payments on a predetermined schedule. In such properties the equity portion of the returns is captured by the residual value of the asset at the time that the lease term(s) have expired. Circumstances such as this create a situation in which a single-real property houses both pure equity and bondlike behavioral characteristics. Some have argued that this comprises a partial explanation for the low volatility observed in real estate returns.

Asset "Lumpiness"

Asset lumpiness refers to the inability of investors to buy or sell an asset in the specific quantities they desire.[6] From a practical standpoint, this usually isn't a problem for equity or fixed-income investments. For real estate investing, however, this problem can be substantial, since as a rule, property is not easily divisible into the smaller economic units that the optimal allocation decisions of many smaller investors may require (e.g., you cannot easily buy 7/100ths of an office building). Thus, asset lumpiness reduces market liquidity by excluding a potentially large number of inves-

---

[5]Richard A. Graff and Daniel M. Cashdan, Jr., "Some New Ideas in Real Estate Finance," *Journal of Applied Corporate Finance* 3, no. 1 (Spring 1990), pp. 79–89.

[6]There are ways around the difficulties brought by asset lumpiness. For example, subunits of commercial real estate can be purchased using real estate investment trusts (REITs), or by participation in limited partnerships. Such methods are not without difficulties of their own, however, and until the direct securitization of property is routine, asset lumpiness is likely to remain a problem.

tors. In addition, the time and cost of the average transaction is lengthened since fewer buyers and sellers are available.

Asset Nonhomogeneity

By definition, no two real estate assets are exactly alike since at a minimum their locations must vary. This is a marked and important contrast to stock and fixed-income markets in which instruments by law are required to be identical. This lack of homogeneity complicates the asset valuation prcess by requiring investors to implicitly impute the effects that different property characteristics have on market value. As a result, unless an investor is fortunate enough to have observed the trading history of an individual property (assuming, of course, that the property has turned over enough times to make this information useful), he or she is forced to rely on the information conveyed by appraisals and by the trading of *comparables* (i.e., properties that may be good substitutes for the investment being considered). Both of these alternative valuation methods have significant shortcomings discussed in Chapter 5, ''Real Estate Appraisal.''

Existence of Market Power

Unlike the market for common stocks and bonds, purchasers of commercial real estate are not necessarily price takers in that buyers are not forced to pay a price consistent with the underlying value of an asset.

Instead buyers may exert considerable influence over price. This effectively drives a wedge between the ''true'' market value of the asset and the price an investor must pay. The reverse situation may exist as well. For instance, through the 1980s sellers enjoyed market dominance in the sale of ''trophy'' properties. In general, commercial real estate markets are typified by smaller numbers of buyers and sellers than would characterize a perfectly competitive market. Whether the existence of market power is really a problem is a matter of considerable controversy, although parenthetically even the most casual observer must be struck by the seemingly inexplicable tendency for the commercial real estate market to suffer through repetitive and protracted periods of apparent under- or overvaluation.

The Data

An unfortunate consequence of the institutional characteristics of the commercial real estate market outlined above is the difficulty in securing consistent and reliable measures of commercial real estate performance. Since a limited public exchange exists, information can only be obtained through the willingness of market participants to voluntarily and accurately report their actions. Due to the competitive nature of the commercial real estate industry, obtaining such information is problematic. Currently one of the most reliable sources of such data is the Russell-NCREIF Property Index.[7] As an alternative to the Russell-NCREIF Index, many researchers have suggested that real estate investment trusts (REITs), particularly those publicly traded, may provide a reliable guide to assessing commercial real estate performance. For example, proponents of using REIT data to estimate commercial real estate performance assert that this information, while flawed, is "certainly more representative of transactions prices than those based on appraised values."[8] Further, since REITs effectively securitize property in the same manner that equities securitize firms, the sophisticated analytical tools used to study the behavior of the stock market can be brought to bear on real estate. It additionally appears that REIT performance may lead "hard asset" performance as measured by the Russell-NCREIF Index. There is increasing evidence that the public markets "wrote down" the value of the underlying real estate appropriately, and in advance of, the private market performance measures.

However, this confidence must be tempered since REIT performance data, though much studied, is not itelf without several serious shortcomings, which, for practical purposes, detract significantly from its usefulness. The first is that REITs may not accurately represent the broader commercial real estate market. In particular, at the end of 1991, the total market value of outstanding shares of publicly traded REITs—including equity, hybrid, and mortgage issues—was approximately \$13 billion. This represents, at best, no more than 1 percent of the total market value of all commercial real estate. This "misrepresentation" can manifest itself in several ways. First, there is the question of how the geographical and property-type distribution of assets secured by REITs reflects the universe of commercial real estate on the whole. Since the asset risk of real estate depends inextricably on both location and property type, inferences based on REIT performance may be biased and deviate considerably from inferences drawn from other samples of commercial property. Further, the

---

[7]A good nontechnical discussion of the difficulties of measuring and interpreting commercial real estate performance statistics can be found in the Volk (1990). For a good general review of real estate performance indexes, see Eatroff, Klessel, and Kohn (1988).

[8]K. C. Chan, Patric H. Hendershott, and Anthony B. Sanders, "Risk and Return on Real Estate: Evidence from Equity REITS," *AREUEA Journal* 18, no. 4 (Winter 1990), pp. 431–52.

nature of financing must be considered. The nature of financial ownership can have a material influence on an assets performance. This is reflected by the finding that the economic characteristics and behavior of equity, hybrid, and mortgage REITs can differ considerably from one another.[9]

There appears to be a general perception that securitized real estate, particularly that held by publicly traded corporations and reflected in the value of the company's stock, is undervalued or in some way "mispriced."[10] That is, the market value of the property which is implied by the REIT stock price is an underestimate of the asset or "breakup" value of the property. This perception reflects a number of factors, centering mostly on the informational difficulties associated with transacting and managing real estate. While it is difficult to reconcile this argument with modern asset pricing theories, it is nonetheless suggestive of some difficulties inherent in the use of securitized property performance.

The final shortcoming is that many studies (such as Gyourko and Keim, and Sagalyn)[11] suggest that REIT returns have characteristics more closely related to those of small company stocks, rather than to commercial real estate. For instance, commercial real estate, as measured by non-REIT data sources, has generally been found to be a good inflation hedge. Studies that have used REIT data to address this same question have reached the opposite conclusion—that real estate, like most publicly traded equities, is a poor inflation hedge. Such contradictory results raise the question of whether the institutional features of the market in which commercial property trades have an effect on the characteristics of the return data themselves.

The Russell-NCREIF Property (henceforth RN) Index is produced through a joint venture between the Frank Russell Company and the National Council of Real Estate Investment Fiduciaries (NCREIF), an organization comprised of approximately 50 large institutional real estate managers.[12] The RN Index used here reports quarterly on the value of an equity portfolio of roughly 1,600 commercial properties with a market

---

[9]Ibid.

[10]See Chew (1990) for a discussion of this issue.

[11]See Joseph Gyourko and Donald Keim, *Risk and Returns of Investing in Real Estate: Evidence from a Real Estate Stock Index* Unpublished Manuscript, (The Wharton School of Business: University of Pennsylvania, September 27, 1992) and Lynn Sagalyn, "Real Estate Securities: Risk and Return over the Business Cycle," FP #2 Working Paper, MIT Center for Real Estate, 1989.

[12]For more information on the construction and composition of this data set, see "The Russell-NCREIF Real Estate Performance Report," (Tacoma, WA.: National Council for Real Estate Investment Fiduciaries).

value of nearly $22 billion. The individual data is gathered from reports filed by each NCREIF member, and represents a broad spectrum of property types and geographies. Specifically, for each property, net operating income and appraised value (or net sales proceeds when appropriate) are reported. From this, an aggregate value index is constructed. Quarterly rates of return are developed by computing the period-to-period percent change in the index. The return data used in this chapter cover the period from the first quarter of 1978 through the fourth quarter of 1989, a total of 48 observations.

The use of this data set is a matter of some controversy within the real estate research community. The principal criticism of this data is that it uses appraisals as measures of market value (so-called appraisal bias). Critics contend that appraisals tend to systematically understate volatility and overstate property values.[13] The empirical evidence on this point is mixed, however.[14] Given the nature of the appraisal process and the apparent propensity of appraisers to most heavily weight current information on rents and values, it would seem possible that appraisals merely lag true market conditions rather than exhibit a systematic propensity to over- or understate values. Cole, Guilkey, and Miles[15] argue that appraisers are competent technicians but poor economists. The paucity of relevant information, along with the expense of searching, collecting, and monitoring information, provide, in part, an incentive to heavily discount the future. As a result of this tendency to look backward, real estate values may appear to lag economic activity rather than lead it, as other asset prices do. This is certainly the conclusion of recent REIT analysis. However, in the long-run, this problem should diminish as more data is recorded over more cycles—the overvaluations of appraisers should be offset by undervaluations.

---

[13]This claim, if true, will lead most portfolio allocation schemes to overrepresent real estate in a portfolio.

[14]See Rebel Cole, David Guilkey, and Mike Miles, "Toward an Assessment of the Reliability of Commercial Appraisals," *The Appraisal Journal* 54, no. 2 (July 1986), pp. 422–32 for a review of this problem. Further complicating matters is the fact that many studies of appraisal behavior were conducted using data only from the 1980s. Arguably this was not a truly representative period for the market. Other studies that examine the question of appraisal bias include David Geltner, "Bias in Appraisal-Based Returns," *AREUEA Journal* 17, no. 3 (Fall 1989), pp. 338–52; and S. Michael Giliberto, "A Note on the Use of Appraisal Data in Indexes of Performance Measurement," *AREUEA Journal* 16, no. 1 (Spring 1988), pp. 77–83.

[15]Cole et al., "Toward an Assessment of the Reliability of Commercial Appraisals."

A more general explanation for the possible shortcomings of appraisal-based data relies not on the difficulties of acquiring and interpreting information, but instead focuses on the economic or contractual relationship between the appraiser and the property owner. Such relationships fall under the general heading of what economists call *principal-agent problems*, or agency theory. The general idea is that the nature of the contract between the principal (in this case the property owner) and the agent (the appraiser) may materially influence the outcome of the appraisal. It is perfectly plausible that a rational, fully informed, profit-maximizing appraiser may not view it in his best economic interest to provide what he or she perceives as "true" appraisals, but instead to provide what he or she thinks the principal will perceive as a true appraisal. As a result, the appraiser has a bona fide economic incentive not to "call them as he sees them," but to "call them as he thinks his clients would like to see them."[16]

On the positive side, these data have much in their favor.[17] In particular, the data reflect the actual transactions of a broad range of major investors, including their choice of location and property type. With the exception of its financial structure bias, the data is reasonably representative of the activities of a significant part of the commercial real estate world, particularly tax-exempt investors. From an econometric perspective, these problems constitute a condition known as *unobservable measurement error*. In and of itself, measurement error of this kind is not necessarily a problem, except that the confidence placed in the conclusions related with the data are weaker than if the error did not exist.

REAL ESTATE IN THE MULTIASSET PORTFOLIO

Real Estate As an Inflation Hedge

An asset with returns that keep pace with inflation at a minimum will ensure that the purchasing power of an investor's income (and hence his or her consumption) does not fall over time. Ideally, if an asset is a perfect

---

[16]See David Shulman, "The Relative Risk of Equity Real Estate and Common Stock: A New View." Salomon Brothers, New York, June 30, 1986, for a comparison of real estate returns with the returns of common stocks generated by an "appraisal-based" approach.

[17]See Susan Hudson-Wilson, "Are Measures of Real Estate Returns Wrong?" *Pensions & Investments Age*, March 1990, for a more complete discussion of this issue.

FIGURE 3–1
Year-Over-Year Property Returns: 1978–1991

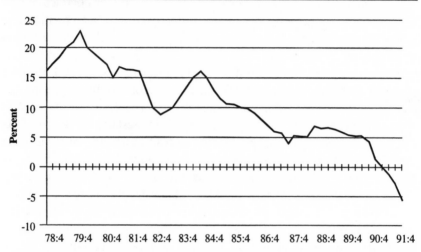

Source: Rusell-NCREIF Property Index.

hedge of inflation, then any increase in inflation will be offset one for one by an increase in the asset's nominal rate of return. To date, most empirical evidence has found that commercial real estate is a good inflation hedge and that stocks and bonds are not.[18] A casual glance at the correlation matrix given in Table 3–1 seems to confirm this: nominal real estate returns have a correlation coefficient with inflation of 0.51, while the correlations of bonds and stocks with inflation are both negative.

Inflation is transmitted to real estate returns via three paths: through rents, through capitalization rates and through discount rates. As inflation, or inflationary expectations, rise landlords will try to pass the added expected expenses through to tenants via the lease rate. If landlords expect inflation to be sustained, they will try to build an inflation index into the

---

[18]See David J. Hartzell, John S. Hekman, and Mike Miles, "Real Estate Returns and Inflation," *AREUEA Journal* 15, no. 1 (Spring 1987), pp. 617–37; Joseph Gyourko and Peter Linneman, "Owner-Occupied Homes, Income-Producing Properties, and REITs as Inflation Hedges: Empirical Findings," *Journal of Real Estate Finance and Economics* 1, no. 4 (December 1988), pp. 347–72; Jack H. Rubens, Michael T. Bond, and James R. Webb, "The Inflation-Hedging Effectiveness of Real Estate," *Journal of Real Estate Research* 4, no. 2 (1989), pp. 45–55; and Charles H. Wurtzebach, Glenn R. Mueller, and Donna Machi, "The Impact of Inflation and Vacancy on Real Estate Returns," *Journal of Real Estate Research* (1991).

TABLE 3–1
Correlation Matrix—Nominal Quarterly Returns

Asset	Property	Stocks	Bonds	T-Bills	Inflation
Property	1.00	−0.16	−0.35	0.49	0.51
Stocks	—	1.00	0.36	−0.16	−0.11
Bonds	—	—	1.00	0.03	−0.35
T-Bills	—	—	—	1.00	0.48
Inflation	—	—	—	—	1.00

Source: Russell-NCREIF.

terms of a lease. This is the dominant form of inflation transmission. The other two paths partially counter the lease rate effect as higher inflation causes both cap rates and discount rates to rise as investor's required returns rise, pushing values down. The notion behind real estate's inflation hedging capacity is that the rise in net operating income more than compensates the downward pressure on value.

In order to more thoroughly evaluate commercial real estate's effectiveness as an inflation hedge, two empirical tests were performed. The first involved computing the elasticity of an asset's return with respect to inflation. Elasticity is an economic concept that attempts to capture the sensitivity of changes in one variable with respect to changes in another variable. Elasticity provides an answer to the question: If variable X increases by 1 percent, by what percent will variable Y change? In the present case, our variable X is inflation, while variable Y is an asset's rate of return.

Computing elasticities is straightforward[19] involving nothing more sophisticated than simple linear regression. Aside from their computational simplicity and ease of interpretation, elasticity estimates can be computed at each point in time that data is available, resulting in a history of how asset prices respond to changes in inflation. These "point-in-time" elasticity estimates are shown for property, stocks, and bonds in Figures 3–2 through 3–4. In addition, Table 3–2 contains point estimates of each elasticity; that is, elasticities based upon the mean values of each asset's return and the mean inflation.

---

[19]The formula for calculating the elasticity of a variable Y with respect to X is: ELAS $= dy/dx \times (x/y)$.

FIGURE 3–2
Point-in-Time Elasticities: Property

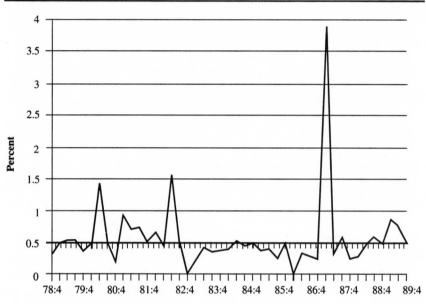

Source: Author's calculation.

FIGURE 3–3
Point-in-Time Elasticities: Stocks

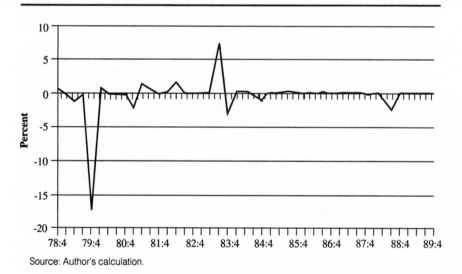

Source: Author's calculation.

FIGURE 3–4
Point-in-Time Elasticities: Bonds

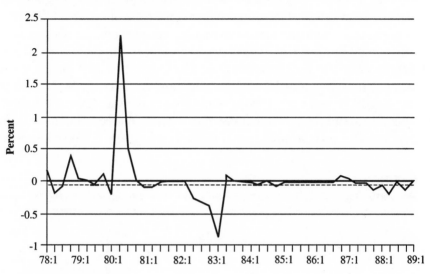

Source: Author's calculation.

The positive relationship between property returns and inflation immediately stands out. According to Table 3–2, on average a 1 percent increase in inflation induces a 0.57 percent increase in nominal real estate returns. The elasticity estimate for stocks is negative, while for bonds it is only marginally greater than zero. This is also confirmed by Figures 3–2 through 3–4. The property elasticity is uniformly greater than zero across

TABLE 3–2
Return-Inflation Elasticity Estimates

Asset	Property	Stocks	Bonds
Elasticity	0.573	− 0.389	0.001

Note: Elasticities are computed using the mean of each asset return series and inflation.

Source: Author's calculation.

the entire sample period, while both the stock and bond estimates fluctuate above and below zero intermittently.

An additional, although somewhat anecdotal, insight may also be gleaned from this analysis. Figure 3–5 depicts the property return-inflation elasticity with the Coldwell-Banker vacancy rate for the national office market.[20] For both data series two regimes may be distinguished. The vacancy rate was very low from 1979 until 1982 and then began a steady climb. In a parallel track the inflation elasticity was high through the later 1970s and early 1980s and dropped as the vacancy rate climbed. This relationship suggests that property's ability to hedge inflation is, in part, a function of the condition of the real estate market.[21] When markets

FIGURE 3–5
Property Elasticities (Left) versus National Office Vacancy Rate (Right)

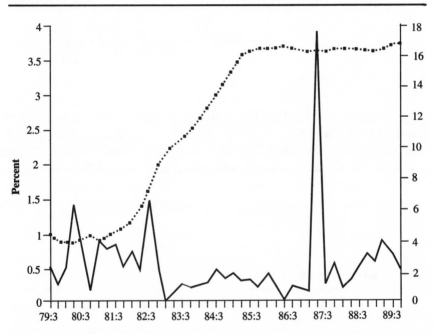

Source: Coldwell Banker Office Vacancy Rate.

---

[20]See Coldwell-Banker Commercial Office Vacancy Index of the United States.

[21]The operational reason for this result is obvious. When markets are soft, lessors are forced to make price and rent concessions to leases, effectively bargaining away the inflation hedge that the lease offers.

are in equilibrium the elasticity is close to 1.0, indicating a very strong correspondence between changes in inflation and changes in returns. When markets are not in equilibrium (or are in disequilibrium), the power of the hedge falls to 50 percent or less of its prior strength. Thus, the overall elasticity of 0.57 is an average. The hedge at any point in time will be subject to the degree of equilibrium in the real estate market. However, it should be emphasized that, in contrast to stocks and bonds, commercial real estate always provides a positive hedge.

The second type of test also involves regression analysis. This test was developed by Fama and Schwert[22] and has been applied to real estate by a number of other authors.[23] The premise behind the test is quite simple. Actual inflation is assumed to consist of two distinct components—expected inflation and unexpected inflation. If an asset is an effective inflation hedge, investors expect asset returns to exhibit a strong, positive correlation with expected inflation.[24] Since asset returns should reflect investors' expectations of future inflation, any changes in expected inflation ought to be reflected in the asset's price (return). To test this proposition, we begin by constructing a historic estimate of expected inflation based upon observed inflation and nominal interest rates. Given this estimate, we define unexpected inflation as the difference between observed inflation and expected inflation. Next, the quarterly return from each asset is regressed on both expected and unexpected inflation. If the regression coefficient of expected inflation is statistically significant and greater than one, we have strong evidence to suggest that the asset is a good inflation hedge for expected inflation.

Table 3–3 contains the results of this test for each of the three assets. Again, these findings support the idea that commercial real estate is a good inflation hedge. The estimated coefficient of expected inflation for property is 1.058. This is not the case for stocks and bonds—neither has an expected inflation coefficient greater than one. The two empirical tests and the anecdotal evidence suggest that real estate does, in fact, provide

---

[22]Eugene F. Fama and G. William Schwert, "Asset Returns and Inflation," *Journal of Financial Economics* 5, no. 1 (1977), pp. 115–46.

[23]Hartzell et al., "Real Estate Returns and Inflation," pp. 617–37. Rubens et al., "The Inflation-Hedging Effectiveness of Real Estate," pp. 45–55.

[24]Notice that we focus explicitly on expected inflation. If an asset were found to effectively hedge unexpected inflation, then an investor could use this information to improve future inflation forecasts, thereby eliminating the efficacy of the hedge.

TABLE 3–3
Results of Hedging Regression Test

Asset	Constant Inflation	Expected Inflation	Unexpected
Property	1.293	1.058	0.328
Stocks	5.884	−1.153	−0.664
Bonds	4.465	−1.149	−2.968

Note: The table gives least squares coefficient estimates.

Source: Author's calculation.

useful inflation hedging power to a portfolio. The power of the hedge does look to be importantly tied to fundamental market conditions, but this is an intuitively satisfying result given the means by which inflation is transmitted to real estate returns.

Reducing Portfolio Risk with Real Estate

The fundamental objective of all "portfolio-based" investment strategies is for an investor to allocate funds across a set of assets in such a way as to become as wealthy as possible. That is, investors seek to construct portfolios that maximize return for a given level of risk, or, equivalently, to minimize risk for a given level of return. Since investors are risk averse, they must be compensated for their willingness to hold assets with uncertain future returns. Since investors dislike uncertainty, the riskier the future return (the larger the possible range of future returns) the higher the premium the investor must be offered to hold the asset.

There are many approaches to portfolio analysis. The most common form is "mean-variance" analysis and usually goes under the name modern portfolio theory, or MPT for short. While the actual determination of an optimal portfolio is an involved mathematical exercise, the fundamental principle underlying the analysis are straightforward.

Two relationships are key. The first is that the expected return (the mean) of a portfolio is simply the weighted sum of the expected returns on the individual assets, where the weights reflect the proportion of the total portfolio investment in each asset. The second is that possible variations of the portfolio's return (the variance) are the weighted sum of the variance of the individual assets, plus the covariation of the assets to each other.[25] MPT uses a portfolio's variance as its measure of risk. Since investors would like to make the variance/risk of the portfolio as small as possible, if they can find assets with returns that are negatively correlated, then by the above definition the portfolio's variance will be less than the sum of the individual asset variances. MPT uses these two principles to mathematically construct a portfolio that has the minimum risk for a given level of return or the highest return at given level of risk.

MPT was used to construct optimal portfolios of the four asset classes shown in Table 3–4. In order to assess the value of commercial real estate in reducing portfolio risk, optional portfolios were formed without real estate using the same return targets as for other assets. Since quarterly real estate returns are negatively correlated with stock and bond returns (see Table 3–1), real estate should exhibit a risk-reducing diversification effect. This exercise was run completely unconstrained. That is, the mean returns, the standard deviations, and the covariance matrix were placed in the mean-variance model as they were actually calculated. The results of this "pure" example may be somewhat unbelievable to consumers of asset allocation models which generally produce different results. The reason that practice often deviates from "purity" is related to the discussion about the real estate data presented earlier in this chapter. It is felt

TABLE 3–4
Nominal Quarterly Returns (Percent)

Asset	Mean	Median	Standard Deviations	Maximum	Mininum	Risk Adjusted
Property	2.83	2.47	1.41	6.43	0.20	2.65
Stocks	4.22	5.73	7.99	21.31	−22.67	2.46
Bonds	2.70	2.09	6.09	22.38	−12.16	2.29
T bills	2.21	2.07	0.66	3.82	1.38	—
Inflation	1.49	1.25	1.05	4.31	−0.43	—

Source: Russell-NCREIF.

---

[25]Formally, the variance of the sum of two assets X and Y can be written as: $VAR(X + Y) = VAR(X) + VAR(Y) + 2 \times COV(X,Y)$ is the covariance between asset X and asset Y. If X and Y are negatively related, then $COV(X,Y)$ is less than zero, and the variance of the sum will be less than the sum of the individual variances.

by many that real estate returns are more volatile (have higher standard deviations) than is captured by the RN data. Thus practitioners frequently raise the real estate standard deviations used in the M-V model from those calculated. Alternatively, practitioners sometimes simply run a constrained version of the M-V model and somewhat arbitrarily hold the real estate allocation down—usually way down. The M-V work in this chapter is unconstrained and the standard deviation for real estate is unaltered. The results below are those resulting from this "pure" calculation. It is not the goal of this chapter to persuade the reader of any version of the truth. It is the goal to expose the process and some directionally sound conclusions. The results are presented in Table 3–5.

Each column in Table 3–5 gives the proportion of the portfolio accounted for by each asset for a given return target. For instance, real estate makes up nearly 85 percent of the optimal portfolio given a 3 percent quarterly return target. The last row of each table gives the risk of each portfolio. For example, the four-asset 3 percent portfolio has a risk of 1.435 percent, while the 4 percent portfolio has a risk of 6.709 percent. The key comparisons to note are the differences in risk between the three-asset portfolio and the four-asset portfolio for a given level of return. For the 3 percent quarterly return, the inclusion of real estate in the portfolio provides a reduction in risk from 3.11 percent to 1.435 percent, a difference of nearly 168 basis points. For the 4 percent return the difference is only 41 basis points.

TABLE 3–5
Optimal Portfolios Weights

| | Quarterly Return Target | | | |
| | 3.0% | | 4.0% | |
Asset	Real Estate	Without Real Estate	Real Estate	Without Real Estate
Property	0.846	—	0.157	—
Stocks	0.125	0.394	0.843	0.892
Bonds	0.029	0.000	0.000	0.000
T bills	0.000	0.606	0.000	0.108
Risk (%)	1.435	3.111	6.709	7.117

Source: Author's calculation.

This same information is shown graphically in Figure 3–6. Figure 3–6 shows the efficient frontiers corresponding to the four-asset portfolio (solid line) and the three-asset portfolio (dotted line). The efficient frontier is defined as the set of optimal risk-return portfolios; that is, it represents the minimum variance portfolio for a given set of possible returns (or the maximum return for a given level of risk). Each point on the efficient frontier represents a different combination of asset weights. The horizontal difference between the two frontiers at a given return level provides an explicit measure of the diversification gain (the reduction in risk) from including real estate. Equivalently, the vertical difference between the two frontiers is a measure of the extra return earned by including real estate in the portfolio for a given level of risk.[26] Clearly for moderate risk-return combinations, the diversification gain from real estate is substantial. For instance, at a risk level of 2 percent, an investor can earn an additional 50 basis points in return by including commercial real estate in their portfolio.

As long as real estate continues to cycle differently from stocks and bonds, it is clear that there will be a role for real estate as a portfolio risk manager for investors for whom risk management comprises a portfolio management priority. The amount of real estate that is necessary in order to obtain these diversification gains remains controversial as it is driven by one's conclusions with respect to the volatility of real estate returns.

Real Estate and the Macro Economy

It is straightforward to see why changing macroeconomic conditions can have important effects on such geographically specific investments as real estate. The most obvious is that the future performance of the asset depends, in part, on the current and future health of the surrounding local economy. In turn, the local economy's well-being is partly linked to the national economy, which is influenced by fiscal and monetary policies, international trade flows, capital market movements, and a host of other factors entirely outside the control (and sometimes the purview) of local investors and local users of space. The risks that are unique to a particular

---

[26]The two portfolios converge at their endpoints since the optimal portfolios are dominated by a single asset at the extremes. For low risk-return outcomes, Treasury bills make up the bulk of both portfolios; at higher risk-return levels, the share of equities dominates.

FIGURE 3–6

The Diversification Gains from Commercial Real Estate Investment

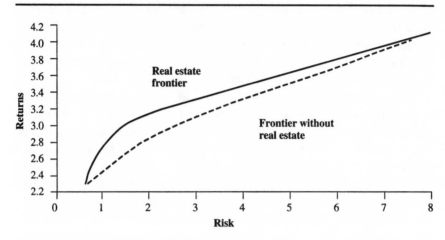

property or local economy are described as *unsystematic* or *unique* and can be diversified away (see Chapter 6 for a full discussion of this). The risks which are not unique, but which apply to all commercial properties are described as *systematic*. The risks associated with the macroeconomy would all be systematic risks. That is, they affect all commercial properties in the system and cannot be diversified away within the real estate portfolio. A second reason can be found in the asset allocation decisions of investors. Risk-averse investors will spread their portfolios across a range of assets, basing their allocation decisions on their assessments of future risk-return trade-offs among combinations of investments. As a result, any event that affects one asset potentially affects all the assets in a portfolio. For instance, consider an investor who holds a portfolio of stocks, bonds, and real estate. If some external event occurs that makes equities relatively more attractive, the investor will increase his or her stock allocation by liquidating some of the bond and real estate positions. This reduces the price of the assets being sold, if enough investors have the same expectations, despite the fact that no changes in the expected future performance of those investments occurred.

This section examines how a variety of important macroeconomic forces have varied over time with aggregate commercial real estate returns. These interdependencies or "co-movements" are useful in uncovering intertemporal relationships that may be difficult to identify or isolate due to the inherent complexity of the economy. To study these dynamics, a technique known as cross-correlation analysis is used. It involves estimating how movements in real estate returns correlate with movements in indicators of economic activity, both contemporaneously and intertemporally. Changes in a number of macroeconomic indicators are associated with changes in property returns. Changes in these variables are examined to determine if they are leading, lagging, or coincident indicators of commercial real estate performance.

Briefly, correlation is one way of measuring the degree of association (not causality) between two variables. Two variables are said to be correlated if changes in one of the variables are associated with consistent changes, either positive or negative, in the other. The correlation coefficient is simply a number between -1 and 1. If two variables have a coefficient between 0 and 1, they are said to be positively correlated; that is, increases (decreases) in one variable are associated with regular increases (decreases) in the other. The closer the correlation coefficient is to one, the stronger the degree of positive association. If the correlation coeficient is exactly 1, then the variables are said to be perfectly positively correlated; that is, if x increases by 10 percent, y increases by exactly 10 percent. Similarly, a correlation coefficient between 0 and -1 indicates negative correlation, meaning that increases (decreases) in one variable are associated with regular decreases (increases) in the other. For instance, changes in mortgage rates are negatively correlated with changes in home sales, since as rates fall, sales tend to rise. The correlation is not perfect, however, since at times, increases in rates are not followed by falling home sales (other forces may come into play that prevent sales from declining).

Finally, if the correlation coefficient is zero, the variables are said to be uncorrelated, implying that changes in one variable are not associated with regular positive or negative changes in the other.

Table 3–6 presents the results of the cross-correlation analysis. The statistics are the correlations between property returns and a set of common macroeconomic forces thought to be important indicators of real estate investment activity. The indicators are grouped by the nature of the activity they reflect such as production, employment, and construction. Since many macroeconomic time series have a strong "trend" component, the macro factors are measured as deviations from their underlying trends. This was done to filter out the common effects of a growing economy, and has been found to yield more reliable and accurate measures of economic interrelationships. Macroeconomic factors are listed down the

TABLE 3–6

Cross Correlations of Property Returns with General Indicators of Economic Activity (Variables Measured as Deviations from Trend)

Indicator	Cross Correlations of Property Returns with Indicator at Time										
	t–5	t–4	t–3	t–2	t–1	t	t + 1	t + 2	t + 3	t + 4	t + 5
Output and Prices:											
Real GNP	−0.02	0.02	0.10	0.22	0.29	0.36	0.35	0.21	0.08	−0.02	−0.06
Real disposable income	0.04	0.07	0.12	0.17	0.16	0.30	0.26	0.14	0.04	−0.01	−0.13
Industrial production	−0.01	0.03	0.10	0.20	0.32	0.41	0.39	0.24	0.14	−0.01	−0.12
Real trade deficit	0.15	0.16	0.15	0.12	0.11	0.08	0.20	0.23	0.24	0.25	0.35
Capacity utilization	0.13	0.14	0.18	0.18	0.17	0.16	0.11	−0.04	−0.14	−0.25	−0.34
Inflation	0.44	0.38	0.50	0.68	0.57	0.51	0.60	0.57	0.45	0.29	0.25
Employment:											
Total (nonagricultural)	0.05	0.08	0.12	0.22	0.30	0.39	0.42	0.36	0.28	0.20	0.10
Manufacturing	0.01	0.04	0.12	0.24	0.33	0.45	0.46	0.37	0.26	0.13	0.03
Nonmanufacturing	0.06	0.09	0.11	0.20	0.27	0.34	0.37	0.34	0.28	0.22	0.14
Construction	0.03	0.05	0.09	0.20	0.26	0.34	0.33	0.27	0.21	0.13	0.05
Construction Activity:											
Housing starts	0.07	0.07	0.13	0.18	0.16	0.07	−0.13	−0.23	−0.23	−0.27	−0.23
Existing home sales	0.09	0.11	0.20	0.22	0.25	0.22	−0.01	−0.10	−0.11	−0.20	−0.21
New home prices	0.19	0.20	0.21	0.37	0.35	0.23	0.10	0.09	−0.02	−0.10	−0.20
Existing home prices	0.16	−0.08	−0.02	0.21	0.23	0.03	0.06	0.32	0.36	0.06	0.12
Contract awards	−0.30	−0.31	−0.30	−0.07	−0.03	−0.02	−0.17	−0.11	−0.07	−0.14	−0.24
Other Assets:											
Stocks	0.02	0.12	−0.05	0.05	−0.11	−0.15	−0.22	0.01	−0.02	0.09	0.07
Corporate bonds	−0.16	−0.12	−0.21	−0.16	−0.24	−0.34	−0.11	−0.04	−0.06	0.08	−0.01
Treasury bills	0.44	0.38	0.50	0.69	0.57	0.51	0.60	0.57	0.46	0.29	0.25
Monetary:											
Real monetary base	0.02	0.03	0.07	0.09	0.09	0.08	−0.01	−0.09	−0.16	−0.26	−0.28
Real M2	−0.12	−0.14	−0.05	−0.05	−0.06	−0.10	−0.20	−0.27	−0.31	−0.36	−0.29
Ten-year Treasury	0.02	0.03	0.07	0.13	0.25	0.39	0.47	0.48	0.52	0.48	0.49
Other:											
Real corporate profits	0.13	0.15	0.21	0.28	0.38	0.45	0.28	0.11	−0.01	−0.12	−0.22
Unemployment rate	0.02	0.06	0.04	0.04	0.04	0.05	0.08	0.16	0.23	0.33	0.39
Real retail sales	−0.03	0.07	0.13	0.20	0.30	0.36	0.22	0.10	0.01	−0.04	−0.11
Population	0.04	0.11	−0.06	−0.14	0.02	0.11	0.04	0.03	0.26	0.41	0.27

Sources: Various.

"Indicator" column, while the timing of the correlations (i.e., the lead or lag of the indicator) are listed across the top. The column labeled "t" gives the contemporaneous correlation between property returns and each macro variable. For example, the contemporaneous correlation between property returns and real gross national product (GNP) is 0.36, indicating that increases in real GNP are associated with increases in property returns. The magnitude of the number does not reflect how large the movements in one variable are with respect to movements in other variables; it only reveals the relative degree of association. If the correlation between variable x and y is 0.75, and the correlation between x and z is

0.50, this does not mean that absolute changes in y are larger than absolute changes in z for given changes in x; it only means that the relative changes are larger: on a percentage basis, y will respond more to a change in x than will z. A correlation coefficient close to one indicates that a series is highly procyclical with property returns, while a number close to -1 indicates a countercyclical relationship. If the correlation is close to zero, the series is uncorrelated with contemporaneous returns.

The other columns of the table reflect intertemporal correlations; that is, the indicator factors have been shifted forward or backward in time from one to five quarters relative to property returns. The columns labeled "$t–5$" through "$t–1$" give the correlation between property returns at time t and the indicator one quarter before t ("$t–1$"), two quarters before "t" ("$t–2$"), and so on. Likewise, the columns labeled "$t + 1$" through "$t + 5$" give the correlation between current period property returns and future values of the indicators, up to five quarters ahead.

While to some extent these measures reflect relative degrees of co-movement, their most important use is to uncover lead-lag relationships. Specifically, we search for the set of time leads or lags at which the correlation coefficients tend to be largest. If the largest correlation coefficients—either positive or negative—of a variable occur in the future, then property returns are a leading indicator of the series, or equivalently, the macro series is lagging indicator of property returns. Current changes in returns are associated with future changes in the macro series. Similarly, if the highest correlations are with past values of the macro series, then changes in property returns lag changes in he macro variable, implying that the series is a leading indicator of returns (or returns are a lagging indicator of the series). If the largest correlation centers at the present—time, t—then the variable is a coincident indicator for property returns.

Table 3–7 summarizes the lead-lag indicator relationships for each of the macroeconomic indicator variables. In some cases, the data reveal a clear intertemporal relationship between returns and the macro indicator. In addition, since relationships are considered pairwise, those variables that simultaneously have been both positive and negative effects on the economy, such as interest rates, are difficult to classify. In these cases, the "Unknown" column is marked. If the cross-correlations are high both contemporaneously and for either the past or the future time periods, then both the coincident and the appropriate time column are marked. The column headings labeled "P" refer to procyclical relationships, while the

TABLE 3–7
Lagging, Coincident, and Leading Indicators of Real Estate Activity

Indicator	Lagging P	Lagging C	Coincident P	Coincident C	Leading P	Leading C	Unknown
Output and Prices:							
Real GNP			X				
Real disposable income			X				
Industrial production			X				
Real trade deficit	X						
Capacity utilization							X
Inflation							X
Employment:							
Total (nonagricultural)	X		X				
Manufacturing	X		X				
Nonmanufacturing	X		X				
Construction	X		X				
Construction activity:							
Housing starts		X					
Existing home sales					X		
New home prices			X		X		
Existing home prices							X
Contract awards						X	
Other Assets:							
Stocks				X			
Corporate bonds				X			
Treasury bills							X
Monetary:							
Real Monetary Base		X					
Real M2		X					
Ten-year Treasury	X		X				
Other:							
Real corporate profits			X		X		
Unemployment rate	X						
Real retail sales					X		
Population	X						

Sources: Various.

headings marked "*C*" refer to countercyclical relationships. Table 3–7 reveals some interesting relationships, some intuitively obvious, others less so.

Business cycles present special dangers and opportunities for commercial real estate. While market timing is not, in most cases, a reliable strategy for commercial real estate in the multiasset portfolio, there are some studies which discuss various aspects of real estate investing during such times. The articles written by Phyrr, Born, and Webb[27] discuss strategies for inflation cycles and market disequilibria during cyclical economic conditions.

Last, there is some evidence that commercial real estate values became divorced from economic fundamentals during the mid-1980s (1984–87) due to the supply of financing available. Giliberto examined commercial real estate lending and construction for the period 1967-1991 and estimated that "$50 to $70 billion of excess construction was undertaken in the 1984-1987 period or about 1.1 to 1.6 billion square feet across all property types."[28] This excess construction may act as a depressant on rents and therefore property values for as long as a decade.

CONCLUSION

This chapter has examined the two most important arguments advanced to rationalize the inclusion of real estate in a multiasset portfolio: inflation hedging and diversification. A third justification, used mainly by noninstitutional investors, is a market timing rationale. This justification holds that investment in real estate should be pursued as opportunities to achieve extraordinary rates of return become available. This is a legitimate approach and may work well for very knowledgeable and responsive investors.

The risk management and inflation hedging capacities of real estate appear sound with the caveats that the transmission of inflation is impeded in some market environments and the amount of real estate needed to generate useful diversification benefits is not yet clear. The analysis of the relationship between real estate returns and macroeconomic forces serves to remind us that real estate is very much subject to influences beyond those of local markets and so, is appropriately analyzed, like stocks and bonds, in the larger context of the macroeconomy. Increasingly, national and international capital market forces will be important to the behavior, and so the role of real estate in the context of the multiasset portfolio.

---

[27]Stephen A. Phyrr, Waldo L. Born, and James R. Webb, "Development of a Dynamic Investment Strategy under Alternative Inflation Cycle Scenarios," *The Journal of Real Estate Research* 5, no. 2 (Summer 1990), pp. 177–93.

[28]S. Michael Giliberto, "Real Estate in the Portfolio: Then and Now," Salomon Brothers, New York, July 8, 1991.

CHAPTER 4

REAL ESTATE IN A CAPITAL MARKETS CONTEXT

S. Michael Giliberto
Salomon Brothers
Sandon J. Goldberg
Medco Containment

INTRODUCTION

Real estate supply and demand are driven by factors in both the tenant market, or the user's market for space to occupy, and the capital markets. Understanding real estate's links to the capital markets is critical for real estate participants. The relationship between these two markets determines rents and prices—both critical to investment and operational decision making. There are important lags in information flows that, once understood, can provide participants in all aspects of the real estate markets with patience and/or an appropriate sense of urgency—as the environment warrants.

In the space market, the interaction of the supply of and the demand for physical space determines rent, which is the price of using a given unit of space for a given amount of time. This price affects decisions about how much space is made available and how much space is leased or purchased. The price (rent) plays a pivotal role in determining the allocation of space among competing users and uses. Similarly, capital markets foster the efficient allocation of scarce capital among competing demands.

This allocation is largely accomplished through the markets' determination of the price of credit (interest rates) and the determination of the minimum yield that an investment must produce, given the investment's risk (the required risk-adjusted rate of return).

In the United States, U.S. government debt is generally thought of as having no risk. That is, the investor who buys a U.S. Treasury security (or another security backed by the full faith and credit of the government) can count on receiving the scheduled payments of interest and principal. Therefore, yields on such securities are regarded as risk-free rates.[1] All securities that admit some uncertainty about the timing and magnitude of future cash flows expose investors to risk. As compensation for bearing risk, investors require an additional yield over and above what is offered on risk-free securities. Such risk premiums take two basic forms: equity risk premiums and credit spreads. An equity risk premium is the incremental yield that the owner of an asset with uncertain future cash flows seeks. A credit spread reflects the possibility that a debt obligation may not be paid off according to the contracted terms and compensates the lender for taking this risk.

The capital markets' determination of yields clearly affects the ability to finance and develop real estate. But interest rates also affect the general pace of economic activity, including businesses' plans to hire more workers, to relocate, to enter new markets, and so forth. Such decisions, which take place on the real—rather than the financial—side of the economy, have obvious, fundamental significance for real estate.

From the investor's perspective, real estate is one of several alternative investment classes; others include such capital market instruments as preferred and common stocks, government and corporate bonds, and money market securities. Real estate's attractiveness to investors, and hence, its pricing and valuation, will depend on how its risk and return dynamics compare with those of other asset classes.

---

[1] Throughout this chapter, the term *risk-free rate* will denote the interest rate paid by the most creditworthy borrower (by definition, the U.S. government). Technically, only securities with a very short maturity are truly riskless, because other securities are exposed to inflation risk. Although nominal interest rates include compensation for expected inflation, unanticipated inflation, which alters the purchasing power of the fixed-dollar amounts received by a bondholder, is a risk. We assume that the capital markets, on average, appropriately compensate investors for this risk as part of the nominal risk-free rate for longer term securities.

RISK AND RETURN BASICS

There are many ways to look at real estate returns, including:

1. Current operating income as a percentage of current value.
2. Stabilized income as a percentage of purchase price.
3. After-tax, after-debt cash flow as a percentage of equity value.
4. Accounting income as a percentage of book value.

None of these, however, is appropriate for thinking about real estate risk and return in a capital market setting. To compare real estate with other asset classes, we need to consider the return or yield that an investor receives over a designated holding period. This *holding period return* (HPR)—also called the *investment yield* or *internal rate of return* (IRR)— is *r* in the following equation:

$$\text{Value}_0 = \sum_{t=1}^{H} CF_t/(1 + r)^t + \text{Value}_H/(1 + r)^H \tag{1}$$

where *t* is a time index, Value_0 represents the current value, CF_t represents the cash flow (positive or negative) at date *t*, and Value_H is the net proceeds from disposition of the property. Thus, an investor's return consists of periodic cash distributions from owning the property, including an initial negative cash flow from purchasing the property, plus a receipt from selling the property, all adjusted to reflect the timing of the cash flows.

After a property has been sold, all the values in equation (1) are known and the HPR actually achieved can be computed. Otherwise, although Value_0 is known (or estimated from an appraisal), the future cash flows (CF_t and Value_H) are generally unknown, so estimated or expected values have to be used to find *r*. The HPR then represents the expected rate of return on the asset. When the future cash flows are not known with certainty, the asset's risk, as well as its expected return, becomes an important consideration. We define the asset's risk as uncertainty about the timing and magnitude of its future cash flows.

The sources of real estate risk can be separated into two broad categories: those that can be managed (''micro'' risks) and those that are systematic and beyond managerial control (''macro'' risks).[2]

---

[2] For a more thorough discussion of real estate risks, see S. Michael Giliberto, ''The Big Picture,'' *Institutional Investor Money Management Forum* (1989), pp. 105–06.

The former include:

1. Lease terms.
2. The degree of operating and financial leverage.
3. Tenant mix and credit quality.
4. A development's positioning within a market.
5. Location.

Clearly, we exaggerate some when we say that all of the aforementioned risks can be controlled at all times. Various local and national market conditions may impede the full exercise of control over lease terms, for example. This list is meant to distinguish areas of possible control from areas where it is always the case that control cannot be exercised. Among the macro risks, which are always uncontrollable, are:

1. Real estate's illiquidity.
2. Taxes and legislation.
3. Competition.
4. The business cycle (local, regional, national, and international).
5. Demographic, employment, and income trends (including housing affordability).
6. Inflation and interest rates.

Typically, risk for an individual asset is measured by the volatility—usually expressed as the standard deviation—of the asset's returns. Measuring risk is more difficult for real estate assets than for financial assets because the inherent illiquidity in real estate markets necessitates the use of appraisal-based return information, and this tends to distort somewhat the "true" level of real estate risk.[3] Although real estate risk is inherently difficult to measure, the relative stability and predictability of future cash flows can be a guide to an asset's risk. Consider two projects, a Class A office building that is 95 percent leased on a long-term basis to A-rated-credit tenants and a 50 percent occupied strip shopping center. Although quantifying the risk of each would be difficult, the strip center clearly is the riskier one of the two investments: its future cash flows are much more

---

[3]Surveys of real estate market participants have indicated that risk measurements based on appraised values understate the riskiness of real estate assets (and portfolios) by a factor of two to three times. See Salomon Brothers, Inc., *Real Estate Risk and Return: 1991 Survey Results* (New York, March 31, 1992).

uncertain. Thus, a project's micro risk, relative to other real estate assets, can often be assessed qualitatively.

In the real estate domain, differences in regional economic performance, property-type performance, lease structures, tenant mixes, and so forth imply that correlations between individual assets' returns are not perfect. As a result, when assets are grouped together in a portfolio, the asset-specific risks will tend to offset one another. This phenomenon is the basis for "scientific" portfolio diversification, or modern portfolio theory (MPT).[4] MPT shows how to construct efficient portfolios that offer the highest level of expected return for a given portfolio risk level, or, equivalently, the lowest risk for a designated return. A portfolio formed according to MPT is desirable because it will nearly eliminate the nonsystematic or idiosyncratic (micro) risk and leave only the systematic or macro risk associated with the chosen real estate assets. Rational investors will always seek to hold efficient portfolios. See Chapter 3 for a more complete discussion.

Whereas the standard deviation of returns is the appropriate measurement of risk for a particular property, an asset's risk in a portfolio context merits a different measure to acknowledge that the nonsystematic portion of the asset's total volatility has been "diversified away." Financial economists have shown that an asset's beta, designated B, is an appropriate risk measure for an asset that is held in an efficiently diversifed portfolio. Beta can be expressed mathematically as:

$$B = \text{Corr}\,(r_a, r_p) * \sigma_a / \sigma_p \tag{2}$$

where σ_a is the volatility of the asset's returns, σ_p is the portfolio's volatility and Corr (r_a, r_p) is the correlation between the asset and portfolio returns. Beta measures the relative risk of a particular asset with respect to the portfolio. The portfolio may be narrowly defined or it can be a broad benchmark, such as the Standard & Poor's 500 Stock Index or the Russell-NCREIF Property Index.

If investors use portfolio diversification to eliminate nonsystematic risk, then they will only be concerned with an asset's portfolio or beta risk. Most importantly, they will base their return expectations on the asset's systematic (beta) risk, not on the asset's total risk. Thus, capital

---

[4]See Harry M. Markowitz, *Portfolio Selection: Efficient Diversification of Investments* (New Haven, Conn.: Yale University Press, 1959).

market yields (returns), which reflect the actions of investors in the aggregate, will provide compensation for bearing systematic risk, but not for bearing total risk. A mathematical statement of the relationship between the expected return on an asset and the asset's systematic risk is called an *asset-pricing model*. One widely used form is the single-factor capital asset-pricing model (CAPM) that posits: [5]

$$E(r_a) = r_f + B_a[E(r_m) - r_f] \qquad (3)$$

In equation (3), the symbol $E(r_a)$ stands for expected value, r_f for the risk-free interest rate, and r_m for the return on the "market portfolio" of all risky assets. A subscript a has been added to B to indicate that it is asset a's beta. The CAPM says that an asset's expected return should be equal to a risk-free rate plus an additional return, a risk premium, equal to the asset's beta multiplied by the differential between the expected return on the market portfolio (the factor) and the risk-free rate.[6] This differential is sometimes called the *market price of risk* because its magnitude reflects the premium over the risk-free rate that investors require for bearing the "market" level of risk.[7] The market price of risk reflects the level of risk tolerance in the capital markets and changes over time. Note that the market price of risk is always greater than zero, because the market as a whole is risky, and risk-averse investors require a risk premium to hold the market.

The CAPM relates the expected or required return on an asset to the asset's specific risk (beta) and to capital market factors (interest rates and risk tolerance). But how is this an asset-pricing model? The answer comes from starting with the standard equation for the present value of a future cash flow to be received one period from today:

$$PV_{CF} = E(CF) / (1 + k) \qquad (4)$$

where k is the required return, given the cash flow's risk. But the required return k is the same as the expected return given by equation (3), so by substituting equation (3) into equation (4) we get:

---

[5]See William F. Sharpe, *Portfolio Theory and Capital Markets,* (New York: McGraw-Hill, 1970).

[6]Multifactor asset-pricing models are also prominent in financial economics. For example, see K. C. Chan, Patric H. Hendershott, and Anthony B. Sanders, "Risk and Return on Real Estate: Evidence from Equity REITs," *American Real Estate and Urban Economics Association Journal (AREUEA Journal)* 18, no. 4 (Winter, 1990), pp. 431–52.

[7]The market portfolio, by definition, has a beta equal to one, as can be seen by regarding the market as both asset a and portfolio p in equation (2).

$$PV_{CF} = E\,(CF) / (1 + r_f + B_a\,[E\,(r_m) - r_f]) \tag{5}$$

A simple example illustrates how the CAPM can be used to value an asset. Assume that the asset has a single cash flow of $1,000 one year from now. The asset's beta is determined to be 1.5. If the current one-year risk-free rate is 4 percent and the market price of risk is 5 percent, the risk-adjusted required rate of return would be:

$$4\% + 1.5\,(5\%) = 11.5\% \tag{6}$$

Thus, according to the CAPM, the value of this asset today is ($1,000/1.115), or $897. The relationship in equation (5) exemplifies several significant factors. First, both the expected cash flow stream and the beta are specific to the particular asset being valued, while the risk-free rate and the market price of risk are determined in the capital markets and will apply to all assets within the market. For a particular asset, an increase in the projected cash flows will induce a higher price. Higher betas, corresponding to riskier assets, will decrease the price of those same cash flows. Second, changes in the general level of interest rates will have an inverse effect on the price of risky cash flows: An increase in the risk-free rate will result in a decrease in the value of a risky cash flow (all else being equal). Finally, changes in the market's risk tolerance level will influence values. Table 4–1 summarizes how a change in any one of the variables on the right-hand side of equation (5) affects the asset's value, holding all the other variables constant.

Consider the asset with the $1,000 future cash flow that we valued before. Suppose that interest rates rise and the one-year risk-free rate increases to 5 percent. The new required return will be 12.5 percent, and the asset's value will decline to $889.

TABLE 4–1
Valuation Effects of Changes in CAPM Variables

Variable	Effect on Value
CF increases (decreases)	Increases (decreases)
B increases (decreases)	Decreases (increases)
r_f increases (decreases)	Decreases (increases)
$E(r_m) - r_f$ increases (decreases)	Decreases (increases)

THE INTERACTION OF CAPITAL MARKETS FACTORS WITH REAL ESTATE: THE MICROVIEW

The valuation equation (1) is a useful framework for understanding how capital markets factors affect real estate. The CAPM provides the required rate of return to value all the cash flows that the property owner expects to receive:

$$\text{Value}_0 = \sum_{t=1}^{H} CF_t/(1 + r_f + B\,[E(r_m) - r_f])^t + \text{Value}_H/(1 + r_f + B[E(r_m) - r_f])^H \tag{7}$$

(We deleted the a subscript of beta for clarity.) Although this looks similar to equation (1), it is conceptually different. In equation (1), Value_0 was known and r had to be determined; in equation (5), the discount rate is known and the value is determined. The asset's risk-adjusted required rate of return incorporates the beta that indicates the risk of the asset with respect to other risky assets in the general market, and the cash flows that are determined by the particular property and market in which it is located. Because equation (7) is simply the summation of a series of separate cash flows, a change in any one variable still affects the asset's value as shown in Table 4–1.

A common way of looking at real estate valuation is to consider the net operating income (NOI) as a fraction of current value. The resulting ratio is called *the capitalization rate*. If we know the property's income and the appropriate capitalization rate, we can determine the property's value:

$$\text{Value} = \text{NOI}/R \tag{8}$$

where R is the capitalization rate. Unlike in equation (7), neither the time pattern of cash flows nor the overall level of interest rates are explicitly taken into account in equation (8); NOI is usually assumed to be a "stabilized" value.[8] But, in equilibrium, the value derived from the full-discounted, cash flow equation (7) must equal the value derived from the simple income capitalization approach, at least if appraisers had identical,

---

[8]One method for computing stabilized NOI would be to value the income stream in equation (7) using the appropriate required return and then convert that present value into an equivalent annuity stream for H periods.

accurate information and expectations about the future. (Chapter 5 presents greater detail on this idea.) Let us assume that this is indeed the case, and that the NOI is constant, or has been converted to a stabilized value. Then we set equation (7) equal to equation (8):

$$\text{NOI}/R = \text{NOI}\{\{ \sum_{t=1}^{H} 1/(1 + r_f + B[E(r_m) - r_f])^t\} + (1/R_H)/(1 + r_f + B[E(r_m) - r_f])^H\} \tag{9}$$

Value was replaced with NOI/R, where R is the capitalization rate that would apply at the end of the holding period. One more step is to remove NOI from both sides to get:

$$1/R = 1/(1 + r_f + B[E(r_m) - r_f])t + (1/RH)/(1 + r_f + B[E(r_m) - r_f])H \tag{10}$$

Why have we gone through these algebraic manipulations? Because equation (10) shows that the current capitalization rate R explicitly depends on both the project's risk and exogenous capital market factors. For example, if interest rates decline, capitalization rates will also decline, holding all other variables constant. The reason we developed this link is that the capitalization rate is a simple way to relate the value of a unit amount of real estate to the income (rent) generated by that unit. This concept will be helpful when we consider the interaction of space and capital markets in an equilibrium setting.

REAL ESTATE DURATION

We have already shown how capital market factors can affect the valuation of a particular real estate asset; specifically, how increases (decreases) in overall interest rate levels can lower (raise) the value of risky assets by increasing (decreasing) the required rate of return on those assets. Taking this analysis one step further, it is possible to quantitatively measure the sensitivity of a particular asset's value to given changes in market interest rates. The measure of this sensitivity is known as an asset's duration. Duration refers to the percentage change in an asset's price resulting from a 1 percent change in interest rates.[9]

---

[9]For a more complete discussion of real estate duration, see David J. Hartzell, David G. Shulman, Terence C. Langetieg, and Martin L. Leibowitz, "A Look at Real Estate Durations," *Real Estate Portfolio Management*, ed. Brian R. Bruce (Probus Publishing Co.: Chicago, IL 1991).

In our earlier example equation (6), the risk-free rate was 4 percent and the market risk premium 5 percent. The asset with the $1,000 cash flow had a present value of $897. Increasing the general level of interest rates by 1 percentage point (to 5 percent) increased the required rate of return to 12.5 percent. The resulting value of $889 represents a decrease of 0.89 percent; thus, the effective duration for this property is 89 years.

The concept of duration can be extended to include changes in property values resulting from movements in inflation expectations, which affect market rent levels over time and which also affect a property's residual value. Additionally, although our examples have focused on unleveraged property, the addition of debt to an asset's capital structure can either extend or reduce its duration and in this way can be used as a tool for portfolio management.[10] Because a lease represents a right to receive a fixed/floating payment and debt is an obligation to pay a fixed/floating payment, these can be combined in such a way so as to alter the interest rate sensitivity of the underlying asset.

AN EQUILIBRIUM APPROACH TO THE SPACE AND CAPITAL MARKETS: THE MACROVIEW[11]

The preceding analysis showed how simple shifts in capital markets factors affect the value of an individual real estate asset. In the illustration, only one variable changed at a time. But we also need to consider what happens when all variables are allowed to change, not only in the capital markets, but in the space market as well.

Links exist between the space and capital markets that, in the long run, move real estate supply and demand toward equilibrium and ensure that the ultimate purpose of real estate—to house people and businesses—is fulfilled (see Figure 4–1). In equilibrium, there is no pressure to alter the supply of real estate, because the cost of constructing another unit of space exactly equals its value to an investor; thus, there are no economic profits to be made.

---

[10]This topic is addressed in S. Michael Giliberto, "Managing Real Estate Duration: A New Perspective on the Use of Leverage," *Real Estate Portfolio Management*, ed. Brian R. Bruce (Probus Publishing Co.: Chicago, IL 1991).

[11]This section was adapted from Jeffrey Fisher, Susan Hudson-Wilson, and Charles H. Wurtzebach, "Equilibrium in Commercial Real Estate Markets: Linking Space and Capital Markets" *Journal of Portfolio Management*, Summer 1993.

FIGURE 4–1
Interaction of the Markets for Real Estate Space and Capital

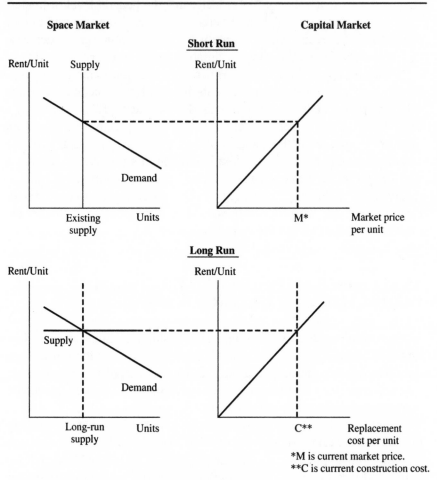

Long-Run Equilibrium

Both the space and capital markets assign values to real estate assets based on the demand for those assets. The two demands arise from space users, seeking the physical "capital," and investors, who supply the financial capital. In the space market in the short run, tenant demand determines rents, because the supply of space cannot be altered. In the capital market, investor demand for real estate assets rises and falls as the rate of return available from real estate investment changes both absolutely and relative to other investment markets. The two markets do not necessarily move in tandem. Although the supply of real estate is fixed in the short run, over the long run the supply of real estate will vary. In short-run situations, there have been periods characterized by tight space market conditions, but relatively weak capital market demand; the converse has prevailed at times as well. To a large degree, tenants are more interested in a property for its own sake and its own characteristics, whereas buyers are (usually) more concerned with the long-run ability of a property to earn a competitive risk-adjusted rate of return vis-à-vis other capital assets. In general, each market has a price into which supply and demand conditions get translated. In the space market, the relevent price is the rent, or the price of leasing a unit of space for a unit of time. In the capital market, the "price" is the capitalization rate, or the price of buying a unit of a property's future cash flow stream. Broadly speaking, it is the dynamics of these two "prices" that determines the long-run equilibrium in both markets and provides the force to move toward that equilibrium.

In order to demonstrate how the equilibrium mechanism works, let us suppose that the capital and space markets both are initially in equilibrium. Any exogenous "shocks" to the system, occurring either in the capital or space markets, are ultimately absorbed so that the markets move to a new and possibly different equilibrium (i.e., no further upward or downward pressure on either rents or capitalization rates). In a full equilibrium setting—in which all factors are variable and the interactions between them can be examined over time—the mechanism works toward equilibrium whether the "shock" originates from the space market or the capital markets. This differs from the partial equilibrium analysis described earlier, which considered only isolated relationships between particular variables and asset values and assumed that all other factors were held constant. Here, those isolated relationships as well as the interrelationships between variables are all examined as a dynamic process. We will begin first by examining a space market "shock" and follow the "chain reaction" of effects on both the value of a particular real estate asset and other capital and space market factors as well.

Suppose the tenant market for real estate is in equilibrium at its structural vacancy level, that is, there is an adequate amount of space for current occupancy and some growth. The structural vacancy rate is that amount of vacant space at which there is no pressure in either direction on real rents; in other words, it is just enough space to accommodate the normal growth in market demand. Unexpectedly, the economy's growth rate accelerates. A strengthening economy increases business profitability, which in turn gives rise to expansionary trends among growing businesses. These businesses grow by adding employees and thereby increase the demand for space. The space market begins to tighten, fueling an increase in rents.

Initially, this event results in increased property values, since higher rent levels translate into additional cash flow. However, the increased cash flows (and values) to property investment attract the interest of investors, who perceive that the value of space exceeds the cost of building it. These investors fund property developers who supply new space to the tenant market; this funding continues as long as the value of the real estate exceeds the cost of constructing it, that is, as long as there are profits to be gained from development (see Figure 4–2).

When investors and developers cease to perceive profits from new construction, the flow of new supply abates. A new equilibrium has been reached at a higher level of supply. Of course, as the supply has increased in response to a demand shock, rents, which initially rose, fall to reflect additional space availability (the supply curve shifts to the right.)

This scenario plays out smoothly, but the process can be subverted by the great uncertainties about future market growth, and the reality that a single, isolated demand shock seldom "plays out" before another shock occurs.

For example, while new space is being constructed, let us assume that the market tightens further—additionally raising cash flows and values—and sparks a full-blown onslaught of investment interest, driving capitalization rates down as investors compete for the most desirable assets. Here, another variable is affected, this time with an inverse relationship to values: investors bid down capitalization rates because they perceive that they have previously underestimated the cash flow growth potential of the asset class, and thus attach a higher multiple to current cash flow, raising property values further (see Figure 4–3). This increased investment interest spills over to the development market, which at the time is clamoring for funds (usually debt) in a new construction cycle. Inevitably, the economic growth that is an inherently cyclical phenomenon begins to slow, and with it tenants' demands for more space. However, the buildings that were started at the peak of the cycle have only just begun to come on-line. Right at the time demand growth is slowing, supply increases dramatically, and the competitive pressure to lease the new space pushes rents down in order to induce tenants to move.

FIGURE 4–2
Short-Term Space Market Shock

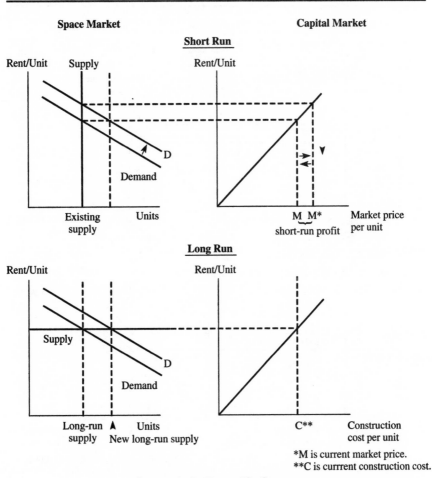

Increase in the Demand for Space

The investors who have funded the new buildings, as well as those who have bought the previously existing properties, begin to realize lower cash flow, and lowering capital values in an unwinding of the earlier trend. New investment interest will naturally begin to wane, and some owners will invariably want to sell. Heightened selling pressure will raise capitalization rates—due to the lower earnings growth environment—and further reduce the market values of all properties. With the incentive (and financing) to develop new properties absent (both from a space and capital

FIGURE 4–3
Short-Term Capital Market Shock

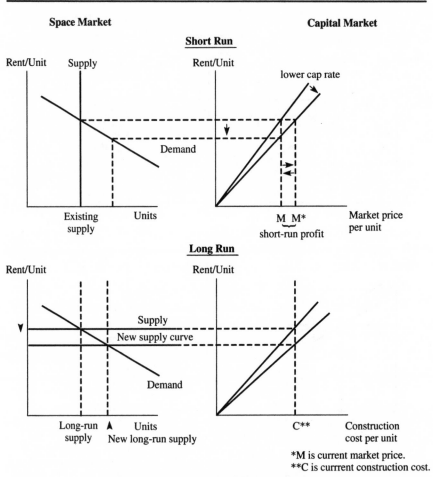

Decrease in the Market Capitalization Rate

markets perspective), developers cease constructing new projects. Economic activity slows to recessionary levels, and space demand withers, which depresses rents, cash flows, and values even further. Investors, who want out, realize that there is little liquidity and additionally raise capitalization rates.

Whereas in the short run, the supply of space is held constant (or perfectly inelastic), in the long run it is perfectly elastic (see Figure 4–4).

Likewise, although the capitalization rate in the short run determines the market value of a property, in the long run the construction or replacement cost for buildings drives values.

A decrease in the long-run capitalization rate for real estate will increase the amount of space being constructed, because real estate's value now exceeds the construction cost. A new lower equilibrium rent level is established. Ultimately, it is the capital markets that will determine the appropriate long-run level of supply, while the space market dictates real estate demand, which tends to be more cyclical than structural. This is intuitive, because construction of a building requires a significant capital commitment that must be procured in the capital markets, while the tenants that fill the space must be found in the space market. Thus, the property must compete in both markets simultaneously, offering a competitive rate of return to the capital market, and a competitive rate of rent (and amenities) to the space market. To be successful, a project must ultimately clear both markets.

THE 1970s AND 1980s: A CASE STUDY IN CYCLICAL EXTREMES

The period from the mid-1970s until the end of the 1980s was marked by cyclical extremes in both the space and capital markets that effectively demonstrate the mechanism through which these markets eventually pull themselves back into alignment. In 1975, the real estate situation was somewhat similar to today, only less overbuilt. Following a severe recession in that year which devastated many major real estate markets including New York City and Florida, construction fell precipitously. Investors had been burned by a debacle involving real estate investment trusts (REITs), and the real estate asset class fell into disfavor, especially among institutional investors. Thus, capitalizaion rates rose and construction funding was scarce.

However, a strong economic recovery in the succeeding five years fueled a pickup in absorption and drove down vacancy rates to extremely low levels. Tightened space market conditions resulted in significant real effective rent increases despite already high inflation at the time (see Figure 4–5). At the same time, the capital markets view of real estate had changed dramatically, primarily in response to four factors:

FIGURE 4–4
Long-Term Space and Capital Markets Trends

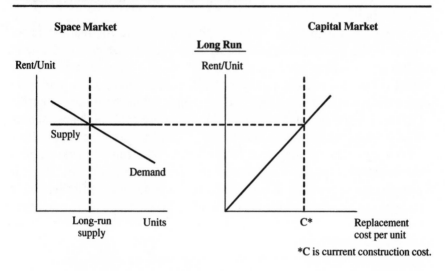

*C is currrent construction cost.

1. The huge returns generated by the swift tightening of space market conditions caught the attention of the institutional investment community.
2. Real estate's perceived characteristics as an inflation hedge whose returns experienced low volatility and only moderate correlation with those of stocks and bonds made it a darling of academics, who trumpeted its underweighted status in institutional portfolios and in doing so, sparked pension fund interest
3. Deregulation of the thrift and banking industries freed up large amounts of debt capital that flowed into real estate
4. Massive liquidity in foreign markets (especially Japan) combined with a weakening dollar brought in significant foreign investment at seemingly higher valuation levels than had been previously encountered.

Thus, capitalization rates for real property of all kinds were driven down to perhaps their lowest levels ever. Yet, at the same time as this trend was playing out, the space markets, which had begun the decade of the 1980s in a state of general undersupply, were being rapidly overbuilt to an unprecedented degree. Although these markets generally move in tandem, divergent trends caused them to temporarily uncouple, setting them up for a major debacle upon recoupling and converging back toward equilibrium. Ultimately, as real estate participants were made aware, capital markets conditions corrected much more quickly than those of the space market, which is still overbuilt and only beginning to move toward a supply-demand equilibrium. Capitalization rates rose swiftly at the same time as cash flows collapsed due to a broad decline in real estate demand, devastating virtually all property market investors. The combination of a softening in yields (the ''return'' from the space market component of a real estate investment) and a sharp decline in capital values (the capital markets contribution) over the past two years has led to the state of shock in which real estate market participants currently find themselves (see Figure 4–6).

FIGURE 4–5
Downtown Office Vacancy Rate and Real Rents, 1970-91

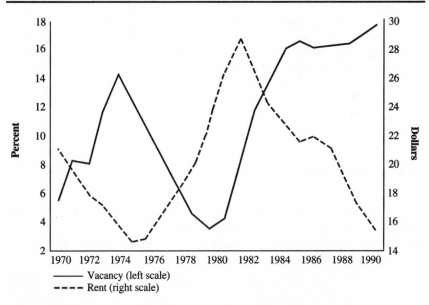

Vacancy (left scale)
Rent (right scale)

Sources: CB Commercial Real Estate Services and Salomon Brothers, Inc.

FIGURE 4–6

Income and Capital Value Components of the Russell-NCREIF Index, 1978–91 (Rolling Four-Quarter Returns)

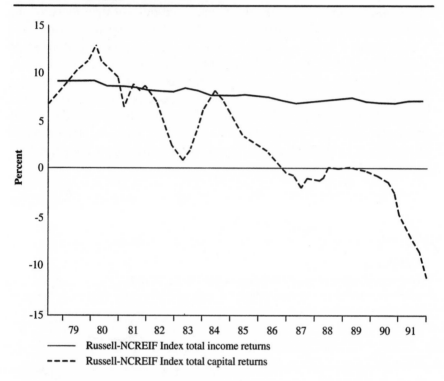

——— Russell-NCREIF Index total income returns

- - - - Russell-NCREIF Index total capital returns

Sources: Russell-NCREIF Property Index and The National Council of Real Estate Investment Fiduciaries.

SUMMARY AND CONCLUSIONS

Real estate as an asset class differs from financial assets in that it must not only provide an efficient risk-adjusted rate of return to the capital markets, but must serve a second role in providing physical space for tenants. Its rent levels are determined by space market conditions, which tend to be more cyclical, while its value as a capital asset is determined in the market for other investable assets with which it competes for funds. It must be priced according to its riskiness relative to other investments.

Because its value is partly determined by interest rate levels, changes in these levels will affect real estate asset values. The relationship between these respective changes is known as the asset's duration, which can be controlled to some degree. Finally, long- and short-run changes in capital and space market conditions will control the supply and demand for real estate both as an asset and a location. The interplay of these factors determines returns from real estate investment. Real estate portfolio managers often are well versed in the space markets, but may lack a thorough understanding of how the capital markets impact real estate. Managers who fail to acknowledge the links between the capital and space markets will both operate and invest at a disadvantage.

CHAPTER 5

REAL ESTATE APPRAISAL

Jeffrey D. Fisher, Ph.D.
Indiana University School of Business.

WHY IS PROPERTY APPRAISED?

Individuals and institutions can invest in stocks and bonds that are publicly traded on an organized exchange where information on the current market value is readily available. In contrast, shares in individual real estate investments do not trade on an organized exchange.[1] Furthermore, because there are a limited number of buyers and sellers in the market at any given point in time, properties sell infrequently. When a property (or an interest in a property)[2] does sell, the price may not be disclosed to the public. This makes it difficult to know how market participants value real estate income property at any given point in time. Even if full information about the transaction price of properties was known, there would be a question as to whether this provides a reliable indication of the value of properties that did not sell. This is because each property is somewhat unique; it is at a slightly different location and may have different physical characteristics and a different lease structure. Furthermore, the character-

---

[1]Shares of real estate investment trusts (REITs) do trade. The price of a REIT, however, represents the value of the portfolio of properties held in the REIT, not a single property. Furthermore, the value of an REIT is affected by the management of the REIT as well as the systematic movement of the stock market.

[2]An example of an interest in a property is a limited partnership interest. There is a very limited market for partial interests in real estate.

istics of properties that investors decide to sell may differ from those of properties that investors decide to hold. For these reasons, the market value of real estate must be estimated by an appraisal process.

The purpose of this chapter is to give readers a general familiarity with the process that appraisers generally use to estimate the market value of real estate income property. The focus is on understanding the key assumptions that the appraiser is making when a particular approach is taken to estimate value. An understanding of these assumptions will contribute to the user's ability to interpret and apply the information in an appraisal. The reader should not expect to be prepared to conduct a professional appraisal based on reading this chapter.

MARKET VALUE

The purpose of most appraisals is to estimate the market value of the property. Market value is defined in the Uniform Standards of Professional Appraisal Practice as follows:[3]

> The most probable price which a property should bring in a competitive and open market under all conditions requisite to a fair sale, the buyer and seller each acting prudently and knowledgeably, and assuming the price is not affected by undue stimulus. Implicit in this definition is the consummation of a sale as of a specified date and the passing of title from seller to buyer under conditions whereby:
>
> 1. Buyer and seller are typically motivated;
> 2. Both parties are well-informed or well-advised, and acting in what they consider their best interests;
> 3. A reasonable time is allowed for exposure in the open market;
> 4. Payment is made in terms of cash in U.S. dollars or in terms of financial arrangements comparable thereto; and
> 5. The price represents the normal consideration for the property sold unaffected by special or creative financing or sales concessions granted by anyone associated with the sale.

Several things should be emphasized from the above definition. First, note that market value assumes a *typical* buyer and seller that are

---

[3]Appraisal Standards Board of the Appraisal Foundation, *Uniform Standards of Professional Appraisal Practice* (Washington, D.C., 1992).

both well informed or well advised. A particular buyer or seller may or may not be typical because of unusual investment motivations or lack of sufficient market information. Thus, market value is not necessarily the same as the value to a particular buyer or seller.[4] Second, market value assumes consummation of a sale as of a specific date. Market value represents a "market clearing price" that would occur if the title were transferred from seller to buyer.

Third, market value assumes that the property is exposed to the market for a "reasonable time." The amount of time that is reasonable varies with property type and market conditions but should not either be unreasonably short or long. If it is assumed that the property must be sold very quickly, the value might reflect that of a forced sale or liquidation value. Alternatively, assuming an unreasonably long marketing time may not result in an estimate of what the property would sell for under current market conditions.

Finally, note that market value assumes that the price is not affected by special or creative financing. This is important because market value represents the value of the real estate. The value of the real estate is not affected by the manner in which a particular transaction is financed. Special or creative financing only changes the way that the value of the real estate is allocated between the debt and equity interests in the property.[5]

INVESTMENT VALUE VERSUS MARKET VALUE

As indicated above, the term *market value* refers to the value of the property to a *typical* investor that is willing to purchase the property at the time of the appraisal. In contrast, the term *investment value* is used to refer to the value of the property to a *particular* investor. Investment value is affected by factors such as the investor's tax status, need for diversification, risk aversion, and other investment motivations. The investment value of a property tends to be influenced by the investor's existing portfo-

---

[4]As discussed later, the value to a particular investor is referred to as *investment value*.

[5]For example, the transactions "price" may be higher if the purchaser assumes a below-market loan from the seller. This premium represents the additional price paid for an equity investment. Because the loan is at a below-market rate, the market value of the loan will be less than its face value. In theory, the lower value of the loan exactly offsets the higher value of the equity. Therefore, the total market value of the property remains constant.

lio. For example, an investor that already has a substantial proportion of his or her portfolio invested in office buildings in Texas may not be willing to pay as much for an additional office building in Texas as an investor who currently owns no office buildings in Texas.

Investment value can differ significantly from market value. For example, an investor may be willing to pay more for a property that is adjacent to his own property because of a need for additional land for expansion. Of course he or she would still attempt to purchase the property at its market value, that is, the price that the typical investor would pay.

The market value of a property is determined by those investors who are willing to enter into a transaction at a given point in time. Real estate markets are very thin and lack liquidity. Thus, sometimes market values are higher than the price that most investors would be willing to pay for the property. An example may be when the Japanese purchased U.S. real estate at a premium over what most U.S. investors were willing to pay. Similarly, market prices can be less than most owners would be willing to accept to sell their properties. This tends to occur in a soft market when there is a shortage of capital for investment in real estate as occurred during the early 1990s.

APPROACHES TO MEASURING VALUE

Because of the inefficiencies in the real estate market and the difficulty in easily obtaining information that indicates market value, appraisers generally have to take several "approaches" to attempt to estimate market value. These approaches are cost, sales comparison, and income. We consider the assumptions and limitations of each.

Cost Approach

The cost approach is based on the premise that the value of the property is equal to the sum of the land value[6] plus the depreciated replacement cost of the building. The economic rationale for the cost approach is that a rational investor would not pay more than the cost of replacing the build-

---

[6]The land value must be estimated by one of the other approaches discussed later.

ing with one that is equally productive on a comparable site. The cost approach can be summarized as follows:

Land value:
+   Replacement cost of building (new).
−   Physical depreciation.
−   Functional obsolescence.
−   External obsolescence.
=   Value of property.

The value found by the cost approach must consider whether there has been physical depreciation in the building (e.g., repairs that need to be done), functional obsolescence of the building (e.g., inadequate or outdated design), and/or external obsolescence (factors external to the property that affect its value). External obsolescence can occur either because a property is no longer (or never was) at an ideal location or because market conditions have changed such that it would not be economically feasible to construct the same building at current rent levels.[7]

There are many factors that make it difficult to apply the cost approach. First, adjustments for physical depreciation, and functional and external obsolescence are hard to measure. Second, consideration must be given to the fact that a developer would not build a building unless an "entrepreneurial profit" could be earned. This profit must be included in the value of a property for the cost approach to make sense. The cost approach also assumes that the buyer can lease the property at current market rents. If there are existing leases on the property that are below market, the estimated value must be lowered to reflect any loss in income.

Sales Comparison Approach

The direct sales comparison approach estimates value by comparing the subject property to other comparable properties that have sold recently. This approach is best used when an adequate number of sales of similar properties exist and data can be retrieved from accurate sources.

---

[7]This latter adjustment is particularly important in soft markets when new construction is not feasible.

The sale price of the comparable properties is adjusted for differences between the comparable property and the property being appraised (subject property). The purpose of the adjustments is to estimate the price at which the comparable property would have sold if it were the same as the subject property. For example, if the comparable property had a better location than the subject property, then, all else being equal, it should have a higher value than the subject property. Thus, the price of the comparable property would have to be adjusted downward to provide an indication of the value of the subject (appraised) property.

The price of each of the comparable properties is often divided by an appropriate *unit of comparison* as a first step in the adjustment process. For example, the price might be divided by the number of square feet of net rentable area in an office building to arrive at a price per square foot. The units used to compare prices differ for different property types.[8] The sale price of comparables must also be adjusted for other factors that would result in a difference in value. Common adjustments include differences in the physical characteristics of the property, differences in location, and any change in market conditions from the time that the comparable property sold.[9]

To estimate the value of the property, a sales adjustment grid is typically created in which elements of comparable properties are adjusted to reflect differences from the subject property. These adjustments can be made through dollar or percentage adjustments. The adjusted sale prices of the comparables will indicate a value for the subject.

When appraisers use the sales comparison approach they usually take a relatively small sample of the market. That is, they tend to use three to five comparables which are adjusted to arrive at the estimated value of the subject property. This is in contrast to using a large sample and statistical techniques such as multiple regression analysis to estimate value. Rather, small samples and "judgment" are used to estimate value.

To illustrate use of the sales comparison approach, information is shown from three office building sales that are similar to the subject property. The effective date of the appraisal is January 1, 1993. The subject building has the following characteristics.

---

[8]Examples of other units of comparison include price per room for apartments, price per cubic foot for warehouse space, and price per front foot for land.

[9]As suggested earlier, the price of the comparable would also have to be adjusted if it included a premium for special financing.

Subject Property

Net building area	42,000 sq. ft.
Age of building	3 years

Comparable Office Building Sales

Property number	One	Two	Three
Date of sale	5/92	10/90	12/92
Age	1 year	4 years	10 years
Location	Better	Same	Worse
Net building area	$3,000,000	$3,500,000	$6,000,000

The sales adjustment grid indicates differences between the comparable properties (comps) and the property being appraised (subject) that require adjustment. In this case the differences are due to differences in market conditions on the date of sale, age, location and net building area. As a first step in the adjustment process, the price of each comparable is divided by the net building area to arrive at a price per square foot (see table below):

Unit of Comparison

Property number	One	Two	Three
Price/sq. ft.	$100.00	$87.50	$75.00

Next, adjustments are made for the other differences. This is based on the appraiser's judgment as to how the differences would affect the value.[10] Recall that the purpose of the adjustment is to estimate what the comparable would have sold for, if it did not differ from the subject property. For example, comparable property number one has a better location. The appraiser has estimated that the comparable would have sold for 5 percent less if it were at the same location as the subject property. Thus the comparable price is lowered by 5 percent for the difference in location. Similarly, adjustments are made for each of the other differences to arrive at an adjusted price per square foot for each of the comparable sales. This is summarized in the following grid:

---

[10] If sufficient data were available, statistical techniques such as multiple regression analysis could also be used to determine the amount of adjustment.

Property Number	One	Two	Three
Price per sq. ft.	$100.00	$87.50	$75.00
Market conditions	+2%	+4%	0%
Location	−5	0	+5
Effective age	−4	+0	+5
Total adjustment	−7	+4	+20

The adjusted sale prices indicate a price per square foot for the subject property in the range of $90 to $93 per square foot.[11] Suppose the appraiser selects $91 as the best estimate.[12] The value of the subject property is now estimated as follows:

$$42,000 \text{ sq. ft.} \times \$91 \text{ per sq. ft.} = \$3,822,000$$

Income Approach

The income approach is based on the income potential of the property. The idea is to determine what the typical investor would be willing to pay for the stream of income that is expected from the property. Appraisers usually analyze the income on a before-tax basis. Of course, the before-tax discount rate used to value the income implicitly reflects any expected tax benefits. That is, if one knows that there will be tax benefits, a higher price can be paid for the property, resulting in a lower before-tax yield.

The appraiser must estimate income for the subject property by considering the market rent for comparable space as well as the impact of any existing leases on the property. The appraiser must also determine what the typical expenses should be for the given type of property. There are many ways of applying the income approach. The most common are discussed below.

---

[11]If markets were perfect and sufficient information were available on each of the properties, the adjusted sale prices might be exactly the same. In practice it is impossible to account for every factor that might result in a difference in sale price.

[12]Rather than simply average the numbers, the appraiser may rely more on property number two which is more similar to the subject property and has a price per square foot within this range.

MARKET-DERIVED CAPITALIZATION RATES

One way of applying the income approach to appraise a property is to use a capitalization rate obtained from comparable sales. The capitalization rate is found by dividing the net operating income (NOI) from the property by its sale price. That is:

$$\text{Cap rate} = \text{NOI} / \text{Sale price}$$

where

Cap rate is the capitalization rate

NOI is the Net operating income

This rate can then be used to appraise the subject property as follows:

$$\text{Value} = \text{NOI} / \text{Cap rate}$$

Used in the manner described above, valuation with overall capitalization rates can really be viewed as a "sales comparison approach." The NOI that is used is the NOI for the first year after the property is assumed to be purchased. The cap rate is usually calculated for several comparable sales. For example, suppose that the following additional information is calculated for the same example as considered above:

	Subject Property		
NOI	$380,000		

Comparable Office Building Sales			
Property Number	One	Two	Three
NOI (first year)	$290,000	$350,000	$620,000
Sale price	$3,000,000	$3,500,000	$6,000,000
Cap rate	9.67%	10%	10.33%

Using the above information, we might select a cap rate of 10 percent for the subject property. This results in an estimated value of $380,000/ 0.10 or $3,800,000. This is about the same answer as was found using the sales comparison approach.

The advantage of this approach is that it is relatively simple to apply. No forecasting of future income is necessary. One of the disadvantages is that often it is difficult to find truly comparable sales. Any differences between the comparable and subject property can cause significant differences in the capitalization rate.

Capitalization (cap) rates are analogous to the reciprocal of price-earnings (P/E) ratios as reported for stocks. That is, they relate the value of the investment to *current* income. Cap rates will differ for investments if the expectation for *future* earnings differs even though current earnings may be the same for the two investments. Just as "growth stocks" have higher P/E ratios, real estate with expectations of higher future income and increasing property values will have lower cap rates.

Because cap rates rely on a single (first-year) NOI, it is important that this rate be consistent with first-year NOIs for the comparable properties from which the overall rate was derived. It is difficult to compare cap rates for investments that will have different future income due to differences in the expected growth in the district or neighborhood where the property is located or simply differences in the leases on the property. Thus, to properly use a market derived cap rate, we must select comparable properties that have similar expectations for future NOI. Using cap rates to compare properties implicitly assumes that the trend in future NOI will be the same for the subject as for the comparable. Because cap rates are based on the first-year NOI, they are also easily distorted by any concessions such as free rent that may show up in the NOI during the first year of the lease.

As a final note about market derived cap rates, we must keep in mind that they are based on historical sales. Ideally, those sales were very recent, which by real estate standards might be within a few months. But clearly markets can change dramatically over a few months if not a few weeks or even a few days. The fact that we do not observe rapid changes in real estate prices, because of the lack of transactions for the same property, does not mean factors affecting value have not changed just as stock prices change daily.

Capitalization Rate Formulas

Another approach to obtaining cap rates is through the use of a formula rather than deriving the cap rate from comparable sales. The cap rate formula expresses the cap rate as a function of the discount rate required by investors and some measure of expected growth in the property's income and resale value. These formulas can be thought of as short-cut formulas for finding the present value of the estimated future cash flows (discounted cash flow analysis).

One common formula states the cap rate as follows:

$$\text{Cap rate} = \text{Discount rate} - \text{Growth rate}$$

where the discount rate is the rate required by investors over the investment holding period and the growth rate is the expected compound rate of growth for income and property value. The property value would be estimated by dividing the first-year NOI by the cap rate. Thus we have

$$\text{Value} = \text{NOI} / (\text{Discount rate} - \text{Growth rate})$$

This formula is analogous to a dividend growth model used for valuing stock. Note again that cap rates are applied to the first-year NOI and thus suffer from the same problems outlined above. This particular formula only works if income and property value are both assumed to be increasing at the same compound rate each year.

To illustrate, recall that the property in the previous example was expected to produce net operating income of $380,000 during the first year. Assume that the existing improvements are expected to have an economic life of at least 75 years. During this time period, the income is expected to increase by an average of 3 percent per year. Assume that a 13 percent investment yield (discount rate) would be necessary to attract an investor to the building.

Due to the long economic life of the building, we can consider the income to be a perpetuity. That is, we can assume that the income will increase by 3 percent per year forever.[13] The present value of an income stream that is increasing at a compound growth rate (g) as a perpetuity is found as follows:

$$V = \frac{\text{NOI}}{r - g}$$

where

V = Present value of the income stream
NOI = the first-year income (NOI)
g = annual growth in income
r = discount rate for present value

---

[13]Although the existing improvements will obviously not last forever, the land will continue to produce income after the existing improvements have been demolished or substantially renovated. Thus, we are assuming that income from the land and/or the building would continue forever. Even if the income decreases substantially after the 75-year economic life of the existing building, the effect on the value we are estimating would be very small because the present value of income received after 75 years is quite small. Thus, whether the income actually continues beyond 75 years or not is practically irrelevant.

or

$$V = \frac{380,000}{.13 - .03}$$

$$V = 380,000/.10 = \$3,800,000$$

Thus, the estimated value of the property is \$3,800,000. This is the price that would result in an expected rate of return of 13 percent over the economic life of the property. It is obviously the same answer as when a 10 percent capitalization rate was found by analyzing comparable sales. There is a conceptual difference, however, in the way that the capitalization rate was determined. In this example, the capitalization rate was based on an explicit assumption about the required discount rate and the expected change in income after the first year. When the capitalization rate is derived from comparable sales, the discount rate and growth rate is implicit.

Holding Period

In the example given previously, we calculated the present value of the income stream over the entire economic life of the property, which was assumed to be at least 75 years. In practice, investors typically hold properties for a holding period that is much shorter than the economic life of the property.[14] Thus, we may want to estimate the value of the property by estimating the cash flow that would be received by an investor over a typical holding period. This should not change the estimated value of the property, however, because the value still depends on its income potential over its entire economic life.

To illustrate, assume that an investor wanted to purchase the property discussed in the previous example with the expectation of selling it after a five-year holding period. In this case the investor would receive the income for five years and at the end of the fifth year the investor would receive cash flow from sale of the property. How much should the investor expect to receive when it is sold? This depends on what the next investor would be willing to pay. The next investor would begin receiving income in year 6. By that time, the income is projected to be \$440,524.[15] This income from year 6 forward is also a perpetuity. Assuming that this inves-

---

[14] The property obviously must be sold subject to any existing leases that extend beyond the holding period.

[15] \$380,000 x $(1.03)^5$ = \$440,524.

tor expects the same discount rate (r) and growth rate (g) the value at the end of year five can be estimated as follows:[16]

$$V = \frac{440,524}{.13 - .03}$$

$$V = 440,524/.10 = \$4,405,240$$

We can now estimate the value of the property by estimating the cash flows over the five-year holding period as follows:

Year	Cash Flow
1	$380,000
2	391,400
3	403,142
4	415,236
5	427,693 + 4,405,240 = 4,832,933

Discounting the above cash flows at 13 percent results in a present value of $3,800,000. As expected, this is exactly the same answer as found when discounting the income over the entire life of the property. This is because the expected resale price includes the present value of the benefits for the remaining economic life. As a result, instead of forecasting cash flows over the entire economic life, we can use a shorter holding period based on the assumption that the sale price reflects the present value of cash flows from that point until the end of a property's economic life.

VALUATION OF A LEASED FEE ESTATE

In the office building valuation example above it was assumed that the property was not encumbered by any existing leases and that it could be leased at a market rate. Thus, the value would be considered an estimate

---

[16]Note that the capitalization rate used to calculate the resale price is still assumed to be 10 percent in this case. A different rate could be used if the discount rate and/or the growth rate is expected to differ at the end of the holding period. The term *terminal capitalization rate* is often used to refer to a capitalization rate that is used to estimate the resale price.

of the value of a "fee simple estate."[17] Properties are often purchased subject to existing leases and the terms in these leases must be honored by the investor. In these cases, "leased fee" estates are acquired by investors. The existing leases may have above- or below-market rental rates which impact the value of the leased fee estate.

To illustrate, assume that the property evaluated in the previous example has an existing net lease with a remaining term of five years at a flat rate of only $300,000 per year. We would expect the value to be lower because the rents will be less for the first five years. The value at the end of the five-year lease term should not be lower, however, because the property may be leased at the market rate at that time. That is, the income for the remaining economic life of the property should be the same as if it had not been encumbered by the below-market lease. Thus, the resale price would be $4,405,240 as for the fee simple value estimate made earlier.

We can now estimate the value of the leased fee estate as the present value of $300,000 per year NOI plus the present value of the estimated value at the end of the lease of $4,405,240. It may not be appropriate, however, to use the same 13 percent discount rate as was used to estimate the value of the fee simple estate because the leased fee estate may be considered more or less risky than a fee simple estate. This depends in part on the creditworthiness of the tenant. The lease represents a contract between the lessor and the lessee. The riskiness of the NOI collected during the term of the lease is dependent on the riskiness of this financial contract. Of course, if the tenant defaults, the owner has the right to attempt to lease the property to someone else at the market rate. The point is that by leasing the property some of the risk of owning the property and collecting current market rents is exchanged for the risk of collecting on the lease contract. Because the existing lease is at a below-market rate, it is less likely that there will be default on the lease, especially if the property could be subleased. Furthermore, it is more likely that the owner could lease the property at a rate that is higher than it is currently leased rather than lower. Thus a discount rate slightly lower than 13 percent might be justified. We will assume that a 12.5 percent discount rate is appropriate. The value of the leased fee estate would therefore be $3,512,766.

In this case, the difference between the value of the fee simple estate ($3,800,000) and the value of the leased fee estate ($3,512,766) should

---

[17]Recall the discussion of the various types of estates in Chapter 2.

reflect the value of the "leasehold estate," which is $287,234. That is, the below-market lease results in the value of the fee simple estate being divided among the leasehold and leased fee interests.[18]

A capitalization rate for the leased fee estate can be calculated by dividing the first-year income of $300,000 by the estimated value of $3,512,766. The answer is 8.54 percent. Note that this is lower than the 10 percent capitalization rate for the fee simple estate. This occurs because the existing leases have more of an impact on the first-year income than they do on the value of the leased fee estate. Because income is expected to increase significantly after the existing leases expire, investors can accept a lower capitalization rate based on the first-year income. It is important to realize that existing leases can have a significant impact on capitalization rates. This is especially important when capitalization rates are obtained from comparable sales illustrated earlier.

Discounted Cash Flow

With the availability of personal computers, spreadsheets, and a variety of software for real estate valuation, appraisers can now do a much better job of attempting to capture investor motivations in the valuation process. That is, they can attempt to analyze the cash flows in the same way that the typical investor would, rather than use oversimplified formulas as previously described. When income is projected and then discounted to arrive at a value estimate, this is referred to as *discounted cash flow analysis* (DCF). Actually, short-cut formulas that express cap rates in terms of discount rates and income growth rates are also in the family of discounted cash flow analyses, but most appraisers have not thought of it that way. Thus, the perception is that DCF is something new. However, all that is new is an attempt to more carefully capture the nature of the income and expenses for the property. This is especially important for leased fee valuation due to the great impact that the specific lease provisions can have on the value of the property.

In general, DCF considers the following:

---

[18]It is sometimes argued that the value of the leased fee estate plus the value of the leasehold estate may not add to the value of the fee simple estate. One reason is that the typical purchaser of a leasehold estate would be a tenant whereas the typical purchaser of a leased fee estate would be an investor.

- Income projected on a lease-by-lease basis.
- Expenses projected by expense type.
- Lease renewals at the market rate.
- Leasing commissions.
- Vacancy based on market conditions at time of lease renewal.
- Estimated resale price.
- Tenant improvements.
- Free rent and other concessions.
- Financing (if desired).
- The impact of taxes (if desired).

It should be noted that whereas DCF does not solve directly for a cap rate, the capitalization rate is implicit in any DCF analysis. That is, once the present value of the cash flows is determined, the resulting value can be divided into the first-year NOI to arrive at the implied cap rate. This cap rate can then be compared with rates obtained from comparable sales (if comparable sales data is available).

The advantage of DCF is that it reflects the way investors make decisions. The resulting value estimate is a market value estimate as long as the analysis is done from the point of view of the typical investor. If the projections are for a specific investor that is not typical, then the result is investment value.

Appraisers sometimes argue that a disadvantage of DCF is that it relies on the projection of the future cash flows. But if investors purchase properties on the basis of expected future cash flows, it is difficult to believe that a reliable estimate of value can be made without making these projections. Appraisers may believe that using market derived capitalization rates from comparable properties does not require forecasting. But as emphasized earlier, to say that comparables (comps) really are comparable to the subject property, the appraiser must implicitly consider whether the future income will be the same for the comps as that of the subject property. Otherwise we know the capitalization rates must differ.

Discounted cash flow has been misused, however, by appraisers who make oversimplifying assumptions when projecting cash flows. During the early 1980s, for example, it was common for appraisers to assume that rental rates and property values would continue to increase at the same rate each year even though markets were becoming rapidly overbuilt, the demand for space was falling, and vacancy rates were rising. That is, appraisers did not consider how the fundamental forces of supply and demand were changing.[19] To be valid, DCF must take into consideration how expected changes in the supply and demand for space will affect rental rates, vacancy rates, and consequently changes in income and property value over a typical investment holding period. Real estate markets are cyclical and appraisers cannot simply assume that past trends will continue. The starting point of a DCF must be a careful analysis of future trends in real estate market fundamentals.

Use of DCF also requires careful selection of a discount rate. One problem with real estate analysis is that we cannot directly observe the yield that investors are expecting on real estate investments. In the case of investments such as bonds, we know the face value and therefore can determine yields from observed purchase prices. For real estate we don't necessarily know what the typical investor had in mind for a resale price. However, we can use several approaches to arrive at a reasonable discount rate. First of all, the discount rate for a free and clear (unlevered) real estate investment should normally be higher than that for a mortgage on the same property due to the additional business risk. To the extent that the property is levered, then equity yield rates would be even higher.

Second, there are numerous surveys done to determine typical yield requirements.[20] This provides an additional way to select a reasonable discount rate.

Third, there are also ways to use comparable sales to help select a discount rate that is consistent with what market participants are projecting for increases in income and property values.[21] Appraisers must be careful, however, to consider how the riskiness of the subject property may differ from the risk of comparables. Differences in risk must be considered when selecting a discount rate. For example, income from existing leases may be considered less risky than income expected from lease renewals or rental of vacant space. If a single rate is used to discount cash flows, the rate must, therefore, consider how these leases affect the overall riskiness of the projected cash flows. Alternatively, different discount

---

[19]Investors were just as guilty of making unrealistic projections, which put pressure on the appraiser to replicate the same assumptions that investors were using.

[20]For example, see the *Real Estate Report* published quarterly by Real Estate Research Corporation, Chicago.

[21] See *The Appraisal of Real Estate*, 9th ed. (Chicago: American Institute of Real Estate Appraisers, 1987), p. 534, for further discussion.

rates might be used to discount different components of the cash flows such as the expected cash flow from existing leases, the expected cash flows from lease renewals, and the expected cash flow from resale of the property.

Mortgage-Equity Capitalization

In the above discussion value was found by discounting the NOI and resale proceeds for the property. The discount rate chosen was so called a "free and clear" discount rate, that is, it did not consider whether the property was to be financed (e.g., how much debt versus equity was used). In effect, we discounted the entire income available from the property as though the investor paid cash for the entire purchase price. We did not consider the possibility of financing and how that income may be split among holders of debt (mortgage lenders) and equity investors. When considering financing, the discount rate used to value a property subject to debt must be consistent with this assumption (e.g., it must reflect rates of return expected on both the debt and on equity invested), that must reflect the *risk* associated with financial leverage. We now discuss how the value of a property can be estimated by explicitly taking into consideration the requirements of the mortgage lender and equity investor—hence the term *mortgage-equity capitalization.*

This method for estimating value is based on the concept that total value (*V*) must be equal to the present value of expected mortgage financing (*M*) and the present value of equity investment (*E*) made by investors. That is,

$$V = M + E$$

To illustrate, suppose that the property considered earlier is expected to be financed with a loan that is based on a 1.2 debt coverage ratio (DCR) applied to the first-year NOI of $380,000. The loan will have an 11 percent interest rate and will be amortized over 20 years with monthly payments.[22] The investor expects to hold the property for five years. As assumed earlier, the NOI is expected to increase 3 percent per year after the first year and the resale price is estimated by applying a 10

---

[22] Financing for real estate income property is frequently based on a target first-year debt coverage ratio.

percent terminal capitalization rate to the sixth year NOI. Investors require a 16.5 percent rate of return on equity (yield rate) for this type of property.[23]

First determine the annual debt service (DS) as:

$$DS = NOI/DCR$$

$$DS = 380,000/1.2 = 316,667$$

This implies a monthly mortgage payment of $316,667/12 = $26,389. The amount of mortgage can be found by discounting the monthly payments at the mortgage rate of 11 percent over the 20-year term.[24] This is the value of the mortgage (M) assuming that 11 percent is the current market rate for the mortgage. The loan amount is $2,556,596.

Project the cash flows over a five-year holding period as follows:

Operating years:

Year	1	2	3	4	5
NOI	380,000	391,400	403,142	415,236	427,693
DS	316,667	316,667	316,667	316,667	316,667
Cash flow	63,333	74,733	86,475	98,569	111,026
Resale:					
Resale in year 5					4,405,241
Less mortgage balance					2,321,746
Cash flow					2,083,495
Total cash flow	63,333	74,733	86,475	98,569	2,194,521

The present value of the above cash flows at a 16.5 percent discount rate is $1,240,237. This represents the value of the equity investors interest in the property (E). The total property value (V) can now be found by summing the value of the mortgage (M) and the value of the equity (E). We have

---

[23]Note that the discount rate is now higher than that used to value the property before financing was considered. The higher rate (16.5 percent versus 13 percent) reflects the additional financial risk to the equity investor.

[24]The present value must be calculated using *monthly* discounting for a 20-year (240 month) mortgage with an 11 percent (11%/12 or 0.9167% per month) interest rate.

$$V = M + E$$
$$V = \$2,556,596 + \$1,240,237$$
$$V = \$3,796,833$$

This is about the same answer as found before ($3,800,000) when the entire NOI was discounted at a 13 percent rate. In theory the answer should be the same because financing does not create value.

CONCLUSIONS ABOUT THREE APPROACHES TO MEASURING VALUE

In theory, in a perfect market, all approaches to estimating value should give the same answer if markets are in equilibrium. In practice, real estate markets are seldom in balance. Even if prices did conform to what would be expected in an efficient market, appraisers (and academics) simply do not have the information necessary to measure (empirically test) that efficiency. Thus, in reality one would be suspicious if an appraiser indicated that all three approaches to estimating value resulted in the exact same answer!

Because all three approaches will not likely give the same answer, it is useful to use all the approaches as separate indications of the value of the property. Depending on the availability of data and the type of property being valued, one approach may be more reliable than another. For example, when appraising apartment buildings in a market where there are a lot of sales of relatively similar apartment buildings in the same area of a similar age and design, and so on, the sales comparison approach might provide the best indication of value. Because apartments typically do not have long-term leases, knowing the rent roll for the building is not as critical as for properties such as office buildings.

If the property right to be appraised is a leasehold estate which depends on the difference between market and contract rents over the lease term, an income approach may be all that can be used. There are not likely to be sales of other leasehold estates that are comparable (same lease provisions, length of leases, and so on) so that a sales comparison approach can be used. Similarly, the cost approach would not be applicable. The appraiser might value the leased fee and fee simple estates separately (perhaps using all three approaches) and then back into the value of the leasehold by subtracting the leased fee value from the fee simple value. However, this can be misleading for the reasons cited earlier under the discussion of leasehold estates.

This chapter discussed the nature of the appraisal process with emphasis on how an appraiser attempts to estimate market value. We saw that there are many assumptions that must be made in order to properly estimate market value. Yet, due to the nature of real estate markets this process is necessary. There is not a sufficient amount of public information about property transactions, nor a sufficient number of sales of the same or similar properties, to adequately judge market values without the use of an appraisal process. Furthermore, the inefficiency of the real estate market requires appraisers to use several approaches to attempt to estimate value.

CHAPTER 6

REAL ESTATE PORTFOLIO MANAGEMENT

PART I—FINANCIAL THEORY REPLACES ANECDOTE*

Charles H. Wurtzebach

INTRODUCTION

Institutional investors have long employed portfolio strategies to set targeted risk and return parameters for their financial asset investments. Financial theory suggests, and financial investment managers have learned, that strategies established at the portfolio level have more of an impact on portfolio performance than does the skill with which individual securities are selected. The purpose of this chapter is to present one view of the evolution of the application of financial theory to real estate which occurred during the 1980s. It is intended as an introduction to Parts II and III of this chapter which detail how a specific portfolio level strategy was successfully implemented by a large, open-ended commingled equity real estate portfolio, and that presents a "stylized" portfolio analysis using a slightly different technique.

---

*The first presentation of many of the ideas in this chapter appeared in Paul B. Firstenberg and Charles H. Wurtzebach, "The Portfolio Construction Process: The Competitive Edge in Managing Real Estate Portfolios," *Managing Institutional Assets*, ed. Frank J. Fabozzi (New York: Harper & Row, 1990).

PRIVATE MARKET INVESTMENT AND PORTFOLIO STRATEGY

Unlike their colleagues in the securities market, real estate investors and their managers have been slow to adopt portfolio strategies based on financial theory. This, in part, reflects the nature of the real estate market. Most institutionally owned real estate is traded in the private market. Entrepreneurs believe that this market offers inefficiencies which can be exploited legally. In particular, information costs are much higher in private markets. Most investors have operated on the assumption that accessing such "inside" information and trading on it through expert intermediaries (i.e., real estate investment managers) will result in higher risk-adjusted returns.[1] However, trading on "inside information" requres a deal-by-deal strategy dictated by the nature of the information and does not logically lead to the development of market-driven portfolio strategies. In fact, modern portfolio theory (MPT) assumes that performance cannot be enhanced by accessing information not available to the market at large. Thus, private market trading, if it in fact delivers higher risk-adjusted returns, may not be consistent with the notion of *portfolio* strategy. However, as Table 6–1 shows, since the early 1980s the performance of equity real estate did not generally deliver returns competitive with financial assets. This suggests that the expected performance benefits of private market trading have not been delivered.

TRADITIONAL REAL ESTATE PORTFOLIO MANAGEMENT

By contrast with recent experience, from 1970 to the early 1980s, real estate did tend to provide very attractive risk-adjusted returns when compared to other financial assets. During this period, institutional real estate investment strategies did not incorporate much in the way of financial theory. Instead, real estate investment managers tended to rely on anecdote rather than financial theory and rigorous research. This approach continued despite a growing body of evidence suggesting that portfolio strate-

---

[1]This varies dramatically from a public market where trading on "inside information" is illegal.

TABLE 6–1
Real Estate Performance versus Financial Assets (Nominal
Total Returns)
(Year-end 12/31/92)

	Year				
	1	3	5	7	10
RUSSELL-NCREIF	−5.0	−3.3	0.6	2.1	5.0
S&P 500	7.7	10.8	15.8	14.6	16.0
3-month T bills	3.6	5.7	6.5	6.4	7.1
Bonds*	7.6	10.6	10.7	10.1	11.5

*Source: Lehman Brothers Gov't./Corp. Bond Index.

gies pay off in managing portfolio risk and return, and despite indications that the fortunes of the real estate investor were about to turn.

Reliance on anecdotal evidence and the search for exploitable inefficiencies resulted in real estate portfolios built one transaction at a time. The prevailing view was that attractive portfolio performance was assured as long as a manager assembled a group of "good deals" in one portfolio. In the 1980s, real estate portfolio performance clearly revealed the weakness in this deal by deal portfolio construction approach. For example, in 1980, if a manager invested in a downtown office building in Houston and one in Denver, little thought was given to the implications of investing in two economies dominated by energy-related activity. In fact, the acquisition officer might well have received important notoriety from completing the "best deal" that year. But, as history clearly shows, an aggregation of best deals can easily turn into a portfolio laden with underperforming assets. This is exactly what happened to numerous pension fund portfolios concentrated in downtown and suburban office buildings located in so-called growth economies. Investors discovered that if they had invested 50 percent to 60 percent of their portfolio in offices, the performance of the nonoffice component of their portfolio was insufficient to overcome the poor performance in the office sector. It became obvious, as performance faltered, that portfolio-level decisions affect returns and that the selection of the correct combination of assets at the portfolio level can materially affect portfolio performance.

Nonetheless, most portfolio managers continued to give little consideration to how individual assets interact within a multiproperty portfolio.

In the absence of a formal portfolio strategy, acquisitions tended to be lined up in the order in which they were discovered. Portfolio managers did not direct acquisition officers toward specific property types or markets based on a fully developed portfolio strategy. In addition, little thought was given to the impact of adding an additional property to an existing portfolio let alone as to how a current acquisition might affect the desired characteristics of future acquisitions, or the ultimate portfolio configuration. By contrast, if a well-developed portfolio strategy is in place, it directs the sequence of asset acquisitions and the level of activity of the real estate acquisition professionals. As individual acquisitions are completed, the universe of possible future acquisitions narrows and may require a stricter acquisition sourcing and transaction selection.

Strategy and Institutional Investor Participation

As portfolio performance continued to decline through the late 1980s, and investors found that they could not exit the asset class due to the illiquidity of the private market, interest in portfolio strategy grew. Institutional investors began to ask their real estate managers hard questions about how investment decisions were made regarding the selection of assets for their portfolios. Unfortunately, acquisition professionals did not have the answers. While institutions were using a strategic approach to managing their multiasset portfolios—in fact, allocation studies were the basis for the decision to include real estate in their holdings—they discovered that once the decision to invest in real estate had been made, no plan had been developed to monitor the real estate investment process. Fee managers essentially were given full discretion to determine how real estate would be acquired, managed, and ultimately sold. These managers, in turn, did not tend to develop portfolio strategies that recognized the importance of diversification within a real estate portfolio or that recognized investor portfolio goals and objectives. Instead managers proceeded to invest in real estate as if it were a homogeneous asset class, making little distinction within the portfolio between property types or locations. Furthermore, while many institutions hired several managers to implement a portfolio strategy expecting that individual managers would exhibit different investment styles, they found little difference in what was actually bought. Consequently, many plans ended up with real estate portfolios highly concentrated by property type and location.

Performance Targeting

As performance continued to decline, institutional investors increasingly requested that their managers develop a portfolio strategy for their real estate assets. The creation of portfolio strategies requires the explicit recognition of investor goals and objectives, generally expressed in terms of minimum targeted rates of return (real or nominal). Once a return target is established for a portfolio, the goal for the manager is to deliver the targeted return accompanied by the lowest possible portfolio risk. Portfolio risk is typically expressed as the standard deviation of the portfolio total return. In essence, pension investors seek targeted rates of return with minimum variability. This approach requires that the investor and the investor's manager agree on the portfolio performance objectives and on an acquisition strategy to achieve those goals.

An investor-driven approach to real estate acquisitions and portfolio management represents a significant departure from how real estate investment opportunities traditionally have been presented to institutional investors. Throughout the 1970s and most of the 1980s, real estate investment managers brought real estate opportunities to institutions based primarily on the *managers'* investment criteria. Opportunities were presented in the form of either open- or closed-end commingled funds, generally in blind pools where investors had no discretion regarding the selection of properties for acquisition. While investment managers convinced investors that the ultimate portfolio would have certain characteristics, the responsibility for determining if the fund met the investor's portfolio diversification needs rested with the investor, not the manager. It should be noted that few institutional investors directed managers to acquire specific property types in specific locations or markets, although they often selected managers based on their property-type specialization. In addition, investors discovered that once they decided to invest they were in essence "locked-in" to the vehicle for an extended investment horizon. While this seemed reasonable at the outset, as real estate markets weakened and performance declined, many investors found they could not exit the vehicles. During the late 1980s, many investors could only watch as the value of their real estate portfolios declined.

Movement toward the use of detailed portfolio strategies materially changed the manager-investor relationship. Complete discretion began to disappear as larger funds moved toward separate accounts and new commingled funds established investor advisory boards that provided the manager with input throughout the investment, asset management, and disposition process.

Strategy and Individual Investor Participation

In Chapters 1 and 2, we described the individual investor's flow of funds into the vehicles available for their participation. These vehicles generally provided a means for smaller individual investors to become involved in real estate assets. That is where the difference between the large institutional investor and the small individual investor ends. The portfolio strategy discipline was exactly the same for small investor vehicles—as for the larger players, it was nonexistent. Portfolios were constructed deal by deal, more in concert with the desires of the investment manager, or general partner, than for most of the investors. As more rigor is applied at the institutional level, the individual investor should begin to see more discipline applied to the vehicles (real estate investment trusts and limited partnerships) available for his or her consideration as well.

Strategy Execution

The move toward applying portfolio strategies to real estate necessitated important changes in the way investment managers carried out their business, particularly regarding the transaction or execution side. Acquisition officers have traditionally focused on finding investment opportunities and executing deals. They tend to view the notion of a portfolio strategy-driven acquisition process as an invasion of their "turf," at least initially. After all, they know where the good deals are! This tension between the development of a portfolio plan and its execution challenges the traditional roles of acquisition officers and portfolio managers.

As the real estate investment management business grew during the 1970s, the successful acquisition officer was generally viewed as the "star" within most firms. After all, income was generated as acquisitions were completed since most manager fees were tied to invested capital. This meant that the acquisition side of the business attracted high-profile, production-oriented professionals who closed the deals. Consequently, as management firms grew, successful acquisition officers were promoted to positions of great importance within the firm. While other important functions were not ignored, recognition of the contributions of asset and property management did not come close to that of the acquisition officer within the culture of most investment management firms. Consequently, as investment management firms grew, successful acquisition officers were promoted to positions of great importance within the firm. Understandably, as institutional investors demanded a portfolio approach to sourcing new properties, acquisitions officers were confused and generally felt threatened.

Dissenters from this view will point out that in fact real estate investment managers have long employed portfolio strategies. Many commingled funds and partnerships did indeed target investments by property types or regions. However, they did not select the targets based on a portfolio's prespecified goals for its risk/return profile. Financial theory suggests that managing the relationship between risk and return is the key to investment success. Targeting a particular property type or geographic location without specifying a risk and return target is not a true financial strategy but an investment process based on anecdotal evidence.

Strategy and Risk-Return Relationships

Until the late 1980s, real estate investors typically ignored the critical relationship between the level of portfolio return and its risk or variability. There was a presumption that the inefficiency of the market all but obliterated the laws of finance. In addition, the varying preferences of institutional investors regarding acceptable levels of portfolio risk and return were rarely considered explicitly. Most of the time, investors discussed expected return at the property level without considering a property's impact on portfolio return. Risk, if addressed at all, was presented as a normative not an objective concept. The notion of off setting risks was not explored. For example, it was quite unusual for an investment manager to discuss the expected standard deviation of an individual property, let alone an entire portfolio. This implied that differences in risk did not exist in a measurable way. At best, return variability was reflected in the pro forma expected performance. However, a truthful real estate analyst will now admit that rent and expense projections were driven by inflation expectations, not by extensive property analysis and market research. Little attention was paid to the reasonableness of rent forecasts. For example, acquisition analysis rarely evaluated the need for tenant increases in sales or fees in order to justify paying ever-increasing rents. Further evidence of this practice of ignoring variation in risk comes in appraisal reports, where the difference between discount rates used to value properties in separate urban areas is minimal.

As a result, real estate investors have generally been hard pressed to explain their investment strategies in terms of financial theory. Some investors attempt to explain risk by referring to property type, financial structuring, geographic region, or market size. But it is rare to find these sources of risk described quantitatively.

The poor performance of most real estate portfolios during the past 10 years, especially when viewed on a risk-adjusted basis, has clearly demonstrated that real estate portfolios are subject to both systematic and unsystematic, or diversifiable risk. Accordingly, investors have become increasingly concerned with structuring portfolios to manage the trade-offs between real estate portfolio risk and return.

Applying Financial Theory of Real Estate Portfolios

Strategies can be designed at the portfolio level to manage a pool of real estate holdings to meet an investor's risk-return preferences. In fact, portfolio management techniques which have been successful in the financial markets are also applicable to real estate portfolios. Zerbst and Cambon[2] and Sirmans and Sirmans[3] present excellent reviews of the early research in this area. More recent empirical work in this area has been completed by Hartzell, Hekman, and Miles,[4] and Hartzell, Shulman, and Wurtzebach.[5] The latter article compared the traditional diversification by four regions approach to a more economically oriented eight-region analysis. Based on historical performance data, these studies suggest that the overall performance (risk and return) of real estate portfolios can be improved by employing specific portfolio strategies.

In 1986, the Prudential Realty Group established an Investment Research team to explore ways financial theory could be applied to real

---

[2]Robert H. Zerbst and Barbara R. Cambon, "Historical Returns on Real Estate Investment," *The Journal of Portfolio Management* 10, no. 3 (Spring 1984), pp. 5–20.

[3]G. Stacy Sirmans and C. F. Sirmans, "The Historical Perspective of Real Estate Returns," *The Journal of Portfolio Management* 13, no. 3 (Spring 1987), pp. 22–31.

[4]David J. Hartzell, John S. Hekman, and Mike Miles, "Diversification Categories in Investment Real Estate," *AREUEA Journal* (Summer 1986).

[5]David J. Hartzell, David Shulman, and Charles H. Wurtzebach, "Refining the Analysis of Regional Diversification for Income-Producing Real Estate," *The Journal of Real Estate Research* 2, no. 2 (Winter 1987), pp. 85–95.

estate portfolios. Prudential's primary pension product, the Prudential Real Estate Investment Separate Account (PRISA), introduced in 1971, had long been considered the standard within the industry. However, by the mid-1980s, PRISA's performance had deteriorated and investor confidence had waned, largely because significant investment bets had been made in the office sector and the "energy belt." An empirically based research effort was needed to address the issue of real estate investment strategy in a theoretically rigorous manner.

Since its inception in 1971, PRISA had pursued what was thought to be a diversified investment strategy. Supporting empirical evidence did not exist at the time, so PRISA's initial diversification strategy targeted five major property types: office, industrial, apartment, retail, and hotel, and four broad geographic regions: East, Midwest, South, and West. While the property-type distinctions were fairly clear-cut, the regional distinctions were less clear. Regional distinctions were made on the basis of state boundaries and were *not* specifically developed to represent differences in commercial real estate markets. Specific target weights for each of the categories were not developed; the approach was to invest in quality real estate while monitoring diversification to see to it that the invested dollars were allocated across the property types and regions. This amounted to naïve diversification at best (i.e., it is better to allocate across some criteria than not). While the intent was clearly to develop an institutional-quality real estate portfolio, expected return and risk were not explicitly addressed. Nor were efforts made to measure the degree to which the portfolio was actually diversified.

The approach of defining real estate portfolios in terms of property type and four geographic regions remained the standard for nearly 20 years. In fact, when the Russell-NCREIF Property Index was introduced in 1978, these diversification dimensions were used to differentiate the performance of commercial real estate. However, it was not until the mid-1980s when real estate performance declined precipitously that investors, consultants, and investment managers began to question the appropriateness of property type and geographic region as diversification classifications.

Principles

Beginning in 1986, Prudential's newly established Investment Research group began to examine portfolio construction methodologies based on Modern Portfolio Theory (MPT). Initial research revealed that in a mean-variance environment, property-type diversification mattered more than the four-region geographic diversification. This conclusion was drawn by comparing the property-type covariance matrix and correlation coefficients to those of the four geographic regions. The analysis suggested that property type was a more powerful diversifier than geographic region. To some, especially real estate acquisition officers, these results were at best counterintuitive. After all, real estate professionals had consistently claimed that the most important element in real estate investment was "location, location, location." Similarly, urban and regional economic theory suggested that local economic activity should directly impact local property performance; that is, when a local economy prospered, so should the individual properties within that economy. These results led the research team to question the validity of geographic regions—until this point, the industry standard for assessing location—as an adequate definition of location at the portfolio level. In other words, the working hypothesis shifted to identifying a more meaningful definition of location, one which was not dependent merely on regional geography.

Economic versus Geographic Location

Well-anchored in urban and regional economics and finance, the initial working hypothesis suggested that local real estate markets could be viewed in an economic context. Further, it held that their economic structure and output could be assessed by their similarities to and differences from the U.S. economy. Just as the U.S. economy filled a specific role within the global economy which could be measured in terms of employment, imports and exports of goods and services, and capital flows, local real estate markets are also appropriate for analysis within an economic model. They can be assessed in similar terms, such as imports and exports of goods and services and capital flows. For example, Houston can be characterized as a net exporter of energy-related products and services and as a net importer of most other goods and services. Local markets can also be analyzed in terms of their employment growth rates: some consistently experience employment growth rates above, below, or close to the national average. While local market relative growth rates vary over time, they can be compared to historical averages or to the U.S. growth rate over a specified period.

These locational characteristics are economic rather than geographic in nature. "Location" at the portfolio level departed from traditional geographic definitions and reemerged as *economic location*, a far more encompassing term which includes broader economic parameters. For example, the economic location of Silicon Valley and Boston's I-28 corridor is similar because both markets are closely connected to global computer chip manufacturing, despite "geographic" locations on opposite coasts. If the world market were suddenly flooded with low-priced computer chips, both these economies would be impaired: geographic location would not be pertinent. If the computer chip market weakened, both local markets and their local real estate markets would be adversely affected because declining tenant revenues would limit both expansion plans and prevailing and prospective lease rates.

The Portfolio Construction Process

In essence, research on MPT produced a process that applies the lessons learned in the financial markets to real estate portfolios while linking urban and regional economics to capital market pricing. As with all portfolio analysis models, the real estate portfolio construction process begins with the careful identification of the investor's investment objectives, expressed in terms of risk and return. In most instances, investors are comfortable with the notion of setting total return targets, but are less comfortable with setting risk targets. As a result, the acceptable level of risk is determined based on the total return target. Since risk and return are positively correlated (i.e., a higher return target requires the assumption of greater risk), most institutional investors have tended to express their expected total return target in terms of a real rate of return. A frequently selected target real rate of return would be 4 percent to 6 percent. Once the target return is chosen, a two-tiered analysis begins which leads to portfolio construction guidelines identifying targeted property acquisitions and/or sales.

Initial analysis is necessary to establish the context within which portfolio performance will be evaluated. This requires an assessment of total portfolio risk, measured as the variability or standard deviation of portfolio returns. First, diversification characteristics of an existing portfolio must be analyzed. (When developing a strategy for constructig a new portfolio this step is not necessary.) The goal is to determine how concentrated portfolio holdings are in economies sharing similar profiles and to suggest alternatives for reducing total portfolio risk.

Diversification is the principal technique for reducing risk without sacrificing return. Diversifying investments among properties whose returns do not move in parallel reduces portfolio total return variability: as one set of returns decreases, another set rises, smoothing the overall return performance. The mission is to identify a set of investments whose returns are not likely to move in tandem (noncovariant returns). Investors may not decide to assemble a diversified portfolio, choosing to accept higher risk in search of higher returns. The point of portfolio strategy, in a risk-return context, is to make this an explicit decision and not to accept higher risk without full understanding of the performance implications.

There is no universally correct portfolio strategy. Portfolio strategies are investor driven. Reasonable strategies can be as diverse as investor goals and objectives. Furthermore, since many investors currently hold real estate in their portfolios, future strategies will be highly affected by the composition of their existing holdings. The attractiveness of a particular property, property type, or market is therefore a function of investor portfolio goals and objectives. All acquisition and disposition decisions must be made within the context of the investor's portfolio strategy. Consequently, an individual investment manager may very well be implementing what seems on the surface to be conflicting strategies for multiple clients. For example, one investor, based on specific goals and objectives, may be acquiring properties in energy-dominated markets while another, with very different objectives, is selling in these markets at exactly the same time.

The second level of analysis focuses on the optimal combination of assets that will produce the most efficient trade-off between risk and return. This selection process seeks to identify classes of assets by property type and economic location that will produce either the highest return for the level of risk the investor finds acceptable or the minimum expected risk for the targeted level of expected return.

Property-Type Diversification

Real estate professionals and investors customarily categorize assets by property type. This kind of classification recognizes the different factors influencing the performance of individual property sectors. For example, typical office and industrial leases do not provide for percentage rents while retail properties do. Apartments have relatively short-term leases compared to most office, industrial, and retail properties. Furthermore, the economic environment affects tenants of different property types in different ways. For example, while an economic recession will most likely depress industrial property performance, apartments may gain as tenants decide to remain renters rather than to buy homes.

Some of the early research in the area of portfolio diversification empirically supports the widely held view that property type diversification can be achieved, but questioned the validity of geographic diversification.[6] As result, research begun in the mid-1980s focused attention on improving the understanding of geographic versus locational diversification while accepting that property-type diversification was also useful. It is the purpose of this chapter to concentrate on locational diversification attributes.

Defining Economic Location

This approach introduces and defines the concept of ''economic location,'' an improvement over the traditional four-region classification. The goal is to categorize individual metropolitan areas on the basis of their underlying economic performance. Economic location is a market-based concept initially defined in terms of *employment performance zones* (EPZs). In the case of EPZs (see Part II of this chapter for a full discussion), employment growth rates for individual markets are compared with the growth rate of the United States as a whole. Differences between markets are statistically measured and similar markets are grouped together.

The EPZ classification scheme resulted in five diversification categories:

1. Cyclical markets, or markets whose employment growth rate matched U.S. rates.
2. Consistently higher employment growth markets, whose growth rate constantly exceeded U.S. rates.
3. Recently higher employment growth markets, whose latest growth rates outpaced the U.S. average.

---

[6]See Mike Miles and Tom McCue, ''Historic Returns and Institutional Real Estate Portfolios,'' *AREUEA Journal* 10, no. 2 (Summer 1982), pp. 184–99; Mike Miles and Tom McCue, ''Commercial Real Estate Returns,'' *AREUEA Journal* 12, no. 3 (Fall 1984), pp. 355–77: Hartzell et al., ''Diversification Categories,'' (1986), pp. 230–54; and Paul M. Firstenberg, Stephen A. Ross, and Randall C. Zisler, ''Real Estate: The Whole Story,'' *Journal of Portfolio Management* 14, no. 3 (Spring 1988), pp. 22–34.

4. Recently lower employment growth markets, whose recent growth rates trailed the U.S. average.
5. Consistently lower employment growth markets, or markets that regularly underperformed compared to the U.S. growth rates.

The second definition of economic location involves identification of dominant employment categories (DEC). The DEC classification scheme focuses on the characteristics of local economies. Individual markets can be viewed as separate economies which import and export goods, services, and capital in a manner similar to the larger U.S. economy. Local economies carry out a balance of trade relationship with each other just as the United States does with the economies of other countries. The portfolio construction process recognizes that the performance of local real estate markets is closely linked to their respective local economies. When the market for energy-related products falls on hard times, the performance of Houston real estate properties suffers and vice versa. This diversification classification scheme ignores geography while stressing economic attributes. Markets with similar economic characteristics are grouped together regardless of their geographic location. For example, though New York City and San Francisco are located on different coasts, they are both considered financial/services markets for purposes of the portfolio construction process. Conversely, some markets which are in close geographic proximity with one another may also be similar in terms of their dominant employment categories. This would include markets such as New Orleans and Houston which are both in the South and dominated by energy-related employment concentration.

The DEC approach resulted in five statistically distinct market categories:

- Energy markets.
- Financial/services markets.
- Government markets.
- Manufacturing and distribution markets.
- Diversified markets.

The employment concentration of each of the categories within each local market was compared to that of the United States as a whole. Markets that had greater concentrations of employment in one area were classified accordingly. Markets that statistically matched the employment concentration of the United States were categorized as diversified markets.

Portfolio Optimization

Following the determination of the economic location and property-type classifications, a data base of individual property performance information is used to calculate the means, standard deviations, and correlation coefficients between property type and economic location. Property type and economic location target ranges are identified utilizing a standard mean-variance portfolio selection technique initially postulated by Harry Markowitz.

The reason for developing the EPZ and DEC measures of economic location was to enhance the understanding of real estate portfolio diversification and improve the risk-adjusted total return of real estate portfolios. Recent research[7] using the performance data of a large institutional commingled real estate fund from the fourth quarter of 1973 through the fourth quarter of 1990 compared the EPZ and DEC methodology with the more traditional four- and eight-region geographical approaches. A sample of the results of the Mueller et al. research are presented in Tables 6–2 and 6–3. While comparing correlation matrices is difficult since no statistical test exists to precisely measure the degree to which one correlation matrix is more attractive than another, a number of normative points can be observed.

- In the four-region correlation matrix, 50 percent of the correlation coefficients were both positive and statistically significantly different from zero.[8]
- In the eight-region correlation matrix, 25 percent of the correlation coefficients were statistically significantly different from zero, six were positive and one negative.

---

[7]Glenn R. Mueller, Barry A. Ziering, and Donna Machi, "Real Estate Portfolio Diversification Using Economic Diversification." *The Journal of Real Estate Research* (Fall 1992).

[8]Correlation coefficients can range from +1 to −1. Positive correlation coefficients indicate that the two variables move in tandem with one another. Negative correlations mean that the two variables tend to move in the opposite direction of one another. For portfolio diversification purposes, low positive or negative correlation coefficients suggest an increase in diversification efficiency. When a correlation coefficient is not statistically different from 0, the actual coefficient sign becomes less important than its lack of statistical significance. Nonsignificant coefficients suggest that the movements of the two variables are not related to one another, which in diversification analysis is preferable to a positive, significant coefficient.

- In the DEC correlation matrix, 20 percent of the correlation coefficients were both positive and statistically significantly different from zero.
- In the EPZ correlation matrix, 20 percent of the correlation coefficients were both positive and statistically significantly different from zero.

TABLE 6–2
Four- and Eight-Region Correlation Matrix

Annual Return	Standard Deviation	Grouping	Correlation of Returns			
			East	Midwest	West	South
		4 Region, 4 Quarter 1973–4 Quarter 1990				
17.53	8.38	East	1.00			
9.61	2.79	Midwest	.308*	1.00		
12.57	4.59	West	.282*	.459†	1.00	
8.73	5.93	South	−.038	.076	.199	1.00

| | | *8 Region, 4 Quarter 1973–4 Quarter 1990* | | | | | | | |

Group	Annual Return	SD	NE	MA	OS	IN	FB	ME	SC	NC
NE	16.35	6.38	1.00							
MA	17.34	9.30	−.212	1.00						
OS	9.88	9.96	−.170	−.077	1.00					
IN	9.78	2.67	−.042	.306†	.025	1.00				
FB	9.28	5.51	−.013	.125	.167	.323†	1.00			
ME	7.04	5.77	−.238*	.070	.126	.177	.205	1.00		
SC	15.28	5.70	.045	.378†	.085	.473†	.361†	.102	1.00	
NC	13.18	5.23	−.007	.095	.139	.207	.139	.145	.371*	1.00

Key:
NE = New England   FB = Farm belt
MA = Mid-Atlantic   ME = Mineral extraction
OS = Old South   SC = Southern California
IN = Industrial Midwest   NC = Northern California

*Significantly different from 0 at 90 level of confidence.
†Significantly different from 0 at 95 level of confidence.

Source: Glenn R. Mueller, Bary A. Ziering, and Donna Machi, "Real Estate Portfolio Diversification Using Economic Diversification," *The Journal of Real Estate Research* (Fall 1992).

TABLE 6–3
EPZ AND DEC Correlation Matrix

Annual Return	Standard Deviation		Correlation of Returns				
			CH	CL	CYC	RH	RL

Employment Performance Zones 4 Quarter 1973–4 Quarter 1990

Annual Return	Standard Deviation		CH	CL	CYC	RH	RL
11.78	4.60	CH	1.00				
16.65	10.58	CL	−.025	1.00			
14.19	4.17	CYC	.130	.251*	1.00		
13.82	5.49	RH	.081	.192	.056	1.00	
7.41	1.89	RL	.258*	.171	.056	.014	1.00

Key:
CH = Consistently higher growth markets.
CL = Consistently lower growth markets.
CYC = Cyclical growth markets.
RH = Recently higher growth markets.
RL = Recently lower growth markets.

Annual Return	Standard Deviation	Group	DIV	Energy	FIN	GOV	MFG

Dominant Employment Category 4 Quarter 1973–4 Quarter 1990

Annual Return	Standard Deviation	Group	DIV	Energy	FIN	GOV	MFG
11.95	5.21	DIV	1.00				
7.12	7.12	ENERGY	.032	1.00			
19.33	12.68	FIN	.014	.022	1.00		
13.40	7.17	GOV	.039	.250*	.180	1.00	
12.68	3.82	MFG	.200	.147	.290*	.114	1.00

Key:
DIV   = Diversified markets.
ENERGY = Energy-dominated employment category.
FIN   = Financial/services-dominated employment category.
GOV   = Government-dominated employment category.
MFG   = Manufacturing/distribution-dominated employment category.

*Significantly different from 0 at 90 level of confidence.
†Significantly different from 0 at 95 level of confidence.

Source: Glenn R. Mueller, Bary A. Ziering, and Donna Machi, "Real Estate Portfolio Diversification Using Economic Diversification," *The Journal of Real Estate Research* (Fall 1992).

A lower percentage of positive and significant correlation coefficients is preferable to a higher percentage. Conversely, while analysts would prefer a high percentage of *negative* and significant correlation coefficients, in their absence, positive nonsignificant correlation coefficients are the next best outcome. However, when analyzing diversification within an asset class, it is unusual to discover a preponderance of negative and significant coefficients. In the correlation matrices presented in Tables 6–2 and 6–3, only 1 coefficient (out of a possible 54) is both negative and significant. When compared to the geographic region approach, the research indicates that using economic location produced lower correlations overall and fewer positive statistically significant correlations and therefore represents a superior diversification methodology.

The portfolio optimization technique relies on a selection model which identifies allocation weights based on each classification's return, mean, and correlation with other asset classifications. The correlation coefficients between the diversification classification categories tend to drive the allocation procedure. Since the application of portfolio modeling to portfolio construction is principally a risk-reduction technique, the optimization model will select combinations of assets which minimize portfolio risk at targeted return levels. Figure 6–1 presents a sample property-type efficient frontier. In this hypothetical example, the efficient frontier represents combinations of property types, in this case office, retail, industrial, and apartment property types, which will minimize risk for any selected level of total portfolio return. Each point on the efficient frontier represents a discrete combination of the four property types which, based on their respective mean total returns, standard deviation, and correlation coefficients, results in the highest return, lowest risk portfolio. Since investment in private market real estate is "lumpy" at best (i.e., it is extremely difficult to acquire a fractional interest in a real estate asset), the portfolio construction process establishes target ranges (rather than point estimates) for the property-type allocation targets. These target ranges are determined by identifying a narrow range of targeted return, say 4 percent to 6 percent real, and then identifying the range or continuum of portfolios which would produce returns within the band. Thus, the portfolio construction process recommends establishing diversification category target ranges, not specific point estimate weightings. For example, the portfolio strategy may target 20 percent to 30 percent office exposure, 25 percent to 35 percent industrial exposure, 30 percent to 40 percent

FIGURE 6–1
Hypothetical Property Type (Efficient Frontier)

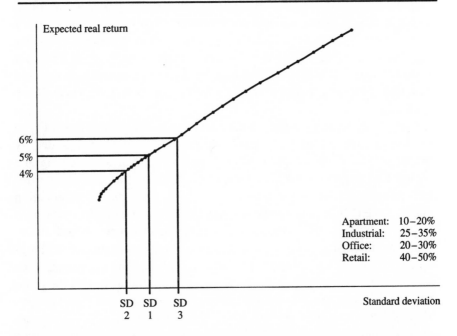

Expected real return

6%
5%
4%

Apartment:	10–20%
Industrial:	25–35%
Office:	20–30%
Retail:	40–50%

SD SD SD
2   1   3

Standard deviation

retail exposure, and 10 percent to 20 percent apartment exposure. When the actual portfolio weights fall within the target ranges, a portfolio manager would consider that portfolio to be properly distributed.

CONCLUSION

The process described above represents a framework for identifying the extent to which a particular portfolio provides the maximum return for any specified level of risk. The result allows the portfolio manager to recommend an explicit strategy to attain the portfolio's specific risk-return position. The last step in the process helps identify those properties that should be held, sold, or acquired. Guidelines for acquisitions or sales can be set that target desired property types within designated markets or economic locations. The development of a specific acquisition or disposition program draws heavily on property analysis conducted at the microeconomic level (i.e., traditional, fundamental property due diligence). This micro-analysis may yield results which are at variance with the portfolio strategy results. For example, the portfolio strategy may show the need to acquire regional malls. However, market circumstances may indicate that initial yields available in the regional mall market are currently unattractively low (this could easily have been the case during 1988–89 when top-quality regional malls were trading at initial cash yields in the range of 5 percent to 6 percent). Under these circumstances, the acquisition program would postpone targeting regional malls until more attractive yields were available.

Portfolio strategy is not intended to act as a straitjacket; flexibility to dispose or invest must be retained which reflects judgments guided by property-specific situations. It is not wise to invest in low-yielding and high-priced properties merely to meet diversification targets. The portfolio optimization technique requires that both yield *and* diversification goals are met. Investors should not sacrifice yield to meet diversification targets or vice versa. Investors and investment managers should understand that the discipline of a solid portfolio strategy will dictate the long-range composition of the portfolio. Sale and acquisition candidates must be consistent not only with the portfolio strategy, but also with the property specific analysis. Microlevel input by experienced real estate professionals adds a critical dimension to the macro approach of strategy development. Part II of this chapter presents a detailed example of how a specific portfolio strategy, the Prudential Portfolio Construction Process (PPCP), was implemented during the late 1980s, and Part III presents a further example of a portfolio-modeling technique.

PART II—WHAT SAVED PRISA? A CASE STUDY

Charles R. Lightner
Institutional Investment Management
Prudential Realty Group

INTRODUCTION

Throughout the 1970s, the first decade of U.S. pension fund participation in the real estate market, Prudential's Property Investment Separate Account (PRISA) was the industry's premier open-end, commingled, equity real estate fund. Initially brought to the market in 1971, PRISA grew in size to $5.1 billion by 1984. Throughout the 70s and into the 1980s the fund's performance was strong. In the early 1980s, however, performance began to falter, and in the middle years of the decade it lagged that of its principal competitors significantly.

Even as PRISA investors were abandoning the fund in record numbers, in response to disappointing performance, changes in strategy, tactics, and operating procedures brought the 300-property account back to life. For the three years ended December 31, 1990, PRISA's performance ranked in the first quartile of all open-end, equity real estate funds tracked by Evaluation Associates, Inc., and exceeded the comparable-period Russell/NCREIF Property Index by a cumulative 10.8 percent.

This chapter traces the changes in PRISA's strategy, structure, and operation that coincided with its return to competitive prominence.

BACKGROUND

The real estate investment management business is in its adolescence. Prior to the 1970s, institutional ownership of equity real estate was not widespread and the management of real estate portfolios for others was virtually unknown in the United States. European insurance companies and pension plans, however, had held equity real estate in their investment portfolios for decades. It was a study of the European experience that led two Prudential executives, Claude Ballard and Meyer Melnikoff, to believe that a product providing the U.S. pension market a convenient means to invest in equity real estate would be attractive.

PRISA was established in 1970 and signed on its first pension client in 1971. While interest in PRISA on a conceptual level was lively, the pace of deposits was slow. Passage of ERISA in 1974, encouraging broader diversification of pension assets, gave impetus to the sale of products such as PRISA. It was not until 1979, however, that PRISA reached $1 billion in net assets. Its largest competitor at that point was half its size. Real estate was clearly still an "experiment" for most pension funds.

In the late 1970s and early 1980s, several factors combined to cause the growth of the new industry to accelerate:

1. The real estate market pulled out of its mid-70s depression: growth in the work force accelerated, vacancy rates dropped, rents and values rose, construction activity increased; there was a pervasive optimism in the market.
2. The experience of portfolios such as PRISA reflected this return to health: total returns moved sharply higher, exceeding 20 percent annually in the 1978–80 period.
3. Influential pension consulting firms began to recommend the inclusion of equity real estate in their client's portfolios.
4. Research on performance during the industry's first decade was impressive. It appeared that equity real estate was not only a very powerful diversifier in a mixed-asset portfolio but also acted as an effective hedge against inflation and produced total returns comparable to, but more stable than, common stocks.

The results of this confluence of positives were dramatic. From 1979 to 1984, PRISA grew from $1 billion to over $5 billion in net assets. Other funds had similar experience. Money was pouring in at such a rate that PRISA actually refused new deposits for a time!

The pension industry was not alone in its sudden interest in the U.S. real estate. The domestic insurance industry moved billions into the equity market in the 80s, as did foreign institutions and investors. Prior to the tax law changes in 1986, additional billions for real estate were generated by promoters and syndicators of tax-motivated investment vehicles.

It was the demand for properties by the pension industry, other domestic institutions, foreign investors, and syndicators, coupled with the seemingly insatiable appetite of banks and S&Ls for real estate financing opportunities that caused the massive overbuilding of the 80s. It was a market driven by excess liquidity and unrealistic expectations: too much money chasing too few good opportunities caused prices to skyrocket and supply growth to explode.

To understand the history of the industry, it is important to keep in mind that the management of real estate portfolios for the pension market from 1970 through the mid-80s was almost exclusively the management of growth. The primary investment task of the manager was the acquisition of properties to absorb the inflow of funds. Portfolio strategy, portfolio structure, and measurement and management of risk were given little attention. As long as property prices continued to rise, yields were acceptable and there was little complaint or question from the pension community, which had not yet had substantial experience with the asset class.

During this period, the composition of portfolios tended to reflect the basic investment view and strengths of the manager and, to some extent, the "accidents" of the marketplace. Prudential, for example, had substantial expertise in office and hotel properties and an institutional bias in favor of the South and West. It was, therefore, not surprising that PRISA grew to have significant concentrations in the office and hotel categories and a large investment in the oil belt cities.

Other funds took on the character of large individual investments which the manager more or less "accidentally" was successful in purchasing. If the acquisition of a large package of retail properties gave a particular portfolio a decided "tilt" in that direction, for instance, it might become known as a *retail fund* and its manager might thereafter adopt a retroactive strategic explanation for its structure. If another manager had been the successful bidder for that same package, its fund might have followed the same path.

The structure of an existing portfolio generally had little impact on the decision to pursue a specific new acquisition opportunity. And, little consideration was generally given to the impact of a new acquisition on the total portfolio or on subsequent acquisitions. What was clearly lacking throughout the industry was a disciplined process of portfolio construction based explicitly on the risk appetite and return expectations of a fund's clients.

PRISA 1986

By the end of 1986, it had become apparent that PRISA's performance problems were significant. Client withdrawals that year fell just short of $1 billion, deposit activity had fallen sharply, returns lagged the competition, and an important segment of the consulting community had lost faith in the fund. It was not difficult to identify the portfolio components causing PRISA's problems:

- PRISA's office buildings were underperforming the office properties in competitive funds, largely because of large bets made in Denver and other energy-dominated markets.
- Hotel performance had weakened at the same time major capital improvement projects were under way.
- The fund's large concentration of oil belt properties had begun to fall in value and further sharp value losses were threatened.
- The portfolio's industrial component contained a large segment of higher risk office/showroom and R&D properties, which were showing signs of weakness.

There were both strategic and operational difficulties as well:

- The fund's strategy was not well defined. It was stated generally in terms of a desire to "mirror the national market for investment-grade commercial real estate." There was no explicit connection between the needs of the client and the composition of the portfolio.
- The lack of clear and direct linkage from client to strategy to portfolio composition made it difficult to define specific investment criteria to guide the acquisitions and sales activities of the organization. As a result, the portfolio management function played less than an optimum role in transaction activities. There was also too weak a connection between property-level operations and the level of fund management.

PRISA was by no means in a class by itself in its shortcomings. Many of its competitors suffered from similar structural and organizational inefficienies. But for a variety of reasons PRISA began to show the ill effects of these weaknesses earlier than others. It was clear that PRISA had serious problems and that timely solutions were required.

The Seeds of Solution

In late 1986, it was recognized that success in meeting the investor's needs would require major changes in operating procedures as well as a solution to the problem of portfolio strategy formulation. A means of explicitly linking client risk/return parameters to the construction of real estate portfolios had to be found, and organizational changes that more closely linked client needs and transaction decisions had to be made.

Of paramount importance was solving the problems of PRISA. Two major organizational initiatives were undertaken in initial response to these needs:

1. A commitment was made to the establishment of unsurpassed real estate investment research capabilities.
2. The Prudential Realty Group's portfolio management unit was strengthened and expanded and its role in the investment process was redefined.

The investment research and portfolio management teams were then charged with formulating a comprehensive strategic framework for the repositioning of PRISA. Importantly, senior management committed itself to aid the researchers and portfolio managers to find the theoretical solutions to PRISA's problems as well as the organizational and operational initiatives needed to implement the plans. Culture would have to change nearly as radically as investment practices and the assistance of senior officers was critical.

THE PRUDENTIAL PORTFOLIO CONSTRUCTION PROCESS

Real estate portfolios are described most frequently in terms of their property-type composition and their geographical diversification. Until the mid-1980s, however, the composition of portfolios was given little serious analytic attention.

Geographic diversification was typically described in terms of the four quadrants of the country. If it appeared that a "reasonable" balance existed among the East, South, West, and Midwest quadrants, it was assumed that a portfolio was effectively diversified. Likewise, if a portfolio's holdings included at least three or four major property types in some apparently rational relationship, there was little question from the investor or consultant communities.

Importantly, in 1987, when the search for solutions for PRISA began, there was no accepted methodology in the real estate industry for linking portfolio composition to portfolio objectives. There was also little research available analyzing locational risk and return probabilities.

It was apparent from the unexpectedly volatile return history of PRISA that the fund had accepted a higher level of risk than it had intended. For example, at one time the oil belt segment of the account exceeded 25 percent. That large an exposure to the risks of one economic variable was unintended, but it occurred because of the industry's definitional conventions: Denver and New Orleans, for instance, fell into different geographic quadrants but certainly responded in lockstep to the fall in fortunes of the oil business. A new method of defining location was required.

Additional examination of the usefulness of property-type diversification was also needed. Several studies done by academics in the early 80s suggested that diversification among the various kinds of properties was an effective means of controlling risk, but many of those results were based on dated or questionable information.

The great advantage enjoyed by Prudential researchers was access to Prudential's own data base of quarterly returns dating back to PRISA's founding. Return series for both property type and locational analyses allowed the research team to measure the risk and return effects of differing portfolio segments and composition alternatives.

By mid-1987 it had been concluded that:

1. Property-type diversification did, indeed, appear to have real merit as a means of managing portfolio risk.
2. Geographic diversification as it had been practiced by the industry did not appear to have significant risk management value.

During the summer of 1987, a variety of alternative approaches to the definition of location were analyzed. One method stood out. It appeared that a two-part definitional framework based on employment data could provide a substantially superior means of defining similarities among markets. Superior, that is, in the sense that similar investment performance was found in properties located in areas with similar economic definition.

- *Employment performance zones* (EPZ) group markets in terms of their employment growth relative to the overall national trends over a 20-year period. Some areas experience job growth at levels consistently higher than national averages, some at consistently lower levels, and some tend to mirror national norms, for example.
- *Dominant employment categories* group markets in terms of significant concentrations of job types relative to national norms. Markets such as Houston have significantly higher concentrations in energy-related employment, for instance, while markets such as New York City have very high concentrations of Finance/Service jobs.

From these studies was born what is called *The Prudential Portfolio Construction Process (PPCP)*. The scope of this paper does not extend a full discussion of the theory and application of the PPCP. *The critical conclusion of the studies, however, was that property investments in these defined locational categories produced characteristically different patterns of returns.* Those categories could, therefore, be used to define a portfolio structure which met given risk and return parameters.

PRISA Diversification: Actual versus Target, 1987

The output of an analysis under the PPCP is a three-part recommendation for portfolio composition expressed as a series of target allocation ranges: one expressed in terms of the five major property types, one in terms of employment performance zones and one in terms of dominant employment categories. Those ranges are produced using a typical asset allocation model of the same sort used in analyzing the composition of mixed-asset portfolios. In the case of the PPCP the asset categories are property types and economic locations rather than the more typical array of bonds, stocks, cash, etc.

A critical element in such an analysis is the selection of a target rate of return. Given a target for return, the model is used to derive an allocation framework which could be expected to produce that return at the lowest possible level of risk. (Conversely, risk tolerance can be specified and likely return level can be derived.)

The specifications of risk and return parameters for a portfolio is the critical link back to the investor! These two characteristics define the motivations of investors. Proceeding from a proper analysis of return requirement and risk tolerance should improve substantially the chances of an investment manager actually delivering the investment results his or her clients desire.

So, before an analysis of the structure of PRISA could be completed, it was necessary to reevaluate the Prudential's perceptions of its clients' motivations. Over the course of the fund's life, based on a combination of empirical analysis and anecdote it had come to be accepted within Prudential that a well-diversified portfolio of unleveraged, investment-grade, equity real estate should produce a real total return, after inflation, of 4 percent to 6 percent over the course of a market cycle.

Conversations were held with both clients and consultants to obtain their views on reasonable return expectations. There was surprisingly little sentiment for a return target outside the range that had been informally adopted over time. The 4 percent to 6 percent range, or a 5 percent average appeared to meet the needs of the investor community.

Given a reasonable definition of return requirement for PRISA the PPCP was used to derive target allocation ranges which would be expected to deliver that return at the lowest possible risk level.

The table below shows the three sets of targets produced for PRISA as well as its actual position at year-end 1987.

It was apparent that the implementation of PPCP recommendations would be no small task. But this was actually just the broadest measure of the task at hand.

Other Structural Considerations

1. PPCP analysis does not differentiate between a suburban office building and a downtown office building, between a government city such as Washington, D.C. and one like Norfolk, Virginia, between manufacturing/distribution areas such as Long Beach, California, and Gary, Indiana. Obviously, examination of holdings among the markets within PPCP-defined categories would be critical.

2. Approximately 36 percent of the portfolio's office space investment was in suburban markets. In square footage terms the proportion was much higher. It was our view that suburban office space had a higher risk level than downtown office space. A specific objective of reducing PRISA's suburban office exposure was adopted.

	Actual	*Target*
I. Property Type:		
Office	49.0%	30–40%
Retail	17.2	20–30
Industrial	16.2	20–30
Apartment	6.4	10–20
Hotel	9.5	5–15
Agricultural	1.7	0
II. Dominant Employment Categories:		
Diversified	17.5%	15–25%
Energy	16.3	5–15
Government	6.2	1–20
Manufacturing	28.3	25–35
Service	28.2	15–25
Unclassified	3.5	0
III. Employment Performance Zones:		
Consistently higher growth	23.3%	25–35%
Recently higher	11.5	15–25
Cyclical growth	34.6	25–40
Recently lower	16.9	5–15
Consistently lower	10.2	5–15
Unclassified	3.5	0

3. The account's industrial portfolio contained a significant component of office/showroom, office/warehouse and R&D space. We viewed this space as having much higher risk than typical bulk warehouse and distribution space. A specific objective of concentrating PRISA's industrial holdings in warehouse/distribution properties was adopted.

4. While empirical studies, based on available data, were inconclusive it was our view that larger properties tended to be more resistant to value loss than smaller holdings. Larger properties tend to be in more populous areas, occupied by larger and more stable tenants, owned by larger and more stable owners, and less subject to unexpected competitive forces. It was decided that smaller properties in all types (except warehouses, which are smaller in dollar terms by their nature) would be avoided.

5. PRISA had held a small portfolio of agricultural properties. Upon reevaluation it was decided that farm properties would, for the foreseeable future, be inappropriate holdings for the portfolio. Liquidation of that segment of the portfolio was scheduled.

6. The PPCP excludes from its methodology cities with populations under 450,000. Holdings in smaller cities appear in the table previously given in the Unclassified categories. Liquidation, over time, of holdings in smaller cities was scheduled. This decision responded to our experience that securing qualified on-site property management services is more difficult in smaller cities and recognized the inefficiency of our attempting to buy, sell, and manage in too many markets.

A RESTRUCTURING DRIVEN BY PROPERTY SALES

A major restructuring of a 300-property portfolio is a daunting task under the best of circumstances. However, PRISA was not in the best of circumstances. The fact was that clients continued to request cash withdrawals and new deposit activity had fallen to an average of $66 million in the 1986–87 period, after averaging $515 million per year over the previous five-year period.

The bulk of the repositioning would have to be accomplished through the property sales process.

The real estate investment management business, as we have pointed out, was an industry on a buying binge. While Prudential had been an active seller in the 1985–87 period, and so was better equipped than most to undertake a very sharply focused sales program, the sell discipline was relatively informal. A new process, more closely tied to the portfolio representatives was required.

New analytic tools were also needed. Historic returns were available, and of some use. Individual property performance was analyzed in terms of absolute income, appreciation, and total returns as well as in terms of quartile rankings among other portfolio holdings. Prospective 1- and 10-year returns were also estimated and played an important role in the selection of sales candidates. Portfolio construction decisions previously outlined gave added direction. But more was still needed.

Two additional new tools to aid in the analysis of portfolio holdings were developed: (*a*) the quality rating matrix, and (*b*) the property-type attractiveness index.

A Quality Rating System

Tools for rationalizing return differentials and measuring relative risk have been available in the securities markets for many years. Bond rating differentials, for example, explain a large portion of the yield spreads in the fixed-income markets. Rating characteristics can also be used to describe relative risk among individual securities and among portfolios. The real estate industry has had no similar tools.

Choosing potential property sales candidates based solely on return history or return projections is a quite hazardous undertaking. Return variations are as well justified among office buildings as they are among corporate bonds, for example, and projections of holding period yields for properties are, at best, less reliable than they might appear. A method was needed to help decide whether a 10 percent projected return on a property in Seattle, for instance, was really more attractive than a 9.5 percent expectation from a similar property in Chicago. A tool for use in that decision-making process was found in the development of the quality rating matrix system.

For each of the five principal property types a system of evaluating the critical attributes of an individual property holding was developed.

For office buildings, for example, attributes fall into five major categories:

- Market.
- Location.
- Physical condition.
- Quality of income stream.
- Ownership structure.

Each of those categories contains a variety of subcategories. The physical condition rating, for example, will include specific analysis of the effects of hazardous materials, if any, adequacy of parking, projected capital improvements needed, and so on. Some of the categories, such as relative macromarket strength, are rated by investment research staff, but most ratings are done by the individual asset managers responsible for the properties.

This system results in the annual assignments of a rating of from 1 to 6 to every property in every portfolio and is among the first steps in the property sales analysis process. Over its relatively short life, the system has proven to produce ratings which are highly correlated to property performance.

The quality rating matrix system provided a means to help choose among properties in deciding which to sell or hold, but some means to help analyze similarly defined markets was still needed. The property-type attractiveness index system was developed for that purpose.

Property Type Attractiveness Indexes

The Prudential Portfolio Construction Process analysis of economic location produces a two-dimensional matrix containing 25 cells. Each of those cells will correspond to an intersection of its two methods of grouping markets. For example, among the markets with diversified employment bases there are some that fall into the ''consistently higher growth'' category, some into the ''cyclical growth'' category, and so forth.

The PPCP definitions are at an extremely aggregate level of analysis, which can result in quite strong and weak markets being grouped together in one of the 25 cells. While the group itself might have a statistically definable relationship to other groups in the system, actual investment decisions require analysis at a more detailed level. The attractiveness index provides that more detailed view.

An attractiveness index system was developed for each major property type. The attributes of a market which might make it attractive for industrial properties would not necessarily make it attractive for apartments, for example. Each index, however, does treat the same three broad categories:

- Supply factors.
- Demand factors.
- Investment factors.

The demand factors for office market analysis will be quite different from those in hotel market analysis.

An example of the value of this system is found in the analysis of office markets in the ''Diversified and Cyclical Growth'' areas. Eleven markets fall into that cell in the PPCP locational matrix; markets as diverse as Birmingham, Alabama, and Syracuse, New York. Among the 11 markets in that cell Columbus, Ohio ranks among the highest rated in the country and Birmingham, Mobile, and Knoxville rank among the very lowest.

This system provides portfolio managers a means to more quickly move from broader strategic analysis to the more refined, tactical level of decision making.

Procedural Changes

Establishment of closer ties between the portfolio management function, as the representative of the client, and the property sales process was needed. The expansion of the portfolio management team allowed that to occur. Selection of sales candidates, approval of pricing and of final sales terms became portfolio management functions. Transactions professionals and asset managers participated in the selection process, however, and pricing, marketing and negotiations were handled by the transactions group. Making the process at the same time more inclusive by requiring participation of all disciplines but more closely tied to strategy and, ultimately, to client interests was essential to the successful management of the restructuring task.

The two tools discussed above, quality ratings and attractiveness indexes, besides being powerful strategic and analytical processes, provided a critical new vocabulary to aid in the interactions between portfolio managers and transactions and asset management professionals.

The implementation of required procedural changes was made much easier for all concerned by the portfolio managers' ability to define more objective decision criteria than had been available in the past.

The Search for the Perfect Sale

The objectives of the restructuring task, as we have seen, were quite diverse. We wanted to change both the property type and economic location structures of the portfolio, reduce smaller holdings, improve overall portfolio quality ratings, and so forth. The process of selecting sale candidates had as a goal the achievement of maximum benefit from each transaction. If an office building were to be sold, for example, it shouldn't just further our objective of reducing office exposure. It should also help move the portfolio toward its economic location goals, perhaps reducing energy belt exposure and exposure to finance dominated markets, for example. A sale of a suburban office building was considered more desirable than a downtown sale, and sale of several smaller properties was more desirable than sale of a major holding. All of those criteria had to be balanced, obviously, against property quality and return expectations, and, lest we forget it, a sale had to be feasible. There had to be a buyer.

The process was predictably one of compromise. There may have been no truly perfect sale, but from 1987 until early 1990 it was still a seller's market. During that period nearly 200 individual sale transactions involving over $1.5 billion were completed on PRISA's behalf. The characteristics of the properties sold is more important than the volume. On average, sales were of smaller properties with below median return history, and median quality ratings, and higher perceived risk.

Aggressively selling poorer properties into a strong market allowed one to move toward diversification targets while at the same time putting upward pressure on portfolio quality and return potential.

Targeted Acquisitions

The contribution of the property acquisitions effort to the repositioning of PRISA was necessarily less dramatic than that of the property sales program. Funds to undertake a major buying effort were simply not available. Getting maximum benefit from the limited funds that were available was, therefore, of prime importance.

Property acquisition procedures were modified to more closely associate strategy and implementation, just as had been done for the sales process. Acquisitions specialists were provided detailed investment criteria specifying desired property types, locations, sizes, financing and ownership structures, initial and projected return requirements, and other selection and pricing parameters. We could not afford to buy a property which did not tightly conform to long-term strategy any more than we could afford to indiscriminately sell.

Only 14 property purchases totaling $236 million were completed over the 1987–90 period (several involved multiple buildings, however). Only industrial, retail, and apartment properties were acquired. Those were the three property categories in which PRISA was underinvested and no acquisitions outside those categories were considered; this brings up the critical points of credibility and accountability.

NOWHERE TO HIDE

In 1987, PRISA was under fire. Clients, consultants, the press, and Prudential's senior management wanted to know what was to be done to solve the fund's problems. The public nature of the account's difficulties proved to contain an important element of its solution.

While much of the strategy which evolved from our analysis was in place and being implemented during the last half of 1987, it was in early 1988 that the entire repositioning program was made known to clients and consultants. Beginning at that time and in every quarterly communication thereafter, we told PRISA's investors precisely what our strategy for the account was, detailing property type and locational targets, and traced our progress toward implementation of that strategy. We analyzed both property sales and acquisitions activity in terms of their consistency with repositioning objectives. Any inconsistency would become obvious and require explanation.

PRISA became an open book; there really was nowhere to hide. Repeated public reaffirmation of our goals provided real incentive to achieve those goals. After all, our competitors were just as aware of our strategy as our clients. Failure to achieve our objectives was not acceptable.

THE NUMBERS TELL THE STORY

Combined sales and acquisitions activity totaling $1.8 billion, completed over the course of four years, was required to accomplish the task defined for PRISA's management in 1987. Figures 6–2 and 6–3 as well as Tables 6–4 to 6–7 in the appendix illustrate:

- The property-type composition of the account was brought within or very close to all target ranges.
- Locational composition was brought within or quite close to all target ranges.
- The combined exposure to lower growth markets was reduced from 27 percent to 17 percent.
- All agricultural properties were sold.
- Holdings in unclassified markets were cut drastically.
- Average gross property size was increased from $18 million to $28 million.
- The percentage of the account in properties with values over $100 million was raised from 33 percent to 56 percent.
- Exposure in suburban office buildings was reduced from 17 percent of the total portfolio to 8 percent.
- Focus on sale of lower quality and lower yielding properties increased the average quality rating of the entire portfolio.

The Results

Movement into or close to target ranges in all PPCP categories has the effect of reducing the calculated risk level of the total portfolio. Backtesting of the PPCP system yielded the conclusion that, had PRISA been structured in accordance with current targets during the 10-year period preceding the study, the volatility of its returns would have been significantly reduced while the actual average 10-year return level would have been little changed.

While only time will tell if this is actually true, it is our belief that PRISA is, in fact, a lower risk portfolio today than it was in 1986. It is also our belief that this risk reduction has not lessened the probability of PRISA producing the level of return considered appropriate by its clients.

The returns produced by PRISA during the repositioning process improved significantly in both absolute and relative terms. Figure 6–2 shows the account's resurgence against the Russell/NCREIF benchmark. Return improvement relative to principal competitors was equally significant.

Demand by PRISA clients for withdrawal of deposited funds (Figure 6–3) fell consistently throughout the repositioning process. New deposits into the account reversed their downward trend in 1988 and rose in both that year and the next.

FIGURE 6–2
Russell/NCREIF Returns versus PRISA, 1978–1990

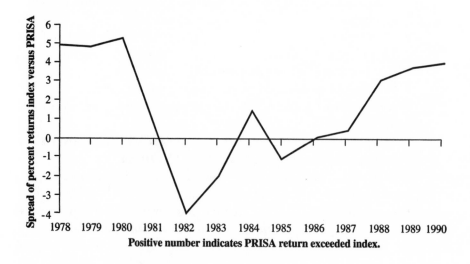

Positive number indicates PRISA return exceeded index.

The total net asset value of PRISA stabilized in 1989. After falling from $5.1 billion in 1984 to $3.5 billion in 1988, net assets at year-end 1989 were within 1 percent of their year-earlier level.

Importantly, PRISA's revival as a viable and competitive vehicle for the client community has been as public as had been its fall from grace. The most important lesson we have learned from the process is the essential linkage from client need to strategy formulation to portfolio construction and management. But the industry itself seems also to have learned the lesson that real estate investment and real estate investment management are different businesses requiring different approaches, practices, tools, and attitudes.

Real estate investment management is undertaken on behalf of others. Those others are, for the most part, not real estate professionals, but they are investment professionals. They understand the value of research and quantitative analysis and generally mistrust the less rigorous analytic techniques characteristic of the real estate industry's past. They understand risk and return even if they don't understand property design or marketing or management. They insist on a higher level of discipline

FIGURE 6–3
PRISA Client Withdrawal and Deposit Activity, 1981–1990

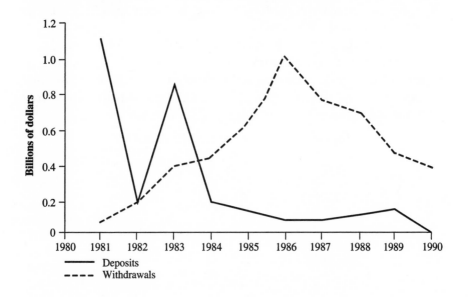

than the industry has been accustomed to as well as a higher level of disclosure. The world of real estate investment has changed, and the change is for the better.

AFTERWORD

The analysis presented in this chapter extends through, but not beyond, 1990. As all observers of the real estate market will know, market sentiment changed radically in mid-1990 and the fundamentals of managing real estate portfolios for others also changed. Nearly every open-end fund has seen the level of requested client withdrawals soar and the level of deposits plummet. Deterioration in the property markets has caused values to fall sharply and portfolio returns to fall to new lows as a result.

PRISA has not been insulated from these difficulties. Returns have fallen, deposits have again turned down, and withdrawals have depleted the account's available cash. The size of the account had fallen to $3.1 billion at September 30, 1991. PRISA's position within the industry, however, remains strong. It was able to maintain liquidity for its clients much longer than most other open-end funds. Its level of withdrawal "backlog" is much lower, as a percentage of assets, than most. Its returns continue to outpace those of the Russell/NCREIF Property Index and to be quite competitive with those of other larger open-end funds. Nothing in the recent performance of the fund leads us to mistrust the efficacy of the steps taken in its repositioning.

We must also add that the analytic tools and processes described here are living and evolving. We learn more about the strengths and limitations of each of them with every use and we continue to rethink, revise, and strengthen each of them as time goes on. That process will undoubtedly continue and we expect that our tools will continue to improve.

APPENDIX

TABLE 6–4

PRISA Portfolio Composition (Portfolio Construction Process Diversification Methodology, 1987-1990)

	12/31/87	*12/31/88*	*12/31/89*	*12/31/90*	*Target Range*
		Property Type			
Office	49.0%	44.6%	41.4%	34.9%	30–40%
Retail	17.2	18.8	21.6	23.3	20–30
Industrial	16.2	15.2	14.6	17.9	20–30
Apartment	6.4	9.8	10.5	11.1	10–20
Hotel	9.5	11.2	11.8	12.6	5–15
Land/agricultural	1.7	0.4	0.1	0.1	0
		Dominant Employment Categories			
Diversified	17.5%	13.8%	20.0%	21.1%	15–25%
Energy	16.3	12.5	11.2	12.0	5–15
Government	6.2	6.3	6.8	8.6	10–20
Manufacturing	28.3	32.3	28.9	29.7	25–35
Service	28.2	33.6	28.9	29.7	25–35
Unclassified	3.5	1.5	0.1	0.1	
		Employment Performance Zones			
Consistently higher	23.3%	22.0%	24.2%	24.5%	25–35%
Recently higher	11.5	13.0	14.7	16.4	15–25
Cyclical	34.6	41.5	43.6	41.2	25–40
Recently lower	16.9	13.9	12.2	12.7	5–15
Consistently lower	10.2	8.0	4.3	4.2	5–15
Unclassified	3.5	1.5	1.0	1.0	

TABLE 6–4 (*continued*)
PRISA—Industrial Properties

Year Ended 12/31	Industrial Portion of Total Portfolio	Bulk Distribution Warehouse		Other	
		Percent of Industrials	Percent of Total Portfolio	Percent of Industrials	Percent of Total Portfolio
1987	16.2%	47.3%	7.7%	52.7%	8.5%
1988	15.2	47.2	7.2	52.8	8.0
1989	14.6	42.2	6.2	57.8	8.4
1990	17.9	52.2	9.3	47.8	8.6

PRISA—Office Properties

Year Ended 12/31	Office Portion of Total Portfolio	Central Business District		Suburban	
		Percent of Office	Percent of Total Portfolio	Percent of Office	Percent of Total Portfolio
1987	49.0%	64.4%	30.9%	35.6%	17.1%
1988	44.6	66.7	29.0	33.3	14.5
1989	41.4	75.7	31.3	24.3	10.1
1990	34.9	77.8	27.2	22.2	7.8

TABLE 6–5
PRISA Property Distribution by Gross Value

	12/31/87	*12/31/88*	*12/31/89*	*12/31/90*
Under $10	14.1%	10.5%	8.3%	9.0%
$10–$19.99	8.7	8.8	7.8	7.0
$20–$49.99	17.8	15.5	12.8	13.8
$50–$99.99	26.7	21.1	17.1	14.3
Over $100	32.7	44.1	54.0	55.8

TABLE 6–6
PRISA Average Gross Property Value by Property Type
(In $ millions)

	12/31/87	*12/31/88*	*12/31/89*	*12/31/90*
Office	$31.6	$36.1	$42.4	$44.9
Retail	29.2	43.6	56.3	53.8
Industrial	5.2	6.0	6.6	7.4
Hotel	74.4	96.6	113.5	117.5
Apartment	31.9	30.4	33.9	35.3
Other	6.1	3.5	8.0	2.1
Entire portfolio	18.4	22.8	27.8	28.4

TABLE 6–7
PRISA Property Sales, 1987–1990

Property Type	Net Proceeds
1987:	
Hotel	10,497,579
Industrial	183,175,326
Land	1,289,992
Office	204,234,602
Retail	188,750,186
Total	587,947,685
1988:	
Farm	20,840,460
Hotel	1,961,833
Industrial	89,311,710
Land	765,460
Office	279,104,951
Retail	56,452,460
Total	448,436,874
1989:	
Apartment	11,290,738
Farm	7,996,543
Hotel	5,208,626
Industrial	108,185,291
Land	916,870
Office	184,231,199
Retail	56,790,802
Total	374,620,069
1990:	
Industrial	8,301,159
Office	122,983,816
Total	131,284,975
1987–90:	
Apartment	11,290,738
Farm	28,837,003
Hotel	17,668,038
Industrial	388,973,486
Land	2,972,321
Office	790,554,569
Retail	301,993,448
Total PRISA Sales 1987–90	1,542,289,603

TABLE 6–8
PRISA Property Acquisitions, 1987–1990

Property Type	City	State	Acquisition Cost
Industrial	San Jose	California	6,700,000
Apartments	Pembroke Pines	Florida	18,800,000
Apartments	North Providence	Rhode Island	15,700,000
Apartments	Scottsdale	Arizona	18,200,000
Industrial	Bolingbrook	Illinois	8,700,000
Retail	Wheaton	Illinois	29,400,000
Apartments	Orlando	Florida	32,000,000
Industrial	Bolingbrook	Illinois	950,000
Industrial	Commerce	California	10,300,000
Industrial	Ontario	California	4,900,000
Industrial	Ontario	California	10,200,000
Industrial	Ontario	California	11,900,000
Industrial	Clearfield	Utah	3,100,000
Industrial	Clearfield	Utah	8,800,000
Industrial	Ontario	California	17,800,000
Industrial	Bolingbrook	Illinois	17,200,000
Industrial	Columbus	Ohio	21,200,000
TOTAL			235,850,000

PART III—"SAMPCO": A HYPOTHETICAL PORTFOLIO ANALYSIS*

Susan Hudson-Wilson, CFA

INTRODUCTION

The SampCo real estate investment portfolio has a net market value of $3 billion and a leveraged market value of $4 billion. This portfolio constitutes 7 percent of the SampCo Master Pension Trust's aggregate invest-

---

*This analysis is compiled from the actual analyses of several portfolios. They are combined to ensure the confidentiality of each. Numbers do not "foot" because of the compilation process.

ment portfolio and has a strategic allocation range of 5 percent to 10 percent.

In this chapter an analytic framework is described that might guide SampCo's participation in the real estate markets. It is clear from our experiences in the 1980s that the mere exercise of assembling a portfolio does not guarantee its successful performance and that there is information available, particularly in the private marketplace, from which an astute investor can benefit. Markets do not all behave similarly. We can use the information imbedded in market fundamentals to assemble and actively manage portfolios of investments. An astute investor presented with an investment opportunity should ask several questions: Is this a good investment and, is this investment good for my portfolio? Does the investment contribute to the goal of return maximization given a level of acceptable risk? Does the investment help me minimize the risk associated with achieving a given level of return? If neither of these, Does the investment represent a "doubling down" or, an assumption of additional, unproductive, risk? Do I wish to deliberately "double down?"

This chapter analyzes the total portfolio and two subportfolios: the "controllable" and the "uncontrollable" portions of the total portfolio. The controllable portion contains real estate investments that can be sold, financed, or expanded at the discretion of the investor. The uncontrollable portion represents assets that are a part of a commingled or partnership structure and, therefore, may not be susceptible to influence by the investor, at least in the short to medium term. This chapter also presents implications and some recommendations for the prospective allocation of the portfolio across property types, metropolitan areas, and financial structures. The "Portfolio Policy Implications and Recommendations" section is designed to be illustrative of the types of analysis the modeling framework permits with respect to the ways in which the portfolio might be restructured. Some obvious restructurings are identified.

A wide range of restructuring possibilities may be explored using the primary analytic framework of efficient frontiers and capitalization ("cap") graphs. Since approximately 80 percent of the portfolio is controllable, considerable restrucuring is possible. All incremental decisions are properly analyzed in the context of this framework. These tools are useful for guiding strategy as well as for the tactical aspects of portfolio management.

The analysis focuses on "the big three" sources of risk and return: property type, property location (described by metropolitan area), and investment financial structure. We strongly believe these variables are the proper focus of the portfolio manager and strategist. If these three sources of risk are aggressively managed at the aggregate real estate portfolio level, the other sources of risk and return (e.g., tenant mix, lease rollover, architecture, tenant credit, and specific property location) may be confidently delegated at the individual asset level. The bulk of the performance of the portfolio will be derived from the active management of the big three.

STATEMENT OF SAMPCO'S PORTFOLIO GOALS

The Context

There is a considerable amount of evidence suggesting that the 1990s present an unusual opportunity to take advantage of the real estate markets. Construction is a fraction of its former peak; demand, battered by the longest recession in post-World War II history, also has plummeted; and institutional investors are reluctant to invest further in the real estate markets. Evidence of the effects of these factors is most apparent in the commercial mortgage markets, where underwriting criteria are the most stringent in years and spreads are unusually high. In this part of the real estate markets (as well as in noninstitutional real estate equity markets dominated by the Resolution Trust Corporation and the Federal Deposit Insurance Corporation) the spread between bid and ask prices has "broken." These markets have provided a clear signal that today's real estate investor can assume less risk and can be more assured of favorable outcomes than was true in the 1980s. In other words, investors can again achieve the risk premium they have historically required for investments in the real estate markets.

The Goal

The principle task of SampCo's real estate portfolio is to capture the systematic behavior of the aggregate real estate asset class for the benefit of the overall investment portfolio. Thus the portfolio should assume risk commensurate with the risk of the aggregate real estate market, should seek returns that are in line with the market average, and should perform on a cycle that is analogous to that of the aggregate market.

This chapter assumes that SampCo recognizes that opportunity exists in the real estate marketplace and seeks to accomplish two objectives: (1) to understand the true composition of the portfolio, and (2) to provide an analytic framework that will allow for the systematic and informed identification of current and potential future major portfolio issues and provide for their resolution.

THE PORTFOLIO

Location and Property Type

The goal of this section is to identify the exposures or the dimensions of diversification (''the bets'') that the portfolio currently has assumed as defined by property type and location. Our analysis is premised upon the assumption that there are three sources of risk and return that dominate all others and that are best managed at the aggregate portfolio level: location, property type, and financial structure. Location is defined as metropolitan statistical areas (MSAs) and primary metropolitan statistical areas (PMSAs), and the property-type categories are: office, retail, industrial, and apartment. The first two risks are analyzed in the context of cluster and efficient frontier analyses, and the latter is analyzed using a portfolio capitalization graph.

A notion central to the mission of portfolio management is the explicit management of risk. It is necessary to assume risk in order to achieve return, but it is sensible to inquire about the risks assumed and about portfolio structures that can efficiently manage and minimize the risks associated with each level of return. The math of mean variance analysis makes it clear that one can achieve improved returns if risks are thoughtfully managed.

An examination of SampCo's holdings reveals some rather large exposures; such as a Seattle retail investment and a Pittsburgh office project. Absent these two investments, the percentage share of the total portfolio associated with any one property type and location drops off considerably. At first glance, this seems reassuring. It appears that the portfolio is spread across a very large number of ''different'' bets. However the question of diversification has not yet been fully explored.

This methodology hypothesizes that because two properties are located in different urban areas or are classed as different property types does not mean that each necessarily brings different risk and return characteristics to the portfolio. Until we have evaluated the comparability of location and property-type investment characteristics, we do not know the size of the bets made, either deliberately or naïvely, by the portfolio. Thus the first step in portfolio evaluation is to discover the dimensions of diversification. How many truly different investment behaviors are present in the portfolio? The second step is to evaluate the interaction of these bets in the context of the portfolio. Below the bets that comprise the investable real estate universe are discussed.

The Dimensions of Diversification

We begin by calculating the total nominal returns (derived market returns [DMR]) for each of a large number of metropolitan areas across the four major property types (office, retail, residential, and industrial).[1] Note that property type and property location are analyzed simultaneously, not sequentially. It is a contention of this methodology that each property type in each location is subject to specific demand and supply influences. It is not appropriate therefore to treat property type as one stage of analysis and property location as a separate stage of analysis. Generalizations at the property-type level of aggregation are unlikely to be appropriate when applied to a range of different locations, each with their own zoning laws, growth rates, economic structures, and economic cycles. We then analyze these DMRs to discover the "dimensions of diversification." We are seeking to discover and to explain the true number of different behaviors available to an investor in the investable universe. Given a universe that

---

[1]Derived market returns are calculated by the researchers at Aldrich, Eastman & Waltch, a real estate advisory firm. These returns are estimated as a function of conditions in the space and capital markets. That is unleveraged, total, nominal returns are assumed to be produced by the interaction of the supply of and demand for space, and the supply of and demand for investment real estate. The modeling process uses the national Russell-NCREIF returns by property type to develop parameters that are then applied to the property categories within a large number of urban areas.

While this DMR modeling process is proprietary it is simply meant to be illustrative. A researcher could substitute a variety of other types of data for the DMRs and would gain some useful insights. For example one could use local vacancy rates by property type, local rental rates by property type, or could construct return series from the property under the researchers' control. This latter approach was used in part II of this chapter. Vacancy and rental rate series may be obtained from the brokerage community, CB Torto-Wheaton and the REIS Reports.

includes all of the largest metropolitan areas and all four major property types, we have discovered 18 separate real estate investment "types" (i.e., 18 separate investment behaviors comprised of two or more derived market returns).[2]

We call the bets "clusters" and define a cluster as containing investment returns that behave similarly to one another. One is neutral among returns within a cluster as each brings very similar behavior to the aggregate portfolio. An investor does not create portfolio diversification by investing in the locations and property types contained within a cluster as it is "combinations" of the clusters that bring return maximization and risk minimization benefits to the portfolio. We will explain the logic of the clusters, characterize their behavior, and note SampCo's exposures to each.

CLUSTER 1
Growth Apartment

Statistics:	
Historical mean return	9.0%
Historical standard deviation	2.2
Forecasted return	8.1
Historical return/risk quotient	4.1
SampCo exposure:	
Total	5.0
Controllable	6.2
Uncontrollable	3.8

The Growth Apartment Cluster (Cluster 1) is characterized by low volatility. This cluster consists of apartment markets that experience strong demand growth complemented with ample supply. Thus, these markets have behaved in a bondlike fashion. Over the forecast period, these markets will experience a slowdown in demand due to disintegrating demographics, accompanied by a reduction in supply induced by the "credit crunch." This market exhibits a favorable return for the level of risk assumed by an investment in it.

---

[2]We use the K-Means clustering algorithm.

CLUSTER 2
Rust Belt Retail

Statistics:
Historical mean return	8.8%
Historical standard deviation	3.6
Forecasted return	8.1
Historical return/risk quotient	2.4
SampCo exposure:	
Total	2.3
Controllable	0.0
Uncontrollable	3.5

Cluster 2, consisting only of retail markets and predominantly located in the Midwest, experiences moderate returns and volatility that is bondlike except in severely recessionary times. Returns during periods of market decline reduce the return per unit of risk; but overall risk-adjusted returns remain average. Supply was quite restrained until the advent of "big box" retail (Wal-Mart). The oversupply of such property brought on by increased construction holds prospective returns down.

CLUSTER 3
Free Land

Statistics:
Historical mean return	10.9%
Historical standard deviation	6.1
Forecasted return	7.6
Historical return/risk quotient	1.2
SampCo exposure:	
Total	7.5
Controllable	7.9
Uncontrollable	6.6

The Free Land Cluster is comprised of satellite office, retail, and industrial markets, and is characterized by high growth. In these markets, high-growth rates have served to balance increased supply, but potential oversupply remains a critical issue. The supply side excesses are severe. No appreciation is expected in these markets. Return per unit of risk is low.

CLUSTER 4
National Apartment

Statistics:
Historical mean return	9.2%
Historical standard deviation	1.9
Forecasted return	5.9
Historical return/risk quotient	4.8
SampCo exposure:	
Total	2.1
Controllable	3.0
Uncontrollable	2.2

This cluster, National Apartment, consists of older, apartment markets exhibiting extremely stable behavior. These markets are characterized by large existing inventories and there has been little net change in inventory per capita during the speculative years. Land costs are relatively high. Demand prospects are poor, making the lack of supply growth irrelevant. These are "baby bust loser" markets that manage to provide good value for the risks assumed.

CLUSTER 5
National Retail

Statistics:
Historical mean return	11.8%
Historical standard deviation	4.1
Forecasted return	9.0
Historical return/risk quotient	2.9
SampCo exposure:	
Total	17.0
Controllable	7.1
Uncontrollable	40.0

The National Retail Cluster includes the majority of the retail markets analyzed. Highly cyclical markets, created by both demand and supply factors, are placed elsewhere. (This is because real incomes are so strongly influenced by national forces such as taxes, safety nets, and economic cycles.) The current recession is more devastating to returns in these markets because it is accompanied by low inflation, high existing supply, and continued construction (mainly large "boxes"). Basic retail continues to provide good value, even with the low inflation. This is good news given SampCo's exposure.

CLUSTER 6
Down Cycle Industrials

Statistics:	
Historical mean return	9.5%
Historical standard deviation	5.2
Forecasted return	10.5
Historical return/risk quotient	1.8
SampCo exposure:	
Total	12.2
Controllable	25.0
Uncontrollable	0.0

The Down Cycle Industrials Cluster includes the large industrial markets that are regularly battered by recession, but tend to recover in a timely and often dramatic way. These markets operate in a fashion very similar to the national average for industrial real estate displaying moderate returns and volatility. The returns per unit of risk are stable and perform only slightly below the median level.

CLUSTER 7
Houston

Statistics:	
Historical mean return	9.1%
Historical standard deviation	6.6
Forecasted return	10.5
Historical return/risk quotient	1.4
SampCo exposure:	
Total	5.0
Controllable	5.0
Uncontrollable	0.2

Cluster 7, Houston retail and industrial, moves along the same extreme cycles. They are both volatile and respond very strongly to changes in the demand side of the market. The cost of land in these markets is negligible so supply constraints are virtually nonexistent. Nonetheless, values have been effectively "marked to the market" enabling a possible recovery. The risk/reward relationship is not as strong here as in some of the other clusters.

CLUSTER 8
Northeast and Midwest Offices

Statistics:	
Historical mean return	8.0%
Historical standard deviation	5.4
Forecasted return	2.4
Historical return/risk quotient	1.5
SampCo exposure:	
Total	4.0
Controllable	7.2
Uncontrollable	3.1

In Cluster 8, these markets are located in the industrial Northeast and the Midwest. There will be virtually no demand growth in most of these markets. In fact, there will be continued contraction in some of them for the foreseeable future. Once a demand peak is passed, these markets tend not to regain their former peak. The returns reflect the wide bid-ask spreads in three markets making valuation especially difficult. One wonders how to value these markets at all. The trade-off of risk and return is among the poorest.

CLUSTER 9
Value Apartment

Statistics:	
Historical mean return	9.0%
Historical standard deviation	2.0
Forecasted return	8.5
Historical return/risk quotient	4.5
SampCo exposure:	
Total	0.0
Controllable	0.0
Uncontrollable	0.0

The markets in Cluster 9 are very stable. They are characterized by steady demand and a pattern of supply that typically reflects prudence given the level of demand. These are bondlike investment markets, with little appreciation potential. The return per unit of risk is one of the best.

CLUSTER 10
Recovering Industrial

Statistics:
Historical mean return	9.0%
Historical standard deviation	3.9
Forecasted return	13.9
Historical return/risk quotient	2.3
SampCo exposure:	
Total	10.2
Contollable	8.9
Uncontrollable	7.0

This cluster, Recovering Industrial, contains solely industrial property types located primarily in major distribution markets. Excess supply created substantial down cycles that were compounded by cycles for poor demand. These markets are very much poised for recovery as supply has been curtailed and demand is improving. These markets generally compensate an investor at a level that exceeds the return/risk quotient median.

CLUSTER 11
Northwest Markets

Statistics:
Historical mean return	10.1%
Historical standard deviation	3.9
Forecasted return	8.7
Historical return/risk quotient	2.6
SampCo exposure:	
Total	7.0
Controllable	10.2
Uncontrollable	8.7

Industrial and retail property types located in Portland and Seattle dominate Cluster 11. Additionally there are some markets in this cluster that are not on the West Coast, but which share an international influence and similar exposure to trade patterns and policies. Risk and return are favorably related in this cluster.

CLUSTER 12
Syndicated Apartments

Statistics:	
Historical mean return	7.4%
Historical standard deviation	2.5
Forecasted return	9.6
Historical return/risk quotient	3.0
SampCo exposure:	
Total	6.5
Controllable	4.9
Uncontrollable	1.0

Intuitively, it would seem that this cluster should be more volatile given that it contains multifamily investments in Denver, Phoenix, and Tampa. However, the observed foreclosure rate in such places was a result of extremely high leverage (very high loan to value ratios applied to unstabilized values and income streams) employed at an unfortunate time in the market cycle. This is a useful cluster with one of the better return/risk quotients.

CLUSTER 13
Distressed Industrials

Statistics:	
Historical mean return	10.4
Historical standard deviation	6.2
Forecasted return	5.3
Historical return/risk quotient	1.7
SampCo exposure:	
Total	12.7
Controllable	10.1
Uncontrollable	5.3

Cluster 13 shows that Riverside, Newark, Sacramento, Philadelphia, and Boston industrial properties are all experiencing severe declines in demand after years of sustained increases in demand. Speculative construction continued in some of these markets for far longer than was defensible. These are high volatility markets where further depreciation should be anticipated. Risk is not well rewarded in these markets.

CLUSTER 14
Distressed Office

Statistics:	
Historical mean return	10.2%
Historical standard deviation	9.0
Forecasted return	5.3
Historical return/risk quotient	1.1
SampCo exposure:	
Total	10.7
Controllable	15.3
Uncontrollable	5.3

These office markets (Anaheim, Atlanta, Boston, Miami, Newark, San Jose, West Palm Beach) face considerable difficulty in the coming three years. These are markets on the East and West Coasts with defense and technology influences. These are the most risky markets and, unfortunately are characterized by poor risk/reward relationships.

CLUSTER 15
Primary Office

Statistics:	
Historical mean return	5.5%
Historical standard deviation	6.9
Forecasted return	9.3
Historical return/risk quotient	0.8
SampCo exposure:	
Total	4.3
Controllable	8.2
Uncontrollable	0.0

Five big Midwestern and Western office markets comprise this cluster. These markets are now overbuilt relative to their ability to produce demand. They were all very popular with institutional investors. The positive demand characteristics in these markets should stabilize these markets now that new supply has been virtually eliminated. The risk/reward relationships are well below the median because of greater than desirable volatility.

CLUSTER 16
Secondary Office

Statistics:
Historical mean return	8.5%
Historical standard deviation	4.2
Forecasted return	12.2
Historical return/risk quotient	2.0
SampCo exposure:	
Total	5.0
Controllable	1.2
Uncontrollable	16.7

The Secondary Office Cluster contains a large number of office markets and two industrial markets that are characterized by a preponderance of "flex" space. Supply has ground to a halt in these secondary markets as institutional interest has cooled. As a result of reduced supply growth, the markets are expected to recover in a timely and appealing fashion. The relationship between return and risk is slowly rising.

CLUSTER 17
RTC Office

Statistics:
Historical mean return	2.4%
Historical standard deviation	4.7
Forecasted return	9.3
Historical return/risk quotient	9.7
SampCo exposure:	
Total	7.9
Controllable	9.3
Uncontrollable	9.7

These markets (e.g., office in Denver, Houston, and Pittsburgh) suffered the most dramatically and visibly during the 1980s. Supply growth has been practically nonexistent for eight years and new construction is unlikely for another five years; in fact, it is questionable whether values will exceed replacement costs in the near to intermediate future. Nonetheless, these markets should experience some appreciation even with the gap between replacement costs and values. As such, an investor's willingness to bear higher levels of risk may be well rewarded in the mid-1990s.

CLUSTER 18
Texas Apartment

Statistics:	
Historical mean return	7.2%
Historical standard deviation	3.3
Forecasted return	7.6
Historical return/risk quotient	2.2
SampCo exposure:	
Total	0.0
Controllable	0.0
Uncontrollable	0.0

The Texas Apartment Cluster has exhibited downside behavior that is consistent with intuition, but the experience on the upside is not nearly as robust as many had anticipated. The appeal of these Texas multifamily markets is diminished by fierce price competition from the single-family home market. The return per unit of risk measure approaches the return/risk quotient median.

Implications of and Relationships among the Dimensions of Diversification

Some interesting exposures to the dimensions of diversification as described are seen. For example, high exposures to Pittsburgh office and Seattle retail, so apparent in the MSA level analysis, are now joined by a significant exposue to Cluster 5. Cluster 5 is dominated by two large investments, but is exaggerated by multiple industrial investments in markets, that prior to this analysis, may have appeared to be disparate and dissimilar.

Some other large exposures can be found in Clusters numbered 7 and 15. Performance of Cluster 7 is expected to continue unchanged for some time, followed by recovery in 1995 and 1996. A similar pattern is evident in the Primary Office Cluster (Cluster 15), except that the cycle has been in a downward mode for far longer and the recovery is expected to be less exuberant.

It is very important to note the exposures to which SampCo is bound. These holdings, assumed "uncontrollable" because of complex investment structures, have a significant effect on the portfolio (as will be made clear). The greatest exposures of the uncontrollable portfolio are to some of the lower expected return clusters such as Clusters 6, 13, and 14.

The portfolio is very significantly exposed to Cluster 11. Fortunately this is a neutral exposure, exhibiting moderate returns and moderate risks. On the other hand, the magnitude of this exposure is large enough to impede the portfolio's returns from approaching a level that would otherwise be achievable. Special attention should be paid to the plans for the controllable portion of this cluster. This will be further developed in the section, "Portfolio Policy Implications and Recommendations."

So far we have only examined the clusters, their rationale and behavior, and the portfolio's exposures. Of equal importance is an understanding of the relationships among the clusters. It is through these relationships that portfolio risk is either managed or magnified. Table 6–8 provides a matrix of correlations among the clusters.

Clusters 7, 9, 12, and 18 all exhibit patterns of low and negative correlation relationships with other clusters. This renders these clusters as potentially extremely useful in the construction of a diversified portfolio. In contrast, Cluster 8 exhibits fairly high positive correlations with other clusters. Free Land, Cluster 3, also presents some high correlations with Northeast and Midwest Office (8), Distressed Industrials (13), and Distressed Office (14). Total exposure to these clusters with poor expected performance comprises 21 percent of the real estate portfolio. Most of this exposure is in the uncontrollable portion of the portfolio. Free Land cities and property types were excluded from some of these less well-performing clusters because the metro areas involved generally have relatively strong demand growth prospects.

The efficient frontier model considers all of the characteristics of the investments introduced into the model: expected returns, correlations, and the relative risk of each cluster. It is rarely intuitively obvious in an 18-asset (cluster) analysis how the efficient allocations will be assigned. In the next section we present the construction of an efficient frontier produced from the inputs just examined. We then show the location of the SampCo portfolio relative to an efficient frontier and an efficient frontier constrained by the portion of SampCo's current investment portfolio designated as uncontrollable.

Efficient Frontiers: Unconstrained and Constrained

The data presented in Table 6–8 (listing historic correlations, standard deviations, and expected returns over a five-year forecast period) were all entered into a standard mean variance model. The efficient frontier produced is presented in Figure 6–4. On the same plot we have included the locations of each of the individual clusters. (We have also included the location of the Russell-NCREIF portfolio to demonstrate its relative merits. Its location should give one pause when considering its use as a performance benchmark.)

As is apparent, there are a wide variety of risk and return combinations available to the real estate investor. The challenge is to combine the choices into efficient portfolios.

The unconstrained efficient frontier presented in Figure 6–4 is the one obtainable by an investor willing and able to invest in the full range of

FIGURE 6–4
Unconstrained Efficient Frontier

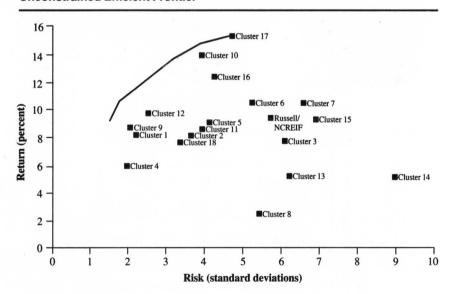

Source: AEW Research.

TABLE 6–9
Cluster Correlation Matrix 1982:1 through 1992:2

Cluster	1	2	3	4	5	6	7	8	9	10	11	12	13	14	15	16	17	18
1	.xxx																	
2	.xxx	.xxx																
3	.xxx	.xxx	.xxx															
4	.xxx	.xxx	.xxx	.xxx														
5	.xxx	.xxx	.xxx	.xxx	.xxx													
6	.xxx	.xxx	.xxx	.xxx	.xxx	.xxx												
7	.xxx	.xxx	.xxx	.xxx	.xxx	.xxx	.xxx											
8	.xxx	.xxx	.xxx	.xxx	.xxx	.xxx	.xxx	.xxx										
9	.xxx	.xxx	.xxx	.xxx	.xxx	.xxx	.xxx	.xxx	.xxx									
10	.xxx	.xxx	.xxx	.xxx	.xxx	.xxx	.xxx	.xxx	.xxx	.xxx								
11	.xxx	.xxx	.xxx	.xxx	.xxx	.xxx	.xxx	.xxx	.xxx	.xxx	.xxx							
12	.xxx	.xxx	.xxx	.xxx	.xxx	.xxx	.xxx	.xxx	.xxx	.xxx	.xxx	.xxx						
13	.xxx	.xxx	.xxx	.xxx	.xxx	.xxx	.xxx	.xxx	.xxx	.xxx	.xxx	.xxx	.xxx					
14	.xxx	.xxx	.xxx	.xxx	.xxx	.xxx	.xxx	.xxx	.xxx	.xxx	.xxx	.xxx	.xxx	.xxx				
15	.xxx	.xxx	.xxx	.xxx	.xxx	.xxx	.xxx	.xxx	.xxx	.xxx	.xxx	.xxx	.xxx	.xxx	.xxx			
16	.xxx	.xxx	.xxx	.xxx	.xxx	.xxx	.xxx	.xxx	.xxx	.xxx	.xxx	.xxx	.xxx	.xxx	.xxx	.xxx		
17	.xxx	.xxx	.xxx	.xxx	.xxx	.xxx	.xxx	.xxx	.xxx	.xxx	.xxx	.xxx	.xxx	.xxx	.xxx	.xxx	.xxx	
18	.xxx	.xxx	.xxx	.xxx	.xxx	.xxx	.xxx	.xxx	.xxx	.xxx	.xxx	.xxx	.xxx	.xxx	.xxx	.xxx	.xxx	.xxx

SampCo Portfolio Weights

Cluster	Cluster Name	Average Return 1982–92	Standard Deviation 1982–92	Expected Return 1992–97	Total Portfolio	Controllable Portion	Uncontrollable Portion
1	Growth Apartment	x.xx	x.xx	x.xx	x.xx	x.xx	x.xx
2	Rust Belt Retail	x.xx	x.xx	x.xx	x.xx	x.xx	x.xx
3	Free Land	x.xx	x.xx	x.xx	x.xx	x.xx	x.xx
4	National Apartment	x.xx	x.xx	x.xx	x.xx	x.xx	x.xx
5	National Retail	x.xx	x.xx	x.xx	x.xx	x.xx	x.xx
6	Down Cycle Industrials	x.xx	x.xx	x.xx	x.xx	x.xx	x.xx
7	Houston	x.xx	x.xx	x.xx	x.xx	x.xx	x.xx
8	Northeast and Midwest Office	x.xx	x.xx	x.xx	x.xx	x.xx	x.xx
9	Value Apartment	x.xx	x.xx	x.xx	x.xx	x.xx	x.xx
10	Recovering Industrial	x.xx	x.xx	x.xx	x.xx	x.xx	x.xx
11	Northwest Markets	x.xx	x.xx	x.xx	x.xx	x.xx	x.xx
12	Syndicated Apartments	x.xx	x.xx	x.xx	x.xx	x.xx	x.xx
13	Distress Industrials	x.xx	x.xx	x.xx	x.xx	x.xx	x.xx
14	Distressed Office	x.xx	x.xx	x.xx	x.xx	x.xx	x.xx
15	Primary Office	x.xx	x.xx	x.xx	x.xx	x.xx	x.xx
16	Secondary Office	x.xx	x.xx	x.xx	x.xx	x.xx	x.xx
17	RTC Office	x.xx	x.xx	x.xx	x.xx	x.xx	x.xx
18	Texas Apartment	x.xx	x.xx	x.xx	x.xx	x.xx	x.xx
					x.xx%	x.xx%	x.xx%

	Expected Return	Risk
Total portfolio	x.xx	x.xx
Controllable portion	x.xx	x.xx
Uncontrollable portion	x.xx	x.xx
Russell-NCREIF	x.xx	x.xx

markets and property types that comprise the investment universe. This hypothetical investor is completely unconstrained and can rebalance its portfolio at will. This is not the case for the typical institutional investor that has been active over the past several years.

To accommodate this, we have run the efficient frontier model with the constraints that reflect SampCo's holdings in uncontrollable investments. This is presented in Figure 6–5. In addition, we have added the plot location which reflects the risk/return characteristics of SampCo's current portfolio (see Figure 6–6), as well as the locations of the uncontrollable and controllable portions of the portfolio (see Figure 6–7).

This work has profound implications for SampCo's portfolio strategy. Two important observations may be made:

1. **The controllable portfolio is better positioned than the uncontrollable portfolio.** It exhibits more return and less risk, for greater efficiency.
2. **The existence, magnitude, and composition of the uncontrollable portfolio reduces SampCo's opportunity set by over 175**

FIGURE 6–5
Efficient Frontier Analysis of Sample Company Portfolio

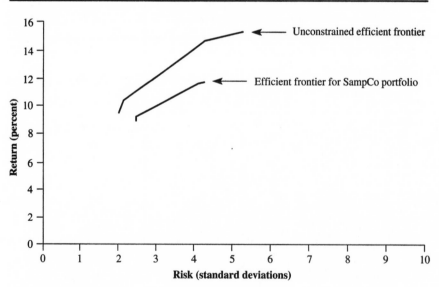

Source: AEW Research.

basis points. This means that, for a range of acceptable levels of risk, SampCo will be denied access to 175 basis points of annual return because it is locked into some assets that are less productive than others might be. The constraint of the uncontrollable portfolio causes SampCo to sacrifice significant mobility; mobility that would greatly enhance the performance of its portfolio.

SampCo is not getting adequately compensated for giving up this mobility. There are real costs (foregone opportunities) associated with being "locked in" to some of the holdings. This observation should cause an investor to rethink the "costs" of obtaining greater mobility.

Even in this constrained environment there is room for improvement. The portfolio could embark on a program to move it closer to the efficient frontier (up and left on the graph), to raise returns while reducing risk. These possibilities are addressed in the policy analysis presented below. This analysis is conducted in the context of the constrained efficient frontier as it best defines the current opportunity set.

FIGURE 6–6
Risk versus Return Analysis of Total SampCo Portfolio

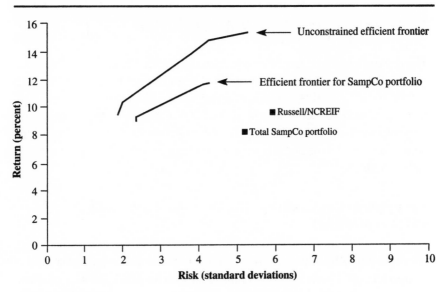

Source: AEW Research.

FIGURE 6–7

Risk versus Return Analysis of Controllable and Uncontrollable Portions of SampCo Portfolio

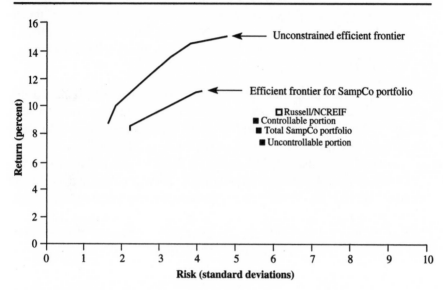

Source: AEW Research.

THE PORTFOLIO: FINANCIAL STRUCTURE

The previous analysis has been conducted solely in the context of the risks and rewards associated with property locations and types. Additionally SampCo should critically assess the aggregate effect of the financial risks it has assumed. Specifically, it should link changes in the location and property type mix to changes in the portfolio's financial structure. SampCo should examine the appropriateness of any given asset's financial structure in light of the risk of its market and property type.

The Portfolio Capitalization Graphs: Total, Controllable, and Uncontrollable

Figure 6–8 presents total controllable and uncontrollable portfolio capitalization graphs. Capitalization graphs are a simple, graphical way of showing how the investor's monies are arrayed along a risk spectrum. Highly

FIGURE 6–8
SampCo Real Estate Portfolio Capitaliztion

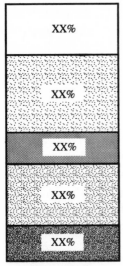
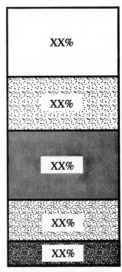

Total portfolio   Controllable portion   Uncontrollable portion

Source: AEW Research.

leveraged investments are housed within the top one or two quintiles of the graph and mortgages reside at the bottom of the cap graph. This helps an investor to see clearly the degree to which they are exposed to the risk of "first-dollar" losses. Leveraged equity will suffer greatly in a property value downturn. Mortgages are far more resilient to property value volatility. The cap graphs illustrate very important differences between the controllable and the uncontrollable subportfolio graphs. The controllable portion is considerably less leveraged and risky than the uncontrollable portion. The difference is significant.

The controllable portion appears more debtlike than equitylike when viewed in its entirety. This is a subportfolio not likely to capture the behavior of the total nominal, unleveraged real estate market.

Recall that, compared to the uncontrolled portion of the total portfolio, the controllable portion also is more efficiently allocated from a property type and location point of view (less risk, and higher returns per unit of risk) and is allocated to markets that are expected to achieve higher rates of return.

Conversely, the uncontrollable portion is substantially riskier from a financial structure perspective. Combine this with the expected performance of the markets in which the uncontrollable portfolio is located and one must think of the value of control and the costs of obtaining it in a different light. The uncontrollable portfolio is not able to be adjusted by the investor, but is perhaps riskier in all three of the "big three" risks than the investor might have wished to be.

PORTFOLIO POLICY IMPLICATIONS AND RECOMMENDATIONS

In this section, we describe some general implications of the analysis conducted above and a few achievable, but fairly minor portfolio restructurings that provide a flavor for the guidance provided by the framework.

Plans of Action

The clearest signal provided by this analysis is that the portfolio is assuming risk in the uncontrollable portion of its portfolio that is greater than in the controllable portion. The location and property-type risks are compounded by the financial structure risks in the uncontrollable portion. The location and property-type risks are more efficiently managed in the controllable portion and the exposure to financial structure risk is less as well.

Thus, SampCo is bearing a substantial opportunity cost created by the immobility of the uncontrollable portion of the portfolio. This is a cost that can produce substantial net gains if the monies invested in the uncontrollable portfolio were able to be "reclaimed" and reallocated. The benefits are twofold: (1) the location of the total portfolio will shift favorably; and (2) the constrained efficient frontier will shift up and to the left, creating a greater achievable opportunity set.

Portfolio Transaction "Option A"

Sell $40 million from the controllable portion of Cluster 13 (Distressed Industrials). This cluster has an expected return of 5.4 percent.

We replace this holding with an unleveraged $40 million investment in Cluster 10 (Recovering Industrial) with an expected return of 13.8 percent. This very minor transaction produces the following results net of transactions costs:

	Return	Risk	Return/Risk
Current total portfolio	8.50%	3.52%	2.41%
Current controllable portion	9.50	3.74	2.54
Current uncontrollable portion	8.32	3.83	2.17
"Option A"—total portfolio	9.00	3.47	2.59
"Option A"—controllable portion	9.82	3.39	2.89

This transaction represents a net gain for the portfolio measured in both absolute and efficiency terms. This is graphically presented in Figure 6–9. The total portfolio has gained an annual absolute return advantage of 50 basis points and a per unit of risk advantage of 18 basis points. (The scale of the graphs has been adjusted to "zoom" in on the effects of the restructuring.) Note that this transaction does not have any implications on the financial structure of the portfolio as both sides were structured as simple unleveraged equity.

Portfolio Transaction "Option B"

Another option would add to the transactions above by selling an additional $40 million from Cluster 5 (National Retail), and purchasing an additional $40 million in Cluster 12 (Syndicated Apartments). The results are shown below, net of transactions costs.

Again, the portfolio would experience a significant net gain in both the absolute annual return (50 basis points) and the annual return per unit of risk for the aggregate portfolio. The efficiency gains are particularly noteworthy. The gains in the controllable portion are even more striking

	Return	Risk	Return/Risk
Current total portfolio	8.50%	3.52%	2.41%
Current controllable portion	9.50	3.74	2.54
"Option B"—total portfolio	9.00	3.53	2.54
"Option B"—controllable portion	9.83	3.20	3.27

FIGURE 6–9

Risk versus Return Analysis of SampCo Portfolio Effect of Portfolio Transaction "Option A"

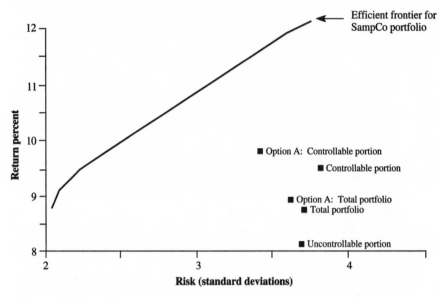

Source: AEW Research.

as this is where all of the adjustments are occurring. The absolute gain is 33 basis points and the efficiency gain is 73 basis points. This simulation is presented graphically in Figure 6–10.

Portfolio Transaction "Option C"

A final example contemplates transactions as described in Option B, the addition of $50 million of leverage to Cluster 5 (National Retail) and the purchase of $50 million of assets in Cluster 17 (RTC Office).

	Return	Risk	Return/Risk
Current total portfolio	8.50%	3.52%	2.41%
Current controllable portion	9.50	3.74	2.54
"Option C"—total portfolio	9.57	3.46	2.76
"Option C"—controllable portion	9.53	3.50	2.72

FIGURE 6–10

Risk versus Return Analysis of SampCo Portfolio Effect of Portfolio Transaction "Option B"

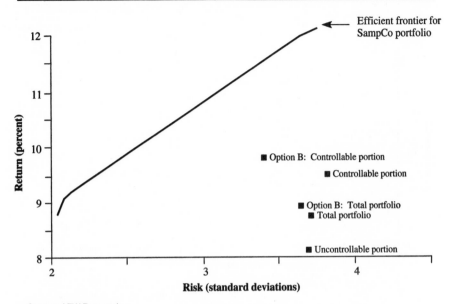

Source: AEW Research.

The gain in absolute return is 107 basis points and the efficiency gain is 35 basis points. This restructuring is presented in Figure 6–11.

This shift has portfolio cap graph implications as well, which are presented in Figure 6–12. The leverage applied to the uncontrollable portion has the effect of exacerbating an already difficult situation. The exposure to first dollar of loss is greater and the portfolio is still riskier from a location and property-type perspective than one would hope. The risk of the overall portfolio increases slightly as well, but the risk of the controllable portion remains essentially unchanged.

This analysis highlights the importance of combining structuring risks with location and property-type risks in a thoughtful and mutually reinforcing fashion. Here we added structuring risks to a portion of the portfolio that is characterized by moderate risk and is projected to generate slightly improving returns. While the addition of leverage was not harmful from an asset perspective or from an aggregate portfolio perspective, a very sizable portion of the portfolio over which SampCo has no control was rendered riskier. This is probably not the most advisable course of action.

FIGURE 6–11

Risk versus Return Analysis of SampCo Portfolio Effect of Portfolio Transaction "Option C"

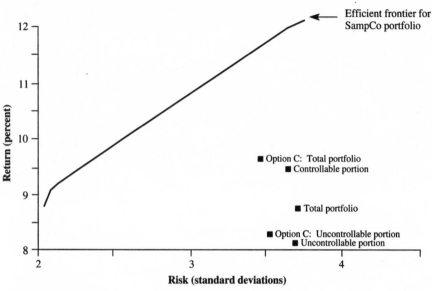

Source: AEW Research.

SUMMARY AND CONCLUSIONS

The analysis has identified several very important issues. The uncontrollable portion of the portfolio is neither efficiently structured nor allocated to markets that are forecast to achieve appealing returns. The uncontrollable portion is causing SampCo to experience a considerable loss of mobility that diminishes its investment opportunity set. This loss of mobility has the effect of denying SampCo access to another 175 basis points of annual return that the market is offering to more efficiently structured portfolios. The inefficiencies in the allocation among property type and location are precariously increased by the financial risk profile of the uncontrollable portion of the portfolio.

FIGURE 6–12
SampCo Real Estate Portfolio Capitalization

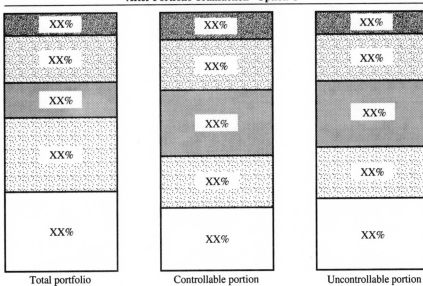

Current Structure

Total portfolio   Controllable portion   Uncontrollable portion

After Portfolio Transaction "Option C"

Total portfolio   Controllable portion   Uncontrollable portion

Source: AEW Research.

An investor can respond to these findings by selecting an approach to achieve a restructuring of the portfolio. The investor would specify which assets would be sold, what would be purchased and how (and if) the new investments would be structured. The investor would likely develop a deeper appreciation for the opportunity costs associated with a lack of control over their investments.

CHAPTER 7

REAL ESTATE INVESTMENT PERFORMANCE MEASUREMENT

Stephen E. Roulac

INTRODUCTION

The accelerating popularity of real estate as both an institutional and individual investment in the decade of the 1980s was fueled by the perception that real estate delivered at least competitive if not superior performance relative to traditional corporate securities investments. Some of these performance expectations were premised upon representations about past as well as probable future performance and employed methodologies whose validity can charitably be described as dubious.

As the performance actually delivered has fallen in many instances far short of the promise, prudent investors are reconsidering the rationale for including real estate in their portfolios. (Refer to Chapter 3.) In a real estate market characterized by disappointment and discontinuity, investors are challenged to determine whether to diminish if not abandon their commitments to real estate, to stay the course with existing commitments, to alter strategies, or to add additional funds to their real estate allocations. This reexamination of the role of real estate as an institutional and individual investment, if it is to contribute to an informed decision consistent with fiduciary standards for institutional investors, should embrace a reconsideration of issues concerning real estate investment performance measurement.

Measuring real estate investment performance has become a priority consideration for investors, real estate investment managers and investment professionals, the broader real estate community, and the capital market in aggregate. Despite its importance, standardization and sophistication are less than optimal, as idiosyncratic, self-serving, even naive approaches dominate the measurement of real estate investment performance. These shortcomings contribute to pension real estate allocations being stuck in the 5 percent range. The allocation is sensibly constrained until the analytic tools have developed sufficiently to support a greater allocation.

A persistent barrier to the broad and enthusiastic acceptance of real estate as a legitimate institutional investment has been its dissimilarities from the familiar and accepted patterns of corporate securities investing, and investors' discomfort with the quality, availability, and reliability of information critical to real estate investing. Unfortunately, rather than building bridges to promote a dialogue and facilitate common understanding, many involved in real estate investing tend to pursue approaches that exacerbate the divergences. The relationship between the broader investment community's views toward real estate and the community of real estate investment specialists' approach to the broader investment issues has been characterized more by dichotomy, inconsistency, bias, self-serving attitudes, conflicting arguments, unsubstantiated claims, and cautionary admonitions resembling more a discordant cacophony than objectivity and understanding. If real estate is to be a legitimate individual and institutional investment, it ultimately must meet the standards and expectations of those investments to which it seeks to be compared.

Performance measurement has assumed growing importance in the financial community over the last quarter century, as the emphasis of investment management has shifted from custodianship to delivering performance. With more funds available to invest and more investors concerned about investing those funds, how well investments perform has gained greater prominence. Recognizing that apparently modest levels of performance variation have profound implications upon the amount of capital required to achieve a designated return objective (or alternatively, the amount of wealth that could be created from a given level of capital), investors, their advisers, investment managers, and other investment professionals have concentrated considerable attention on the question of how well different asset classes and specific investments actually do perform. Interest in performance measurement has been accentuated by the proliferation of investment alternatives, the discontinuity of fundamental economic and business relationships as well as the variability of performance between and within different classes of investment.

Although insisting on "equal treatment" by the mainstream investment community, and therefore expecting proportionate allocation of investable assets, the proponents of real estate often insist that because real estate is "different," its performance cannot be assessed in the same way as that of corporate securities. Thus, the real estate investment management community seems to advocate the direct transferability of its version of performance measurement for purposes of comparison to corporate securities investment performance only when such comparison serves its purposes.

Those investment traditionalists specializing in corporate securities assert that because the fundamental attributes of real estate investing differ materially from those of corporate securities, comparisons of relative performance between real estate and other asset classes should not be attempted. But since institutional and individual investors committed extraordinary amounts of capital to real estate in reliance upon claims of superior investment performance, it would be irresponsible not to examine the reality of that investment performance.

As challenging as real estate investment performance measurement may be, it is an undertaking that is performed implicitly if not explicitly. Decisions concerning investment policy, manager selection, performance monitoring, financial reporting, performance evaluation, and compensation all depend on real estate investment performance measurement. There is a fundamental need to integrate real estate into overall investing programs for individual and institutional investors, and such integration requires meaningful and reliable performance measurement information.

The divergent interpretations that can be drawn from multiple-period information on a group of managers' performance is amusingly depicted in an essay by J. M. Brew, "The Trustees' Meeting—A City Daydream."[1] The manager with the highest overall absolute performance achieved it through an outstanding first period result followed by substantial underperformance of the index thereafter. A second manager, after a very weak first period, then outperformed the index and all the other managers in all subsequent periods, although that manager's overall result lagged all other managers. Another manager showed less variability than

---

[1]Reprinted in *Classics II—Another Investor's Anthology*, ed. Charles D. Ellis with James R. Vertin (Homewood, Ill.: Business One Irwin, 1991), p. 325. Originally appeared in *Journal of the Society of Investment Analysts* (June 1971), p. 14.

the index, an attribute that certain trustees favored. But then a different set of managers showed more variability than the index, which some trustees preferred, thinking such a pattern would be beneficial, as they expected the markets to perform well in the future. Yet a different manager was favored by some because he outperformed the index every time, even though several other managers had better aggregate performance.

As this story effectively illustrates, the assessment of investment performance remains an undertaking susceptible to broad interpretation—even when the data reliability, representativeness, and timeliness are not in question. Without clear prior specification of investment objectives, evaluation of subsequent performance inevitably will reflect personal prejudice and priorities as well as varying degrees of sophistication and náiveté—circumstances that frustrate effective decision making. Since the data quality and maturity of real estate investing markedly lag that of corporate securities, clarity of investment objectives and the criteria by which the performance will be measured for purposes of comparison to those objectives merits the highest priority.

Although many seek a single universal measure that would capture all factors influencing an assessment of investment (and investment manager) performance, the reality is that the quest for the Holy Grail of performance measurement is a journey rather than a destination. Given the inherent complexity of the process, the discontinuity of markets and the economic environment in which investments and decisions are made, the plethora of investment options, the escalating complexity of investment instruments generally, and the accelerating pace of innovation of investment products specifically, performance measurement cannot be a mechanistic and straightforward structured process. It involves a high degree of interpretation and judgment. Therefore, understanding those factors that influence performance measurement generally and real estate investment specifically is fundamental to effective participation in real estate and other investment markets.

DIFFERENCES BETWEEN REAL ESTATE AND CORPORATE SECURITIES

Since real estate investments properly are viewed in the context of the overall investment universe where corporate securities are the dominant traditional investment form, consideration of how real estate investing differs from corporate securities is useful. A holder of stock buys an indirect position removed from involvement in and influence over the business decisions of the company. The owner of real estate and/or his or her managing agent is in direct control of the asset and all the business decisions associated with that asset. Growth in the securitization of real estate, which allows investors to acquire an indirect interest in real estate via the purchase of shares of an entity holding title to the property places that part of real estate investing on more of a parallel with corporate securities investing.

In the nonsecuritized real estate market, the investor generally owns 100 percent of a real property asset as contrasted with the fractional ownership held by the corporate securities investor. This distinction is significant. In the securitized market substantial information is made available on a somewhat objective and consistent basis to all owners, as well as the overall market. In the case of an asset held by a single, direct owner, such information is not readily available to nonowners, and consequently questions of measuring investment performance are compromised. Lacking information and the motivation to generate analysis for multiple-existing and prospective owners, analysts complete little analysis of real estate investments, relative to that which is done concerning corporate securities investments. Few analysts and lesser analysis contribute to both market inefficiency and pricing variability in real estate relative to corporate securities, which further affect the real estate investment performance measurement process.

Beyond the significant implications that follow from these differences, there are also profound implications on the pricing process that applies in a narrow, negotiated market (such as real estate) as compared to a near-perpetual broad auction market, such as corporate securities. The valuation of corporate securities is based upon the latest transaction, whereas the valuation of real property is based on an appraisal, which amounts to an estimate of the value of the asset. (Refer to Chapter 5.)

As the pricing mechanism for corporate securities is continually incorporating all known information that influences the future performance prospects of that business, prices can change continually and often by dramatic amounts over relatively short time periods. Real estate is valued much less frequently, generally on an annual basis, with the result that values appear to be more stable. In fact, this apparent stability is attributable more to the inherent "smoothing" processing of infrequent appraisals rather than how market forces influence property values.[2] Not

---

[2]David Geltner, "Smoothing in Appraisal-Based Returns," *Journal of Real Estate Finance and Economics* 4, no. 3 (September 1991), pp. 327–43.

appreciating the implications of appraisal smoothing and reliability considerations, many reach the mistaken impression that real estate values are inherently subject to a lesser degree of price fluctuation than corporate securities, and therefore that real estate is a less risky investment.

Still, it should be recognized that the valuation and reporting for corporate securities is not without certain problems, including whether to choose as a value the bid, ask, or a close price; the potential distortions introduced by abnormal transaction volumes; or the effects of year-end pricing distortions resulting from "ex-dividend" status concerning stock prices.

FUNDAMENTALS

Basic to real estate investment performance measurement is an understanding of certain basic terms (identified and defined in Table 7–1) and their interrelationships. Primary considerations are that *performance measurement* is concerned with calculating changes, expressed either in absolute numbers or, more usefully, in a relative quantitative measure, over a specified time period; *performance evaluation* involves an assessment of the performance delivered and comparison to some standard or benchmark. The data used are derived from the income statement, which reports the results of operations; appraisal reports, which are estimates of value; and documents reporting the purchase, financing, and sale of specific assets and interests.

The consequences of direct ownership of properties and pricing by an appraisal process allows substantial variation, and therefore the potential for at least influence if not overt manipulation, of reported income and property values. Consequently, real estate investment performance measurement is both more subtle and more susceptible to distortion than corporate securities performance measurement. Even though corporate securities performance measurement is quite susceptible to such manipulation, consumers of real estate investment performance measurement information must be both more skeptical and more sophisticated than consumers of corporate securities performance measurement.

In evaluating real estate investment performance measurement, it is appropriate to ask the question of performance relative to what? Among the possible points of reference for measuring performance are absolute standards unique to the investor or relative standards relating to other

TABLE 7–1

Basic Terminology of Real Estate Investment Performance Measurement

---

Appraisal—an estimate that measures value at a particular point in time.

Income statement—a report of the results of operations for a particular period, with the income being the difference between revenues collected and expenses paid.

Gain—the change of value over a given time period, with the value figures at given dates determined either by transaction prices, as reflected by purchase or sale of the property, or appraisal values.

Income—the difference between revenues and expenses over a given time period.

Cash return—a return reflected in actual cash without consideration of noncash accrual or unrealized items.

Accrual return—a return that gives consideration to noncash items, such as revenue and expense items that are paid or scheduled to be paid in other than the period being measured.

Unrealized gain—the change of value reflected by the amount the appraisal value exceeds the purchase price of the property, which difference is yet to be realized because the property is yet to be sold.

Nominal return—an investment return reported in current dollars without consideration of changes in the purchasing power of the dollar over time.

Real return—an investment return reported in constant dollars, adjusting the returns realized in subsequent periods for changes in the purchasing power of the dollar, or other currency as appropriate, to account for the effects of inflation or, more rarely, deflation.

Return net of currency adjustments—an investment return for cross-border investing calculated *after* adjusting for effects of currency price fluctuation.

Total return—the overall return realized on the investment as a result of income realized in each period and the change in value of the investment from date of acquisition to date of measurement and/or disposition.

Pre-tax return—a calculation of a return without consideration of tax consequences, which usually reduces the level of return but may in some instances of specialized tax-oriented investments increase return.

After-tax return—the total return reflecting consideration of tax liabilities for a designated tax bracket, which generally must be stipulated, inasmuch as tax rates can vary significantly depending upon an investor's circumstances over time as well as changes in the tax law.

Performance measurement—a calculation of how an investment performs, involving consideration of both income generated by that investment and the change in the value of the investment over time.

Performance evaluation—an assessment of performance, generally involving a comparison of the performance measured to the performance delivered by other investments, investment managers, benchmarks, or market indexes.

---

investment types, investment programs, and investment managers. Investor-specific standards can include specified investment objectives expressed as nominal and real returns and various measures of investment risk. It should be recognized that the objectives of a particular investor may vary materially from those embraced by the investment manager charged with implementing the investor's program. Such variances are not necessarily inappropriate, as many managers may internally have aspirations that exceed those of the investor. If, however, the investment manager aspires to a lesser level of performance or a very different strategy than does the investor (i.e., the aggressive pursuit of capital appreciation when the investor desires a more conservative emphasis on current income), misunderstanding and disappointment are the quite likely consequences.

Beyond what a particular investor may seek as a return for its own purposes, comparisons to how an investment portfolio and an investment manager perform in the context of the larger universe are inevitable. Here, consideration may be given to performance relative to investors with similar circumstances, to investment programs pursuing similar strategies, to the aggregate of investments of that particular class, or to a broader universe of investments. Such comparisons involve consideration of using some type of external performance benchmarks, which often can take the place of a market index.

PRIMARY CONSIDERATIONS AND ISSUES

Among the primary considerations and issues that influence the real estate investment performance measurement process are:

Measuring Performance for Particular Properties or Portfolios in Aggregate

In the corporate securities context, performance is measured at the portfolio level, rather than focusing on particular winners or losers. The practice in real estate tends to involve attention both to performance overall and to the implications of particular problem properties. This emphasis on the status of individual assets results because real estate involves direct as opposed to indirect investing. Further, the considerable incidence of problem properties in the latter 1980s and early 1990s necessarily demands more attention. Nonetheless, there is a disproportionate emphasis on particular properties at the expense of the overall portfolio, which emphasis may represent a disservice to the investors' ultimate objective.

Measuring the Performance of Real Estate Assets versus Return on Overall Real Estate Portfolio Investment

Many real estate investment managers advocate concentrating on the real estate per se and considering only results achieved from the date when a property is acquired. Such *real estate-only* proponents favor disregarding consideration of the effects of cash not invested. Although such a real estate-only orientation is a useful and potentially illuminating refinement, properly it should be secondary to how the investor's ultimate portfolio performs: the investor receives a return on the total commitment of capital to the investment program, *not* merely on how that capital performs during the period it is invested in property.

Desired Precision and Reliability

For a number of reasons, some of which are developed in greater detail below, there are inherent limitations as to the degree of precision that can be achieved in measuring real estate investment performance. It must be recognized that the objective of achieving a highly precise calculation is somewhat specious, since performance numbers are compared to other performance numbers that are characterized by disputable precision. Similarly, reliability must be viewed in the context of the range rather than an ultimate standard. Consequently, concern about results reported in much beyond a rounded real number is largely misplaced.

Impact of Financial Structure

Emergence of institutional real estate dominated by pension funds has revolutionized the financial structure of real estate investing, with a predominantly all-cash orientation replacing investment structures that traditionally were heavily leveraged. It is important to recognize that the returns generated by the real estate overall may diverge from the returns delivered to a particular investment position in that real estate. Although investment managers aspire to devise financial structures that enhance returns for particular investment positions over what the real estate itself generates, some structures, especially those designed for various highly leveraged, aggressively tax-oriented limited partnerships, deliberately deliver materially lower returns for the investor's position than the real estate itself generates.

Inflation Influences

Real estate gained great popularity as an individual and institutional investment in the late 1970s and early 1980s when inflation was a dominant investment concern. Many investment managers were beneficiaries of the fortunate confluence of a high ratio of debt financing, priced at long-term fixed rates that effectively amounted to low if not negative real interest costs, and substantial overall inflation at the very time that real estate rents, occupancy levels, and therefore, values were increasing dramatically in real terms. As a result, highly impressive but temporary track records were created.

Tax Influence

While the tax-exempt institutional investor is generally not directly concerned with tax factors, except where leveraged investment arrangements are employed, tax considerations loom large for the individual investor. Real estate tax considerations are generally more complicated and less readily understood than corporate tax considerations from the perspective of most investors. Indeed, an individual investor receives a different K-1 tax form for each limited partnership investment and files a separate tax schedule for each investment held directly. As there may be major divergences between pre-tax and after-tax returns, careful consideration of the tax consequences of each investment and the portfolio in aggregate is fundamental to real estate investment performance measurement.

Performance Attribution

As highlighted in the discussion above concerning the effects of financial structure, inflation, and taxes, understanding the true source of the investment return merits a high priority. This important subject is explored in a subsequent section.

Divergent Objectives

The objectives of various consumers of real estate investment performance measurement information can diverge materially. The institutional investor generally approaches investment decisions with a process orientation derived from a long-term, going-concern attitude. Pension investors are most concerned about the relationship of their investing program to long-term actuarial and benefit payout assumptions and decisions. Necessarily, institutional investors tend to be risk averse, with the consequences of loss being of much greater concern (and, therefore, dominating their thinking), than the potential benefits of a superior result. Such investors are most concerned about how performance is reported in the context of certain identified goals and regulatory compliance requirements, thereby making optimizing or satisfying objectives more important than maximizing concerns.

Individual investors typically work with a shorter time horizon than do their institutional counterparts. Further, some of them are likely to be more risk aggressive and transaction specific in their approach.

Managers of real estate investments tend to employ a deal orientation, often emphasizing a specific transaction over the portfolio in aggregate. Such managers may be motivated to maximize the near-term return on investment, as a means to attract more deals, rather than long-term, overall performance. This shorter term orientation can result in a manager promoting the isolated performance of a single asset over a very short-time horizon as representative of the entire portfolio over the long term.

Past versus Future Performance

The accounting tradition of recording past financial results in financial statements, rather than looking to the present and future, constrains consumers of financial information to emphasize *what has been* rather than *what may be* in using financial information. This constraint also influences investment professionals to put an emphasis on *what has been* as contrasted to *what may be* in the future. This orientation has been reinforced by the Securities and Exchange Commission's emphasis on reporting past financial information and discouraging the reporting of future-oriented financial information.

More sophisticated financial and investment professionals recognize that past performance may not be a meaningful predictor of future performance. Nonetheless, human behavior and market practice place a predominant emphasis on drawing conclusions about what the future likely will be based on what has been. This is generally done without adequate adjustment for differences in the overall environment, financial markets, and the specific circumstances of the investment and investment management in question. Consequently, investors should be cautious in relying too heavily on conclusions drawn from past measures of investment performance without adequate consideration of how the future environment may diverge from that of the past.

Audience Sophistication and Investors' Needs

Dramatic variability characterizes the relative sophistication and needs of different types of investors and audiences for performance measurement information. Full-time investment professionals approach the interpretation of information on investment performance quite differently from lay individuals, who, although lacking in investment training, may serve part-time on the board of a pension fund, and quite differently still from individual investors who are neither trained in nor committed to an ongoing monitoring of their investments. These divergent circumstances influence what type of information might properly be provided to what audience and how that audience might be expected to employ that information.

Timing and Frequency

Questions of timing and frequency of real estate investment performance measurement are influenced both by consideration of the appropriate time period to adequately measure real estate investment performance, and the pressure to provide information on a time horizon that is comparable to that for other asset classes. Generally speaking, the pressure for parallelism with other asset classes causes more frequent and shorter duration readings of real estate investment performance than may be warranted, given the nature of the measurement process and the time horizon over which real estate investment performance is legitimately delivered. The pressure for more frequent, short-term readings is very real, and must be recognized by those delivering, measuring and interpreting real estate investment performance.

Of particular note in the real estate investment setting is the inherent delay in real estate financial reporting relative to corporate security reporting. Information is readily available for purposes of measuring return on corporate securities in the form of dividends and price adjustments, and accordingly such information can be processed expeditiously through computerized evaluation models, the relative timeliness of real estate information reporting and analysis lags dramatically.

It often takes several months for information to pass from the property level through various steps until reported to an investor. Then, considerable effort is involved to verify and validate the information and to organize it in a format amenable for analysis. Consequently, the reporting and assessment of real estate investing performance can lag six months or more from the date of the economic events being evaluated.

As a review of the above considerations indicates, real estate investment performance is characterized more by complexity than simplicity. If a single, universal measure is unachievable for corporate securities, such a standard is even more remote in the instance of real estate investment. But if performance measurement for real estate investment is much more difficult than for corporate securities, the problem is aggravated by the substantially lesser amount of analytic resources and sophistication applied to real estate.

WHAT PERFORMANCE SHOULD BE MEASURED?

The measurement of real estate investment performance can be captured at multiple levels:

1. *Real Estate as a Asset Class*
2. *Component Classifications of Real Estate*—including different types of property and property-based enterprise activity that involve the management issues and risks of business operations in addition to the tangible assets. Among the component classifications of real estate are:
   a. Core properties: comprised of office, industrial, retail, and multi-family.
   b. Specialized properties: including noncore, income-producing property types, ranging from primary property types such as hotels to specialized properties such as retail franchise facilities; nonincome-producing unimproved land, agriculture, and timberland.
   c. Different investment positions: including equity, debt, and hybrid instruments.
   d. Development: embracing an array of strategies ranging from passive, joint-venture equity positions financing a development project to active direct involvement in the development process.
3. *Geographic Market*—involving country, region, metropolitan statistical area, and submarket.
4. *Investor*—embracing all of an investor's real estate involvements including multiple types of real estate, managers, and manager relationships.
5. *Manager*—including all of the real estate investments managed for all types of accounts.
6. *Fund*—containing a discrete investment program or product organized and managed for a single or multiple investors.
7. *Component of a Portfolio*—consisting of all properties of a particular type or located in a particular region within a fund.

8. *Single Property*—in some instances this may be a relevant unit of performance, if that sole asset is being managed by a manager on behalf of
   an investor or group of investors. As noted above, however, it is more
   appropriate to look at the real estate investment portfolio involvement
   in aggregate rather than on an asset-by-asset basis.

Critical to real estate performance measurement is who does the
measurement. As noted, most investors rely upon agents, either an
internal investment staff, or third-party professionals, to assist them in
the interpretation of the investment performance information. In the
instance of major institutional investors, the investment staff, often
assisted by real estate and pension consultants, will analyze the information provided by the manager to achieve a presentation that is both
internally consistent and consistent over time. Again, the customized
performance measurement process often is supplemented by, or draws
upon information provided by third-party professionals or investment
management reporting services.

To the extent an institutional investor is self-managed, generating
and overseeing its real estate investments, without the involvement of a
third-party manager, the performance measurement process generally will
lack the arm's-length objectivity that exists where third-party managers
are involved. To the extent the performance of a pension fund's staff is
being reviewed by a board of directors, that board of directors often
retains a consultant to assist it in evaluating the performance of its staff,
both for reasons of objectivity and comparative sophistication.

PERFORMANCE MEASUREMENT PURPOSES

Real estate investment performance measurement can serve many purposes including:

- Investment policy.
- Manager selection.
- Performance monitoring.
- Financial reporting.
- Regulatory compliance.
- Performance evaluation.
- Property disposition decisions.
- Compensation determination.

- Market selection decisions.
- Client communications.
- Promotion of new investor relationships.

These varied purposes reflect the diverse objectives and concerns of the multiple participants in, and audiences for, real estate performance measurement.

The assumptions about proper levels of real estate investment performance have major investment policy implications for asset allocation, target return objectives for financial planning, and tactical implementation decisions. The importance of real estate performance measurement in the investment policy context is underscored by the thesis that investment performance is more dominantly influenced by investment policy decisions than by portfolio construction and security and/or individual investment analysis. Since expectations about the levels and attributes of investment performance drive determinations of how much of an investor's portfolio should be allocated to particular classes of investment, the relative quality and reliability of performance information assumes extraordinary importance. To the extent that investment policy decisions are premised upon misperceptions of investment performance, then the performance of the resulting portfolio will be inherently, and possibly adversely, influenced by such misperceptions.

Beyond the determination of how much of a portfolio might be allocated to a particular asset class, the level of return that can be expected from a class of investment drives financial planning decisions. These decisions apply in the institutional setting in the form of how much of a contribution is needed by the sponsor of a pension fund to ensure that retirement benefits can be paid to beneficiaries. In the individual investing setting, target return objectives determine the amount of funds that must be set aside to achieve a given wealth target.

With a plethora of real estate investment managers, investment products, and investment strategies from which to choose, the selection of manager, strategy, and investment product is influenced by an assessment of probable future performance. Those offering real estate investment management services employ research on historic and future real estate investment performance to market real estate as an asset class and to promote the specific strategies that the manager proposes to employ. Indeed, manager self-promotion to date has been the dominant form of the application of real estate investment performance measurement. Consequently, those who are concerned with selecting and evaluating real estate investment managers, cannot expect to make such decisions responsibly and reliably unless they have strong understanding of real estate investment performance measurement. Such understanding must extend beyond the concepts and generalities to embrace not just the details but also the nuances and subtleties that are susceptible to manipulation, distortion, and even deception.

Beyond decisions concerning investment policy and the selection of real estate investment managers, monitoring real estate investment performance depends heavily on how real estate performance is measured. Among the issues of concern in real estate performance monitoring are the performance of real estate as an asset class, as well as the performance of subcategories of real estate including property type and geographic regions, with such subcategories amenable to more finite specification and classification. Applications of information derived from performance monitoring apply to decisions concerning particular securities interests such as common stocks, real estate investment trust shares, and limited partnership interests. At the property level, these decisions involve the property management and leasing functions as well as acquisition, financing, and disposition decisions.

Financial reporting is an important purpose of real estate performance measurement. The results of real estate investment performance are manifested in periodic financial statements, which in most instances are prepared by management on a quarterly basis and audited on an annual basis. Both the basic financial statements and *repackaged* forms of the financial statements are employed to communicate to investors and for regulatory compliance. Depending upon the nature of the investment arrangement, federal and state agencies are involved, including the Department of Labor in the instance of pension funds, and the Securities and Exchange Commission and state securities regulatory agencies in the instance of publicly held securities such as real estate investment trusts and public limited partnerships.

Recipients of performance information employ that information both to evaluate performance generally and to make a series of specific decisions. Among these decisions are: how real estate performs against other asset classes; how certain segments of real estate perform against other segments as well as real estate in aggregate; how management is doing generally and against particular objectives; the due diligence process of evaluating manager's representations; and comparisons of multiple managers working on behalf of a common investor. Depending upon circumstances generally and the nature of the performance, the result of performance evaluation may be translated into decisions about investment emphasis, the number of investment managers and the allocation of capital among those managers.

A very important purpose of performance measurement from the perspective of both the investor and the manager is that of compensation. In the institutional setting, the majority of compensation arrangements are based upon a certain percentage of the value of assets under management. Consequently, the higher the value of the portfolio's properties, the higher the level of compensation that is paid. Investors and managers have congruent goals in this regard, so long as the property values reported are real rather than illusory.

The economic significance of performance measurement is magnified to the extent compensation is performance based. There has been considerable interest on the part of both investment managers and institutional investors to embrace performance-based compensation. As a practical matter, implementing that objective has proven rather difficult. In the instance of individual investors, by contrast, the preponderant number of compensation arrangements for real estate limited partnerships and to a lesser degree real estate investment trusts do involve incentive-based compensation arrangements.

Since some compensation incentive arrangements can be considerably complex, it is critical to consider how the formulas work in practice, and whether a particular incentive structure promotes decisions that are, in fact, congruent to the investor's objectives. As a case in point, many incentive compensation arrangements designed by sponsors of real estate limited partnerships in the 1970s and 1980s were tied to the realization of investment objectives expressed in nominal terms, which during a period of accelerating inflation proved to be a virtually instantaneous wealth transfer from limited partners to general partners on the formation of the investment program, independent of what performance ultimately may have been delivered.

WHO IS INTERESTED IN PERFORMANCE MEASUREMENT?

The audience for performance measurement embraces investors and their representatives, investment managers, the financial community, regulatory agencies, and those involved in the real estate markets in general.

While these audience segments share some common needs, they differ markedly in their objectivity, sophistication, and specific needs.

While some investors may be considered primary consumers of real estate investment performance measurement information, the majority tend to be represented by agents who review, interpret and act upon the performance measurement information on the investors' behalf. In the institutional setting, the pension funds' beneficiaries are represented by a board of directors or trustees that oversees the work of the officers and staff of the pension fund in question. Generally, the sophistication and time spent by those consuming performance measurement information is inversely related to their relative authority and responsibility. Consequently, staff presumably is more knowledgeable and spends more time interpreting real estate investment performance information than would the officers of the pension fund; officers, in turn, are likely to have more background and devote more attention to working with the real estate investment performance information than would the members of the board.

Individual investors usually are represented by an account executive affiliated with an investment firm and/or financial planner who sold the investment to the investor originally. In some instances the financial planning function, concerned with developing an individual's financial plan and then monitoring its implementation, is separate from the product sale function. A financial planner who emphasizes creating and monitoring the performance of an investment program generally brings a different orientation and skill set to the task than does the representative whose main source of compensation is tied directly to product sales. Because most individual investors lack the sophistication, resources, and inclination to delve into the details of their investments, especially investments as complicated as many real estate interests can be, individual investors tend to rely upon their representatives to review, distill and interpret real estate investment performance measurement information.

Beyond investors and their representatives, the team of professionals working for the investment management organization represents a primary audience for real estate investment performance measurement information. Executive management of investment management organizations is concerned with integrating the multiple considerations of client relationships, acquisition strategies, and portfolio management with the often cold and sobering quantitative measurement of a process that is characterized by dynamism, high emotion, and highly subjective behavioral patterns and motivations. Property managers are concerned with information that relates to how specific properties are performing. Similarly, portfolio managers are concerned with information relating to the portfolio's properties, just as a fund manager is concerned with how the aggregate of properties and portfolios that comprise the fund for a particular investor or group of investors is doing.

The financial community is a primary audience for real estate investment management performance information. Financial analysts and rating agencies tracking investment programs and managers as well as real estate as an asset class pay attention to the measures of real estate investment performance. The media, wanting to keep the financial community informed and being on the lookout for any provocative story concerning extremes of performance is an audience whose impact may well exceed its sophistication. Finally, academics and researchers employ performance measurement information in their various studies, some of which have profound import and some of which, unfortunately, more serve the publishing imperative of academic promotion than legitimately advancing knowledge creation.

Users of real estate represent another audience for performance measurement information. To the extent real estate is delivering a high level of investment performance, it is because those who utilize real estate as tenants are paying rent sufficient to provide substantial cash returns from properties relative to what investors originally paid for those properties. Thus, indications of high levels of financial returns from real estate investment may motivate tenants to own real estate rather than lease it.

Similarly, strong levels of investment performance motivate developers, at least according to theory, to create more buildings, although the reality is (particularly in recent times) that developers seldom need any more motivation than available financing to undertake more real estate projects. Of course, the very evidence of superior real estate investment performance that motivates investors to commit capital to developers to create more inventory of real estate virtually ensures that future levels of returns will be lower than the perceived returns that motivated such investment.

Organizations and professionals that provide services to the real estate markets, including accounting, tax, legal, consulting, property management, transaction support, and the like, are all influenced by performance of real estate investments. Higher returns generally translate into greater incidences of market activity and, therefore, more demand for professional services, especially those related to deal promotion. Conversely, negative returns translate into both a reduced level of demand for professional services and importantly, a very different type of demand for professional services.

Finally, those organizations and officials serving the public sector are influenced by and concerned with levels of real estate investment performance. Particularly in the instance of multifamily residential property, and those jurisdictions where rent stabilization or variations of rent control apply, the perceived level of return from real estate investing has important public policy implications in terms of the process by which allowable rents are determined. These deliberations in turn influence housing affordability and have implications for social service demand, fiscal policy, and municipal economics in a jurisdiction.

SOURCES OF INVESTMENT RETURNS

Real estate investment returns are in the form of both current income, analogous to dividends paid on corporate securities, and change in asset value over time. The current return that is the focus of performance measurement in real estate investing is derived from operating results of the property enterprise, rather than by a decision of management to pay out dividends. Therefore, consideration of the source of investment returns assumes a higher priority in evaluating real estate performance.

Real estate returns are of two basic types: those that are the result of operations and those that ensue from a change in the value of the initial equity investment. Operating results are composed of both cash flow and tax effects. Changes in equity value are derived from paying down mortgages and appreciation, with tax effects being an important consideration as well.

The investor's tax status has a greater impact on investment returns in real estate than in corporate securities. The taxpaying and tax-exempt investor receive the same form of returns in corporate securities investing but just treat the returns differently for tax purposes and determining the true, after-tax investment return. In real estate, by contrast, the nature of the tax law that governs real estate investing causes very different results for taxpaying and tax-exempt investors. Depending upon the nature of the investment structure, the investment return on an after-tax basis may be *higher* for the taxpaying investor than the tax-exempt investor.

In real estate investing, the current return is comprised of both cash flow and tax effects. Depending upon the structure of the investment, the nature of the property performance, and the investor's characteristics, the tax effect can be positive or negative, meaning that either it can increase or reduce cash flow on an after-tax basis. The tax consequences of sale for the taxpaying investor reduce the proceeds available by the amount of tax liability, except in certain specialized exchange transactions.

To the extent an otherwise tax-exempt institutional investor employs borrowed money to finance its investment activities, it may be subject to tax on unrelated business taxable income. Further, it should be recognized that this discussion relates to the tax treatment of an investor who is participating in real estate investing either directly or through a legal entity that achieves *flow through* tax treatment, such as a partnership, so that taxation is calculated at the investor rather than the entity level. Real estate investors who participate through the ownership of corporate shares will be treated in a manner comparable to their treatment of corporate securities. Current returns will be received and measured in the form of dividends and the change in equity value will reflect the difference between what was paid to acquire the shares and the value at the measurement date.

Thus, in considering the sources of investment return for both the taxpaying and tax-exempt investor, the three basic components of real estate returns are cash flow, tax effect, and change in equity value. Each is described more fully:

1. *Cash Flow.* Cash distributions are from operations. There are usually several claims on the operating income that take precedence over the claims of investors. These include debt service on the mortgage, reserves, and sponsor compensation. Some in the industry prefer to call the figure remaining after payment of debt service and sponsor compensation, "cash available for distribution."
2. *Tax Effect.* Tax benefits that result from the fact that the taxable income, because of depreciation deductions, usually is less than the cash flow. The tax effect is calculated by multiplying the taxable income by the specific effective tax rate. There is a different tax effect for each separate tax rate. Cash flow in excess of the taxable income is tax sheltered. To the extent that the taxable income is negative, as it often is in the early period of an investment cycle, there may be additional opportunity to shelter the investor's other income. Of course, once taxable income is positive, the tax effect is negative and thereby reduces rather than increases the annual benefit from operations.
3. *Change in Equity Value.* The increase in the value of the investment that results from the amortization of the mortgage debt on the property as well as the increase in the value of the property over time. While traditionally many have viewed principal pay-

ments, often termed *equity buildup*, and appreciation as important components of return, they are in fact returns only when realized. They really should be thought of as deferred, conditional, and tax-contingent returns. They are deferred in the sense that they are available only when the property is sold or refinanced, and may be even further delayed if, in the event of a sale, secondary debt is involved, or, in the event of refinancing, the funds generated are used for reinvestment in the property. They are conditional because they are available only if the value of the property is maintained. Given the risks associated with any investment in today's dynamic and uncertain business environment, there is no guarantee that today's values will not change dramatically. Perhaps most significant, changes in equity value are realized only after the associated tax liabilities are paid. Funds obtained by mortgage refinancing would not give rise to a taxable event, but a sale or foreclosure would cause taxes to be due, providing a gain had been realized. Investment benefits from operations could be significantly reduced by a tax liability in excess of cash proceeds at sale.

It is important to distinguish the timing of the various returns. Cash flow and tax effect are current returns since they are immediately available. Changes in equity value are deferred, conditional, and tax-contingent returns, since their realization is delayed, uncertain, and quite possibly nominal, if not negative. The sum of the cash flow and the tax effect is called the *total current benefit*. It represents the total benefits, consisting of cash flow (plus tax shelter or minus tax liability) that are available in the current period.

MEASURING INVESTMENT RETURNS

There are a number of approaches used to measure the return on real estate investment. Most are simplistic and can result in misleading information and undesirable decisions. Among the measures of investment return employed are:

1. Free-and-clear return.
2. Payback period.
3. Accounting return.
4. Profitability index.

5. Internal rate of return.
6. Adjusted rate of return.

In truth, most of these so-called return measures are really indicators of financial relationships, and thereby more properly classified as financial ratios, rather than rate of return measures.

It is appropriate to identify the considerations that should be incorporated in an accurate and reliable measure of return. These include:

1. The amount, timing, and full tax consequences of the initial investment.
2. All cash flows from operations over the entire life of the investment.
3. All tax effects, both tax shelter and tax liability, if any, over the entire life of the investment.
4. The cash proceeds (or obligations, as the case may be) from sale after giving effect to all tax considerations, including capital gains tax as well as the ordinary income tax liability on the recapture of the excess of accelerated depreciation (over straight-line depreciation), and the refund of any unused prepaid expenses or reserves where appropriate.
5. Recognition of the time value of money. As a dollar received today has more value than a dollar to be received tomorrow, money has a time value. When payment is deferred, the ultimate recipient must sacrifice the regular "savings rate of interest" that could be earned at the bank as well as forego special new investment opportunities that may be available.
6. Expression of the return as an index figure that permits comparison of different projects. It is desirable that projects involving different amounts of invested capital, different tax consequences, and different termination dates be readily comparable.

Consideration of the degree to which various of the so-called profitability measures meet these criteria yields insights as to their efficiency, as highlighted in the discussion below.

Free-and-Clear Return

The free and clear return is defined as the annual cash flow available to the investor divided by the equity investment. Two critical questions are involved. First, what components of "return" does it include?

- Cash flow?
- Cash flow plus tax effect?
- Cash flow plus tax effect plus equity buildup?
- Cash flow plus tax effect plus equity buildup plus appreciation?

Second, How is "equity investment" defined?

- Original cash down payment only?
- Original total cash payment including principal down payment plus such other items as prepaid expenses, underwriting commissions, and legal fees?
- Original total cash payment plus such other items as prepaid expenses, underwriting commissions, and legal fees, adjusted for the tax effect of the deductible items?

For both "return" and "equity investment" there are a number of additional possible definitions. To illustrate the impact of alternative definitions of return, consider the following example. For an apartment building requiring a $100,000 equity investment, there was a $7,000 cash flow, $4,000 of tax effect (resulting from a taxable loss of $10,000 for an investor in the 40 percent tax bracket), $3,500 of equity buildup, and $4,000 of appreciation (reflecting a 1 percent increase in value on the $400,000 initial purchase price). The impact of alternative definitions of return is highlighted in Table 7–2.

Clearly, the definition of *return* has a marked impact on what the return on investment turns out to be.

TABLE 7–2
Impacts of Alternative Definitions of Return

	Dollar Return	Return on $100,000 Equity Investment
1. Cash flow	$7,000	7%
2. Cash flow + tax effect	$7,000 + $4,000	11
3. Cash flow + tax effect + equity buildup	$7,000 + $4,000 + $3,500	14
4. Cash flow + tax effect + equity buildup + appreciation	$7,000 + $4,000 + $3,500 + $4,000	18.5

Payback Period

The payback period is defined as the amount of time required to recover the investment. For example, a project requiring $10,000 in equity with annual distributions of $2,500 per year would have a four-year payback period. While the payback method usefully identifies the period of time over which the invested funds are at risk, investors are interested in receiving a return beyond mere recovery of the investment. Using this method, it is possible to mistakenly select an investment that achieves a rapid payback of invested funds but no more, while rejecting an investment that has a slower payback but generates substantial total payments above and beyond the initial investment.

Accounting Return

The accounting return is defined as an average return over the entire holding period. It is derived by determining the sum of all returns less the initial investment and then dividing that figure by the term of the investment expressed in years, all divided by the initial investment amount. If the project described immediately above returned $2,500 per year for five years, the accounting return would be calculated as follows:

$$\text{Return} = \frac{\dfrac{5(\$2,500) - \$10,000}{5}}{\$10,000}$$

$$= \frac{\dfrac{12,500 - 10,000}{5}}{10,000}$$

$$= \frac{\dfrac{2,500}{5}}{10,000}$$

$$= \frac{\dfrac{500}{10,000}}{} = 5\%$$

The accounting return has the advantage over the payback method in that it considers all flows over the entire term of the investment.

The above-described profitability measures all leave much to be desired. Their chief shortcomings include recognition of equity buildup and appreciation prior to the time they are actually realized in cash; use of average figures; failure to consider all flows of both cash and tax effects over the entire investment cycle; and disregard of the time value of money.

Profitability Index

The profitability index is defined as the ratio of the present value of all positive flows divided by the present value of all negative flows at a given interest rate. Turning to a specific situation, an investment has cash flows over four years of $100, $400, $900, and $1,200, with an initial investment cost of $1,300 in year zero, and the investor must pay out $500 in year 5. The calculation of present value at a 10 percent discount rate of the positive cash flows is:

Year	Cash Flow	Discount Factor	Present Value
1	$100	.909	$ 91
2	400	.826	330
3	900	.751	676
4	1,200	.683	820
Total	$2,600		$1,917

The present value of the payouts (negative flows) is calculated as follows:

Period	Flow	Discount Factor	Present Value
0	$1,300	1.000	$1,300
5	500	.621	310
Total	$1,800		$1,610

Then, the profitability index can be readily calculated:

$$PI = \frac{\text{Present value of positive payments}}{\text{Present value of negative payments}}$$

$$PI = \frac{\$1,917}{\$1,610}$$

$$PI = 1.2$$

Since the profitability index at a 10 percent interest rate is greater than one, the investment has a rate of return in excess of 10 percent. If a 10 percent return were the criteria for selection, this particular investment would be acceptable. While the profitability index facilitates comparison of different investment opportunities, many investors want to know what *rate of return* they are earning on their investment. The internal rate of return, which is an extension of the profitability index, provides this information.

Internal Rate of Return

The internal rate of return is defined as that interest rate at which the present value of all positive inflows equals the present value of all negative outflows. All of the considerations identified above as basic for an accurate and reliable measure of investment performance are incorporated in the internal rate of return. Calculation of the internal rate of return requires information for the full investment cycle. The numbers that are used in the calculation should be expressed on an after-tax basis. The internal rate of return adjusts all flows to their present values and it expresses the returns as an index figure that facilitates comparison of one investment to another.

The internal rate of return is essentially a variation of the profitability index. With the profitability index, the interest rate is fixed and the unknown is the ratio of the positive inflows at that interest rate to the negative outflows at that interest rate. If the profitability index is equal to 1.0, the investment has an internal rate of return equal to the designated interest rate. If the profitability index is more than 1.0, the investment has an internal rate of return in excess of the designated interest rate.

Advances in computer technology have vastly simplified financial calculations and especially the rate of return. The procedure is *virtually automatic*, even though many making and interpreting such calculations lack a true understanding of the process and would be hard pressed to explain the methodology. Still, it is important to understand how the internal rate of return is actually calculated. To compute the internal rate of return, the profitability index (i.e., the ratio of the present value of positive inflows to the present value of negative outflows) is fixed at 1.0, and the unknown is the interest rate that is required to make the present values of these two flows equal to each other. Thus, the internal rate of return is that interest rate at which the present value of the positive inflows is equal to the present value of the negative outflows.

While the computational process of determining the profitability index is relatively straightforward, the calculation of the internal rate of return is cumbersome. This is because a series of repetitious calculations must be undertaken to arrive at the interest rate that is the internal rate of return. The process is one of trial and error, and the sheer number of calculations can be very time-consuming unless a computer is used.

It was determined for the illustration above that since the profitability index at a 10 percent interest rate exceeded 1.0, the internal rate of return for the illustration exceeded 10 percent. As the internal rate of return is defined as that interest rate at which the profitability index is equal to 1.0, to calculate the internal rate of return we must first select a trial interest rate of return. While with experience one can gain skill at selecting the appropriate interest rate, the process generally is one of trial and error. An interest rate is selected and used to calculate the present values. If the sum of all discounted flows exceeds zero, the interest rate selected was too low and a higher rate is needed. If the sum of the discounted flows is negative, the interest rate selected was too high.

This process of selecting an interest rate and calculating the present value of all flows continues until a rate is chosen where the sum is zero, that rate being by definition the internal rate of return. For our example, we will start with a rate of 19 percent. The calculation is shown in Table 7–3. Since the sum of the present values of the separate flows is negative ($11), the rate selected was somewhat higher than the internal rate of return for this particular investment. Continuing, a somewhat lower rate— 18 percent—is chosen and the calculation is again shown in the table. As seen, the sum of the present values is $20, indicating that the internal rate of return is between 18 percent and 19 percent.

When carried to several places to the right of the decimal point, such tables are of questionable validity and utility. They would tend to imply more accuracy in measuring returns than is warranted in most circumstances. From Table 7–3 it can be seen that the absolute difference between the present values at 18 percent and 19 percent interest rates is

TABLE 7–3
Illustrative Calculation of Internal Rate of Return

Period	Amount	Discount Factor	Present Value
18% Internal Rate of Return			
0	(1,300)	1.000	(1,300)
1	100	.847	85
2	400	.718	287
3	900	.609	548
4	1,200	.516	619
5	(500)	.437	(219)
			20
19% Internal Rate of Return			
0	(1,300)	1.000	(1,300)
1	100	.840	84
2	400	.706	282
3	900	.593	534
4	1,200	.499	599
5	(500)	.419	(210)
			(11)

31. The internal rate of return by straight-line interpolation, is equal to 18 percent plus 20/31 or, to express the same value in a different way, 19 percent minus 11/31. Straight-line interpolation is used here for simplicity; in fact the relationship between one discount rate and another is *not* linear. Consequently, the internal rate of return for the illustrative investment is approximately 18.64 percent, derived by subtracting .36 [11/31] from 19 percent, or adding .64 [20/31] to 18 percent.

Adjusted Rate of Return

The internal rate of return has the disadvantage that for nonsimple investments—whose flows have multiple changes of sign—there are nonunique solutions. Thus, multiple returns are indicated for some investments. Further, with the internal rate of return it is implicit that all flows during the investment period are invested and reinvested at the same *internal* rate earned by the project. Where returns are particularly high or low, the reinvestment rate to be actually used for the released cash must be close to the internal rate of return; otherwise there will be a distortive effect, and good projects will look better, and poor projects will look worse, than they really are. This "overstating" effect can be particularly pronounced where the initial contributions are *staged* over time.

While many in the real estate business still rely on unsophisticated profitability measures, there is evidence of considerable progress toward higher standards. The involvement of more sophisticated investors, accustomed to advanced capital budgeting and securities analysis techniques, has been an important influence as has been the concern of securities regulators and the Association for Investment Management and Research. With increasing attention to the communication of the expected and achieved results of real estate ventures, more emphasis has been directed to the appropriate measure of investment results. Indeed, an often reliable indicator of a real estate company's competence in modern institutional real estate is its attitude toward, and familiarity with, the more sophisticated profitability measures.

RELEVANT TIME PERIOD

A critical consideration is the time horizon for performance measurement. Pertinent factors influencing the time horizon consideration include the frequency, timeliness, and reliability of information; the facility with which purchase and sale transactions might be implemented; and the appropriate duration of the holding period, reflecting the reasonable life cycle of the economic activity of the investment program.

In the corporate securities investment environment, the combined influences of the going-concern concept for corporate enterprises and the ongoing daily trading for most securities, provide both the information for frequent readings and the ability to implement the prompt purchase or sale of an entire portfolio. By contrast, real estate assets and markets reflect divergent attributes. The real estate investing process is inherently more complex because of the direct acquisition of properties. The inevitable distortions reflected by recent chaotic conditions pose particular challenges in specifying the relevant time period for real estate investment performance measurement.

Properties are often purchased with deliberate end-game strategies in mind—perhaps implementing some physical value-enhancement through refurbishment or introducing a repositioning of tenancy and restructuring the leases—with a sale objective in 5 to 10 years for many assets. Additionally, improved real estate is, by definition, a wasting asset, with the physical structure susceptible to depreciation, including physical deterioration and functional obsolescence, and often requiring either substantial refurbishment or replacement.

Time lags in collecting, processing, and reporting information on specific properties, then validating the reported information and combining it to gain a reading on portfolios, result in reporting that is approximately one-quarter in arrears of the events reported on. Transactions similarly involve considerable time from the decision to sell a property until a transaction is consummated, given such factors as the function and structure of markets, due diligence, documentation, and regulatory compliance. While information is available and performance is measured on a periodic basis, the time lags and distinctiveness of time horizon, often customized to the manager's objectives and circumstances, compromise comparability within the real estate investing sector and between real estate and other asset classes.

The nature of real estate investing makes it inherently less amenable to short single-period assessment than to longer multiple periods of evaluations. As a general guideline, unless the subject investment is functionally a bond surrogate whose performance is primarily determined by movements in interest rates in the capital markets rather than by the performance of the underlying real estate, the relevant time period for performance assessment should parallel that appropriate for the implementation of the manager's strategy.

The determination of the relevant time period generally involves consideration of a property's performance over multiple cycles of market conditions as well as the opportunity for the manager to put in place a new lease structure for the property. Depending upon the nature of the property and the structure of leases in place at the time of its acquisition, a period of at least 5 years, and more reasonably 10 years, is required for a given property's tenancy to reflect a manager's strategy for that particular property rather than the strategy in place at the time the property was acquired. The chaos and discontinuity characterizing many real estate markets suggests that at least equivalent periods are required to reflect the manager's performance in both up and down markets.

Institutional investment management is much less mature for real estate than corporate securities. Because institutional real estate investment management for both individual and tax-exempt investors is of relatively recent origin, few managers have meaningful track records covering an extended period of time. Rather, most track records are of a shorter rather than longer duration. With regard to relatively shorter track records, the adversities that have plagued the real estate markets since the mid-1980s have an inevitable depressing and prospectively distorting impact on assessing how effectively management may have performed. With regard to managers with relatively longer track records, the composition of the professional staff and strategy employed today may be very different than that which prevailed in other times.

Given that performance measurements should cover multiple periods, an inherent question concerns the appropriate frequency of taking and reporting measurements. The resolution of the frequency issue is largely influenced by information availability and information reliability. As noted above, there is an inherent lag between the timing of the economic event reported upon and the availability of information reflecting how that economic event has affected investment performance. The role of appraisals in setting valuations has major implications for timing frequency, inasmuch as appraisals are generally prepared on an annual basis, yet the investment community is accustomed to quarterly reporting of corporate performance and daily indications of stock prices. Some managers resolve this timing dilemma by staggering their property evaluations so that 25 percent of their portfolios are appraised each quarter. Others appraise all properties on an annual basis and estimate valuation adjustments on a quarterly basis or, alternatively, record valuation adjustments when the next appraisal is available.

Whether appraisals are conducted on a staggered schedule or concentrated in time, the issue still exists of how to deal with valuation adjustments for reporting periods between appraisals. To the extent that such valuation changes are recognized based on estimates in each period as contrasted to annual appraisals, or alternatively only reflected by a disposition of the property, both the smoothness and overall level of returns reported can vary markedly. The more conservative the value change recognition, tying it to the appraisal date or in the extreme case, the realization of sale proceeds, will reflect more stable reported returns in initial reporting periods but then more abrupt return adjustments in the later period(s). Even though the measure of realized returns is common, the performance recognized on a ratable basis will appear both smoother and higher than performance resulting from a more conservative, value recognition methodology. This issue, in truth, is nothing more than a variant on the classic realization question of income recognition in accounting.

Beyond questions of timing in recognition of appreciation, there are also key questions of timing in recognition of income. Whether income is presumed to be received on a monthly, quarterly, semiannual or year-end basis can move the overall level of reported returns by multiple basis points. Of additional concern is the disposition of cash collected but not distributed to the investor. The interest rates in the capital market applicable to the investment of cash may have the effect of increasing or decreasing the overall portfolio return. Presuming that all cash is effectively and aggressively managed on behalf of the investor, he or she will be the ultimate beneficiary of funds collected but not yet distributed. This assumption may not necessarily apply since some managers may employ cash held on behalf of investors as part of compensating balances for their corporate credit lines and thereby not invest such funds as aggressively as might be the case were they not so motivated. Thus, the measure of the return should recognize cash when available to the investor as contrasted to when it is collected at the property level.

A further performance measurement timing concern has to do with the circumstances under which a disproportionate amount of the overall portfolio was held in cash funds, especially during the start-up phase of an investment program and/or prior to the reinvestment of proceeds from a sale or refinancing. To the extent interest rates are low and property returns high, real estate managers may advocate that the investment performance should be measured at the level of real estate and for the funds that are invested in real estate. But when the reverse relationship applies— where yields on cash funds exceed those on real estate—real estate managers seem to object less to measuring the performance of the total investor commitment as distinguished from those funds directly invested in real estate. The preferred approach is that the real estate investment manager be evaluated for what has been done with the capital entrusted to the manager from the perspective of the investor. This issue can be resolved by application of performance attribution, as discussed in a subsequent section.

It should be noted that the measure of return on a fund can differ meaningfully from the performance of real estate alone, because additional cash contributions or withdrawals may have the effect of increasing or decreasing overall return. Consequently, care should be taken to assess those elements of the investment program that the manager has the ability to influence and those elements that are in fact derivative of decisions made by the investor concerning cash contributions and withdrawals.

Concerning time horizon considerations, it is pertinent to address whether the relevant time horizon is: (1) that elected by the manager, which presumably would relate to the strategy for the particular asset or portfolio; (2) that specified by the investor, which would reflect that investor's particular financial planning horizon; or (3) some other criteria, which might be an arbitrary 3-year, 5-year, or 10-year period, as preferred for measuring other types of investments. As much as real estate managers would advocate that only their overall performance over the full-time horizon should be measured and assessed, intermediate readings are most prevalent and inevitable. Analysis of data on interim performance can yield insights as to a manager's style and direction.

IMPLEMENTATION OF PERFORMANCE MEASUREMENT

The process of real estate investment management performance measurement starts with results at the property level, which are reported on monthly and/or quarterly financial statements for each of the properties in the portfolio, and periodic, usually annual, appraisals of each of the properties. Then, the property level information is aggregated to provide a composite base of information for the portfolio. Next, nonproperty level items must be accounted for, including interest income and expense income from sources other than real estate, portfolio expenses that apply to the aggregate of all the properties and the entity rather than a specific property, professional fees, allocated overhead, if applicable, and management fees and reimbursement of costs. The next step in the real estate performance investment management process shifts the initiative from the investment manager, who packages the information described above into a financial report, to the investor.

With the financial reports from various managers that oversee different elements of the investor's portfolio, the investor is now in a position to implement its part of the real estate investment performance measurement process. Although not broadly recognized, a primary and substantial task for the investor (that is often implemented by the investor's advisers and professional consultants) is confirmation of the accuracy of the information presented in the manager's reports. Once the accuracy of the information is confirmed, the multiple reports are consolidated into a format that reflects the performance of the investor's portfolio in aggregate. To the extent the investor has not insisted that its various managers employ a common format, substantial additional work is required to translate the myriad divergent formats employed by different managers into a common methodology, terminology, and presentation to facilitate consolidation and comparison.

Once consolidated information is available, the investor then proceeds to calculate performance measures, as discussed previously. With the information on measures of performance in hand, the investor is then in a position to analyze the performance generally and compare it to various benchmark reference points specifically. Part of this comparison involves consideration of attribution to determine what the manager did to influence performance, as contrasted to what degree performance is attributable to other factors and forces not susceptible to the manager's control and influence.

The investor and its representatives then evaluate the overall results of the investment performance and the analysis thereof to reach conclusions and determine any actions that may be indicated. Properly, this evaluation and review process should involve communication from the investor to the managers as to how the investor assesses their performance and any desired shifts in priority and emphasis. By the time the cycle is completed, the investment managers will be involved in generating information from accounting reports and beginning the sequence again. Thus, the implementation of real estate investment management performance is an ongoing process rather than a one-time event.

A major challenge in implementing real estate investment management performance measurement is the extraordinary variability in format and reliability of the information employed. Although some investors are passive consumers of the information provided by their investment managers and the professionals involved, others take a more proactive and directive posture in stipulating what procedures and formats should be applied. To highlight the implications of this issue, consider a portfolio whose appraisers employ widely divergent discount rates for essentially common capital market conditions. To ensure consistency and uniformity of presentation, both across investment managers and over time, some investment managers and investors have implemented appraisal management systems, specifying a common format to enhance the reliability of appraisal information employed in the real estate performance measurement.

In assessing the reliability of various reported real estate investment performance measurement information, it should be recognized that while information derived from audited financial statements is generally comparable, information from appraisals is subject to much greater variability. Further, it should be recognized that in calculating measures of performance, information derived from appraisal reports lacks the objectivity, reliability, and uniformity of audited financial statements. The methodology that may be elected, the particular computer systems that may be employed to implement that methodology, and the actual implementation of calculations themselves are subject to extraordinary variability as a consequence of conscious choice, unconscious deviation, and inadvertent mistake.

As suggested earlier, the measurement challenges can be daunting. Among these measurement challenges are considerations of partial periods, lag effects from when money is committed to managers and when it is actually invested in real estate, dissimilar time periods, and therefore properties of widely varying maturity, divergences in the proportion of funds that are actually invested, and disproportionate scale in terms of size of assets and the aggregate size of the portfolio.

Among the communications issues of consequence are those having to do with the desired level of detail, the presentation format, and the degree of explanatory comment. The communications issues are complicated by the inherent desire of investment managers to tell their own version of their story on their terms. The investment managers argue, and not without some inherent logic, that standardization forces a rigid presentation that oversimplifies and obfuscates what really is happening concerning that particular portfolio. Great tension exists between a consistent objective presentation of information and consideration of the nuances and special circumstances that are of particular concern to the manager. Necessarily and understandably, some investment managers, if allowed to present their version of their performance, will provide reports that are inherently self-serving if not misleading or even highly distorted. Few consumers of the reported results of real estate investing have sufficient sophistication, resources, and inclination to distill this cacophony of discordant information in a manner that contributes to informed and responsible decisions.

Considerations that influence how the results of the real estate investment performance measurement process are communicated to investors include desired levels of detail in terms of reporting the basic findings, comparing those findings to the investor's particular objectives and other benchmark points of reference, evaluation of the performance absolutely and relative to such comparisons, performance attribution to identify what the manager did and did not do to influence the performance actually delivered, and the decisions that may be derived from the evaluation process. Effective presentation of the information properly involves a combination of text, tables, and charts, emphasizing clarity and consistency from period-to-period, so that consumers of the information can proceed down a learning curve over time rather than starting afresh each period. To this degree, it is important that the presentation of performance measurement information includes appropriate explanation and documentation of the methodology employed to facilitate assessment of the presentation.

PERFORMANCE ATTRIBUTION

Astute students of the investment markets recognize that forces beyond those that investment managers can directly influence, or even control, often exert considerable impact upon the performance actually achieved. Sophisticated investors are interested in knowing how much of a particular manager's performance is attributable to what the manager actually did, as contrasted with being attributable to independent market forces.

The concept of performance attribution involves identifying those factors that influence the ultimate realized investment performance and determining the relative contribution to each of the total result achieved. By way of simplistic illustration, if a manager delivered a 15 percent return pursuing the acquisition of assets from a class that provided a 12 percent return in a market that overall yielded 10 percent, then in attributing the manager's performance to the influencing factors, 10 percent of the overall return was attributed to the market, with a 200 basis point premium for the strategy that the manager elected to pursue by the type of assets selected plus a 300 basis point premium for the manager's execution of that strategy in terms of the particular investments acquired.

As much of performance measurement tends to reflect a bland, nondiscriminating approach to isolating how a manager really did, performance attribution is fundamental to understanding what drives performance and what value the manager really added. Essentially, performance attribution seems to provide a finer screen of assessment beyond the concept that "a rising tide raises all boats" by giving consideration to which type of boat was selected, which particular boat was chosen, which course was charted, and how well the boat was skippered.

Simply stated, performance attribution seeks to isolate what the manager can do and did do to influence performance from the other forces that determine the ultimate performance of the investment portfolio. Certainly, the selection of what strategy to pursue can add value in influencing the results ultimately achieved. Then, how well the managers perform in implementing that strategy is an important source of value added.

Among the factors that influence investment performance are:

- *Inflation*. Many real estate investment managers deliver performance that represents no more than an "inflation ride" and often, if inflation effects are netted out, is in reality a less than impressive result.
- *Market*. Consideration of how the real estate market does overall, how a particular property type does, how a geographic region does, and how a submarket performs, is critical.
- *Financial Structure*. As discussed previously, financial structure can meaningfully enhance or impede the investment return. Unless a performance attribution assessment is undertaken, understanding the degree to which the financial structure contributed to the overall return will be a mystery.
- *Tax Considerations*. While tax factors are generally of limited direct concern to the tax-exempt pension investor, they loom large in import for the individual tax-paying investor. How an investment is structured for tax purposes, especially where leverage and creative tax structuring are employed, can be of significant consequence. Although the current tax laws materially limit the opportunities for tax structuring, application of performance attribution analysis for tax factors in assessing track record is still of critical import, since many managers seeking investment capital do so in reliance upon a track record of past performance that was achieved largely by their creativity in designing tax-favored strategies rather than their excellence in acquiring real estate or merely by their having invested during periods when the tax laws virtually assured certain basic return levels.
- *Management Decisions*. The decisions by management concerning real estate, having to do with its acquisition, disposition and leasing structure, are critical elements of performance attribution, with the objective being to strip out those factors over which the manager had no control from those which it did.

To implement the performance attribution to isolate the influence of the key factors discussed above, it is helpful to employ the concept of decomposing the rate of return. This process involves identifying what portion of the return is attributable to current yield, both cash flow and tax effects, and what portion to changes in the value of the property.

Although performance attribution is clearly of great value in assessing an overall track record, especially for purposes of evaluating how a manager has done with portfolios for which it had responsibility, performance attribution is most powerful in application when used on an ongoing basis to assess, monitor, and manage the real estate investing process. The application of performance attribution has important applications in selecting managers, monitoring their performance, and then evaluating the manager's overall performance. To the extent a performance attribution system is set up as part of an ongoing performance monitoring process, signals can be detected that suggest deterioration of performance so that corrective action can be taken.

When the patterns of a manager's performance reflect a discernible change, it is appropriate to discern whether such a change is random, or whether there is an explicit reason why the change may have occurred. Reasons why a manager's performance might change include:

- *Market Conditions.* A management style that worked in one set of market conditions might achieve different results in another set of market conditions.
- *Strategy.* To the extent the manager's investment strategy changed, then its performance might be expected to change.
- *Decision System.* Employing different means to make decisions, as reflected both by analytic techniques and methodologies as well as the way that decisions are made—centralized or decentralized, individually or by committee—could influence performance.
- *Staffing.* Change in the composition of the individuals implementing the investment management are crucial, since the output of an organization is a function of the people that work in it.

Although a sophisticated performance measurement concept, performance attribution is fundamental to responsible institutional investing.

CONSIDERATIONS IN COMPARATIVE ANALYSIS

Although information on investment management performance is valuable and useful in an absolute sense, the value of real estate investment management performance measurement information is enhanced by a context for the assessment of the information. Such a context is provided by comparison to indexes and benchmarks generally and for real estate specifically.

Implementing the comparative investment analysis involved in indexes and benchmarks is a difficult undertaking if the results are to be meaningfully representative and free of bias. Among the important considerations are:

1. That similar investments in fact are used in the analysis.
2. That the investments studied are "representative."
3. That the implicit and explicit investment policies are logically formulated and consistently implemented.
4. That appropriate cash reinvestment policies are used.
5. That purchase and sale prices are reasonably derived.
6. That reasonable policies regarding tax treatment, leverage, and transactions costs are consistently employed.
7. That the significance of timing is given proper recognition.

In general, it is quite difficult to develop any research program such that the results support reliable generalizations. This problem, which for corporate securities is acute, is especially troublesome in the real estate sector. Consequently, most comparative analyses of real estate investment performance yield information that is interesting but of only limited applicability for decision-making purposes. While reviewing certain of the problems and primary considerations inherent in comparative analysis, it is well to mind the classic research trade-off between abstraction from the real world at the input stage and validity and application to the real world at output.

At the outset it is essential to verify that what is studied is, in fact, the specific investment type that is desired to be studied. In considering real estate investments, it is essential to focus on how the investment interest is defined. Different types of investment interests have different risk characteristics, as do different positions within the same investment. A deal involving an actual conversion of land use—as in land speculation in anticipation of selling the land for development—will have a totally different risk profile from one that consists of a passive investment in an established income property.

Further, some types of properties, by the very nature of the enterprise that is conducted on them, should not in the strictest sense be considered as equivalent to pure real estate investment. While it is true that every property must be viewed as a business unto itself, some, primarily hotels and motels, are so dependent upon management that they reflect the attributes of operating businesses rather than income-producing properties. Comparisons without making appropriate adjustments can be misleading. While a passive real estate investment position can parallel the purchase of stock in a solid growth company, the "activity-oriented" real estate conversion ventures are comparable to investing in start-up, venture capital situations. Clearly, it is misleading to compare the probable returns from such highly heterogeneous investments without adjusting for their differences.

Comparisons of investment results between alternative investment media require the development and aggregation of information on past investment results for the particular media under study. Developing such information must utilize samples, and this factor is too often underplayed. Samples are necessary for two reasons: first, it is often an impossible task to obtain data on an entire population of investments; and, second, even when data are available, the data cannot be analyzed efficiently.

If any sample is to possess credibility, it must be representative of the entire universe under consideration for that particular investment type, and it must accurately reflect all such available investments. Unfortunately, the majority of investment studies represent only a narrow and weighted slice of major investment spectra. If a sample of common stocks is to be representative, it must avoid omitting industry types, companies of certain sizes, geographic locations, and business practices such that its reliability would be biased. If a real estate sample is to be representative, it must include varying property types, geographic locations, and financing and ownership arrangements. Most real estate studies do not validly represent general investment results but rather provide exiguous evidence of some small universe. Illustrative of this point would be an investment study of apartment houses of a certain age and rent level in a specific town.

Any consumer of research information will do well to demand, and examine, the probabilistic significance of the numbers before considering the study findings. Where a study and its results are significant, there is a high degree of certainty that if the entire universe were analyzed, or if the study were duplicated for a similarly constructed sample, results very close to those indicated by the current study would be found. Three common problems exist with regard to the establishment of credibility and representativeness: the universe is insufficiently defined, the sample is too small or biased, and the research design or implementation is inadequate or sloppy. To the extent that it is not possible to verify the credibility or representativeness of a sample by statistical measures, then such verification must be based on qualitative considerations and the results will be less generalizable.

The best analysis of realized investment returns will be based on consideration of actual results achieved by investments held in specific portfolios. Here, we are talking about what actually happened as opposed to a simulation of what might or could have happened. Unfortunately, in most cases, information on historical investment performance must be reconstructed from aggregated or separate bits and pieces of disparate data rather than retrieved from detailed actual results of market participants.

Reasons for reconstruction rather than retrieval of historical data include the reluctance of investors to disclose information, the general dearth of accurate records, the varying and often short-lived investment participation by investors, the difficulties in isolating the impact of specialized factors, such as a particular management orientation, and the influence of "noninvestment" objectives, and the lack of comparability across cyclically affected heterogeneous time periods.

Along with the management factor applied to choice of individual investments, there must be an explicit investment policy in terms of how investment funds are allocated to individual investment opportunities, within the particular investment class. Is it on a proportionate basis weighted according to asset value, net worth or equity value, or earnings? Or, should investment funds be allocated equally among all investments within the sample? If the latter policy is elected, should adjustments be made for changes in the values of the individual investments over time? While it is impossible to generalize as to which approach is best, it is emphasized that the method selected must be rational. In assessing any empirical investment study, it must be recognized that the investment policy selected is very influential in determining the indicated results.

Other important considerations regarding the representativeness and credibility of the investment performance research are the derivation of the purchase cost and the derivation of the terminal value of the investment. The research model must "manage" these events carefully so as to avoid distortion. As a minimum criterion, a uniform procedure is necessary. Thus, in the case of common stocks, purchases might be made at the opening price on the first trading day of the year and sales at the closing price on the last trading day of the year. Absent a record of transactions such as exists in securities markets, great care must be used in determining the purchase and sale prices to be used. As a minimum standard, there must be a close parallel to actual transactions that occurred at the particular time in question. In such circumstances, it must be recognized that reliance on estimated transaction prices, absent carefully controlled verification and substantiation, may prejudice the research results.

The reinvestment policy used for each investment within the class and for one class of investment compared with another must be identical. The reinvestment policy selected for the research can involve constant reinvestment of all dividends and investment benefits in a mechanical or managed fashion, or it can provide for no reinvestment. It must be recognized that reinvestment in real property interests is generally possible only with investments in the securities form where additional small increments of the subject investment class may be purchased. It should also be noted that transaction costs for a small increment may be so great that the investor would do better by placing the funds into an alternative investment medium, particularly a savings account, where the return would be undiluted by the substantial transaction costs associated with small investments. It can be argued that such a reinvestment policy is counterproductive unless the financial commitment to the investment in question is adequate to achieve reasonable transaction costs.

PERFORMANCE INDEXES AND BENCHMARKS

As noted earlier, an index measures the overall financial results, reflected by current income and changes in value, for a defined segment of the capital market. A benchmark, on the other hand, is a reflection of how a specific participant or group of participants performed in that market segment. Thus, an index can be considered to reflect the overall investment environment while the benchmark reflects the actual performance of enterprises in that environment.

In interpreting investment performance indexes, it should be recognized that by definition the *mean* of investment results of all investors must be *less* than the results indicated by indexes for the reason that the indexes omit significant costs incurred by investment management organizations. Specifically, indexes do not include transaction costs, management fees, overhead, and cost reimbursement for the management organization, and professional fees for legal, accounting, and consulting services as well as costs incurred in communicating the investment performance results to investors, regulatory agencies, and the financial community. Consequently, for purposes of comparing the results of an investment manager, the indexes must be adjusted for these costs, or in the alternative, the point of comparison can be a benchmark performance measure reflecting a composite of a universe or sample of investment managers.

A benchmark of investment performance reflects the results of what managers and investors operating in a specific market achieve from actual investment strategies implemented in that market over that time period. Consequently, a benchmark reflects current returns actually delivered as well as overall returns including consideration of changes in asset values. As stated earlier, if the performance of all investors in a market is measured and consideration is given to transaction costs as well as the other costs involved in managing the investment portfolio, by definition the composite benchmark performance of the aggregate of managers must be *less* than the market index, for the reason that for purposes of evaluating performance one is dealing with a zero-sum game. Those who outperform the market do so at the expense of those who underperform the market. Since both managers outperforming and underperforming the market incur transaction costs and the overhead for their investment management organization, the aggregate results achieved by all investors will be less than the indicated performance of the market in which they invested. This point is eloquently made in Charles Ellis's classic article, ''The Loser's Game.''[3]

Among the points of reference are popular stock market indexes including the Dow Jones Industrials, the Standard & Poor's 500, the New York Stock Exchange Composite, and the Wilshire 5000. Measures of bond market performance include various indexes maintained by Salomon Brothers and Shearson Lehman Brothers.

Various financial reporting services provide information on the performance of specific programs. Organizations covering results of mutual funds include Lipper Analytical Services and Wiesenberger. Private research organizations that track the performance of real estate securities

---

[3]Charles Ellis, ''The Loser's Game,'' *Financial Analysts Journal* 31 no. 4 (July/August 1975), p. 19.

intended for individual investors, specifically real estate limited partnerships and real estate investment trusts, include Audit Investment Research, Robert A. Stanger, and Greenstreet Advisors. The performance of institutional investment managers is tracked by various of the pension consulting organizations who advise pension funds on their investing programs, such organizations as Evaluation Associates, SEI, Callen, and Frank Russell. Many of the pension consultants maintain databases tracking the performance of real estate investment managers, with those most active in this area including Evaluation Associates and Institutional Property Consultants.

Real estate investing performance benchmark information differs dramatically from that available on corporate securities in several significant ways, including the length of past historical data, methodological sophistication and consistency, the general availability and accessibility of what indexes are prepared, as well as their general reliability, representativeness, investability, and acceptability. Among the reasons for these divergencies are the relative maturity of institutional real estate investing. The information complexity resulting from the direct form of real estate's economic performance delivery as contrasted to the comparative simplicity associated with the indirect nature of securities investing, the nature of real estate transactions as distinguished from corporate securities transactions, information availability and reliability as well as participant sophistication.

While the indexes of real estate markets are neither as established nor as accepted as those for corporate securities, several do exist, the more popular being the Russell-NCREIF Index, which has tracked the real estate investment market for approximately the last 15 years. A more recent real estate market index is the Liquidity Fund Index. These real estate indexes differ from those covering the corporate securities markets in that they are based not on dividends paid and prices reported in an auction market but rather on reports of property operating performances and appraisals of property value.

The reliability of indexes based on reported information must be considered as potentially diverging from that of indexes based on market data reflecting the results of multiple transactions in an auction market. In contrast to indexes for corporate securities markets, all of which source data is objectively provided by a third-party exchange mechanism and involve a composite of multiple transactions, real estate information is voluntarily provided by the reporting party.

Even in the instance of an actual sale of a property, there may be motivations for the reporting party to present an "edited," if not dramatically distorted, view of the true economics of the transaction. Such forces as financial reporting objectives, compensation and other contractual factors, and income and property taxation can motivate a presentation of other than the actual sales price or the true economics of the transaction. Given that many of the critical pieces of information are based on appraisals rather than actual transactions, it must be recognized that their reliability is inherently questionable, inasmuch as the appraisals are provided by among the least regulated segments of the financial services marketplace, specifically investment management organizations and life insurance companies.

Given the questions and controversy that surround performance indexes in real estate investing, it is not surprising that similar issues exist concerning the benchmarks of real estate investment manager performance. Some of the questions concerning real estate investment management benchmark data are not unique to real estate investing but rather common to the entire investment field. Specifically, these questions embrace the broader scale, public policy issue of information as a public good and the relative role of public purpose, nonprofit organizations as contrasted to private sector, profit-motivated organizations in creating, maintaining, and disseminating information to guide important decisions. As information availability and reliability is crucial to a well-functioning market economy, a primary priority and a major thrust of various government agencies concerned with business activity is to provide information on overall levels of economic activity, and the performance of particular markets so as to facilitate more informed decisions. At the same time, government information is plagued by certain problems and shortfalls, which have motivated private organizations to create and disseminate important information measuring economic activity.

Some private sector organizations are motivated by the resulting visibility that can be translated into prestige and ultimate economic benefit that creating and disseminating such information provides. As a case in point, the Dow Jones publishing organization is a substantial beneficiary of the considerable publicity resulting from broad use of the Dow Jones 30 average measure of performance of the stock market in aggregate. Similarly, within the institutional investing community, the Wilshire 5000 composite measure of the overall market performance has gained a broad following and thereby generated visibility that is beneficial to the organization that prepares and disseminates it.

But in the realm of benchmark data, private sector involvement takes on a different slant, inasmuch as the broad applicability of the information is more limited and the financial consequences of how a particular manager appears in the context of the information is much more significant. Fundamental in preparation of private sector benchmark measures of institutional investment performance is the question of who should pay for the information provided: those who are evaluated or those who are using the information? Necessarily, the party that writes the check expects to exert some influence, at least indirectly and implicitly. In the instance of payment to a proprietary firm that provides investment performance information on a group of companies, the manager supporting that service would expect the consultant to look more favorably on it than if it did not support that service. Similarly, the support of that service may be perceived as a precondition to being considered by certain investors who might be advised by that consultant. Thus, questions of monopoly market position and competitive advantage loom large in how performance benchmark data are prepared and utilized.

Presently, questions of data reliability and interpretation are of pressing concern. Not surprisingly, issues of relative market position and competitive advantage tend to be more dominant than those of how the information is used to make more informed decisions. These are concerns that those involved in real estate performance measurement need to be aware of, both because they are important in their impact, and also because they are unlikely to be readily resolved in the near term.

CHAPTER 8

INTERNATIONAL REAL ESTATE

Charles H. Wurtzebach
JMB Institutional Realty Corp.

Andrew E. Baum
University of Reading

INTRODUCTION

While international real estate investing has been a part of the global business environment since the beginning of recorded history, leading institutional investors are relatively recent entrants to the field. To date, U.S. institutions have participated in international real estate investing in a very limited way. Few U.S. pension plans are currently adding international real estate to their portfolios. However, non-U.S. institutions initiated large-scale, long-term international real estate investment nearly three decades ago, when the Dutch began acquiring major urban properties in New York City, Boston, and Washington, D.C. British insurance companies and pension funds entered the process in the early 1970s, followed by Middle Eastern and South American investors in the 1970s. The Japanese emerged as leading international real estate investors during the 1980s. While much of the international activity has in the 1990s included U.S. investment, they have also invested in Europe and Asia. Most U.S. institutions have focused on U.K. investments followed by continental Europe and Asia.

Initially, non-U.S. institutions pursued international real estate investment to satisfy a range of investment objectives which were similar to the original reasons they invested in domestic real estate. International real estate typically became attractive when investors discovered they could not achieve all of their real estate investment objectives within their home countries. For some investors (e.g., the Dutch), the availability of quality domestic real estate assets was extremely limited. International real estate investment opened whole new investment markets for their consideration. For others (e.g., U.K. investors), diversification of their real estate portfolios enhanced the attractiveness of international real estate investment. Diversification could be achieved since international markets did not tend to follow identical rent growth, vacancy rate, and capitalization rate trends. Nearly all international investors sought prime quality properties which would provide stable, long-term investment growth, attractive risk-adjusted returns when compared to financial assets, and protection against unanticipated inflation. These very same factors initially prompted leading U.S. institutions to consider, for the first time, major long-term real estate investments in the United Kingdom, Canada, Europe, and the Far East.

This chapter will review the rationale used by U.S. and U.K. institutional investors, to invest in commercial real estate outside of their domestic markets. To date, a strong real estate research and investment tradition, combined with active and large real estate markets, are found primarily in the United States and the United Kingdom. Hence, while we recognize that new markets and research initiatives are springing up in other global markets, we have presented the evidence from the traditional U.S. and U.K. markets. We begin with a brief discussion of the investment objectives identified by U.S. investors for investing in domestic real estate, followed by a more detailed discussion of the reasons that U.S. investors consider non-U.S. real estate investment. The view of U.K. institutional investors toward nondomestic real estate investment will then be presented.

RATIONALE FOR NONDOMESTIC REAL ESTATE: U.S. PENSION PLANS

The U.S. institutional investors turned to non-U.S. real estate during the late 1980s as a reaction to the condition of the U.S. commercial real estate market at that time. Specifically, high-market vacancy rates resulted in underperformance and significantly low returns in both office and hotel properties. To a lesser extent, certain industrial and retail markets were also adversely affected by oversupply which led to poor performance. Unlike other property-type markets, the U.S. apartment market experienced falling vacancy rates as new construction starts lagged increases in demand.

In many ways the rationale for U.S. pension plan investment in non-U.S. real estate paralleled the rationale developed for investment in U.S. real estate. Examination of the performance of the overseas investment market during the mid- to late-1980s revealed the following characteristics:

- Attractive historical absolute total returns.
- Non-U.S. office vacancy rates have been more stable.
- Global real estate portfolio diversification opportunities.

Attractive Historical Absolute Total Returns

Although performance data for non-U.S. real estate, especially outside the United Kingdom, are not as widely available as performance data for U.S. real estate, a number of data sources indicate that during most of the 1980s non-U.S. real estate earned higher total returns than U.S. real estate.[1] As shown in Table 8–1, during much of the 1980s, U.S. office performance clearly trailed that of the United Kingdom, Spain, France, Germany, and Japan. However, the spread between U.S. and European investment returns has narrowed during the late 1980s and early 1990s, if not entirely disappeared. Unfortunately, the declining spread is the result of the erosion of non-U.S. performance from recently lofty levels, not improvement in the performance of U.S. commercial real estate. However, in spite of recent declines in performance levels, this research indicates that historical returns for European property investments have generally performed countercyclically to U.S. property returns, and have provided negatively correlated or modestly positive correlations with U.S. property returns, thereby reducing portfolio volatility.

However, as analysts have repeatedly cautioned, investors must carefully consider possible biases in historical data, such as period-specific currency trends and market results that raise questions about the future sustainability of key relationships. For example, the risk-reduction

---

[1]See Charles H. Wurtzebach, "Looking at Non-U.S. Real Estate," *Real Estate Review*, Spring 1991, pp. 48–54.

TABLE 8–1

Performance Data: U.S. Office Buildings compared to Office Buildings in Selected Foreign Countries, 1985–1989

	United States	United Kingdom	Spain	France	Germany	Japan
Capitalization rates	7.0%	6.0%	5.5%	4.5%	4.0%	2.0%
Five-year rental growth	(2.0)	11.0	11.0	11.0	8.0	11.0
Five-year International Rate Return	7.0	15.0	30.0	20.0	25.0	40.0

Source: Reprinted with permission from Charles H. Wurtzebach, "Looking at Non-U.S. Real Estate," *Real Estate Review*, Spring 1991, published by Warren Gorham Lamont, a division of Research Institute of America Inc., Boston; Copyright 1991 Research Institute of America.

attributes of international investments have derived from low correlation levels between foreign and U.S. markets and the assumption of a continuation of recent return variability levels. However, as markets become more globally integrated, this could mean diminishing benefits from international diversification. This caveat can be applied to a wide range of investment research topics. The key to relying on empirical research that does not cover a substantial period of time is to understand the context within which the authors developed the work. Naturally, as new and more accurate information becomes available researchers and investors alike must evaluate the impact upon previously held interpretations of historical data.

Non-U.S. Office Vacancy Rates Had Been More Stable

Throughout the 1980s, the level of operating risk as measured by the volatility of office vacancy rates in non-U.S. real estate markets has been very low. Figure 8–1 shows that during 1978–89 office vacancy rates in London, Frankfurt, and Paris indicate that operating risks in those cities were generally lower than in New York City. Not only did New York office vacancy rates consistently exceed those in the three European cities over the period, but New York office vacancy rates were more volatile. In fact, except for 1989, the three overseas markets experienced approximately half the reported New York vacancy-rate variability.

These patterns of office vacancy rates imply that there may be distinct differences in the market structure of non-U.S. markets that result in increased stability. The property markets in most European countries have generally been in better supply and demand balance than those in the

FIGURE 8–1
Office Vacancy Rates in Selected Cities, 1978–1989

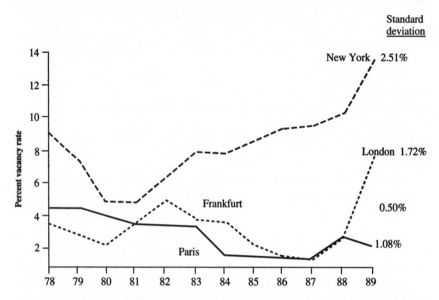

Source: Reprinted with permission from Charles H. Wurtzebach, "Looking at Non-U.S. Real Estate," *Real Estate Review*, Spring 1991, published by Warren Gorham Lamont, a division of Research Institute of America Inc., Boston; Copyright 1991 Research Institute of America.

United States. This may be because new construction in European real estate markets has typically been demand driven, in contrast to the capital and tax-motivated projects which were built in the United States throughout the 1980s. In short, tighter land-use control and the general lack of legislatively encouraged development has historically kept speculative building in Europe in check. Institutional investors must bear in mind, however, that although the past performance of an investment category is instructive, it cannot be relied upon as a forecast of future performance. The very existence of the recent interest by U.S. developers in non-U.S. markets may lead to additional supply in those markets. Indeed, the significant increase in London office vacancy rates during the late 1980s and early 1990s suggests that a near-term change may have taken place in that market. In Paris, on the other hand, strict development and building limitations may protect the supply and demand balance in that office market.

In addition, as we move through the 1990s, European employment markets will become more service sector oriented and therefore demand for office space will rise. This is the opposite of the employment trends currently being experienced in the United States where service employment growth has fallen dramatically from the mid-1980's peaks. Consequently, one would expect that European tenant lease-up rates would generally exceed those reported in the United States. Furthermore, given the relative oversupply of vacant U.S. office space, little new speculative office construction is expected during at least the first half of the decade. These trends are not expected to reverse themselves soon and suggest that U.S. office vacancy rates may remain above those typically found in Europe for some time.

Global Real Estate Portfolio Diversification Opportunities

Non-U.S. real estate performance trends have led investors to consider the diversification benefits attained by investing outside of the United States. Analysis has shown that a combination of non-U.S. and U.S. office building investments produces attractive portfolio diversification gains for U.S. institutional investors. Figures 8–2 through 8–5 indicate that diversification benefits have been shown to exist in the areas of office market vacancy rate volatility, rent levels, capitalization rate volatility, and, perhaps most importantly, office market returns.

A global real estate portfolio would exhibit reduced vacancy-rate volatility if the markets and property types represented in the portfolio exhibit different vacancy rate cycles. Figure 8–2 indicates that over certain periods of the 1980s, an equally weighted portfolio of New York, London, Frankfurt, Paris, and Sydney office buildings demonstrated reduced vacancy-rate volatility. In essence the building cycles in these markets did not move in tandem. From the U.S. investors' perspective, the addition of the London, Frankfurt, Paris, and Sydney markets added stability to the more volatile (in terms of vacancy rates) New York office market. This simply means that by adding a selection of non-U.S. markets to an all-U.S. portfolio has the potential to reduce the portfolio vacancy rate volatility of the entire portfolio.

As one would expect, the diversification benefits of a global portfolio resulting from varying vacancy rates results in more stable portfolio rent changes (Figure 8–3). Again, an equally weighted global office portfolio would have achieved a more stable rental stream than an all-U.S. office portfolio. Similar results were also observed when office market capitalization rates were examined (Figure 8–4). An office portfolio including a

FIGURE 8–2

Office Vacancy Rates in Five Cities Compared with Vacancy Rates in a Global Portfolio with Equally Weighted Investments in Each City, 1980–1989

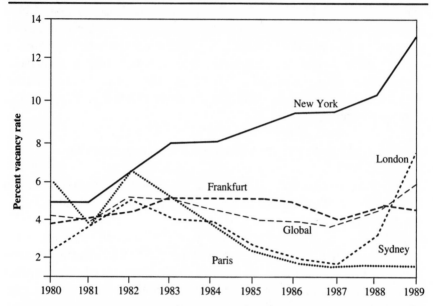

Source: Reprinted with permission from Charles H. Wurtzebach, "Looking at Non-U.S. Real Estate," *Real Estate Review*, Spring 1991, published by Warren Gorham Lamont, a division of Research Institute of America Inc., Boston; Copyright 1991 Research Institute of America.

portfolio of U.S. East Coast properties (Washington, DC, New York City, Boston, and Philadelphia), London, Frankfurt, Paris, and Sydney would have demonstrated less-volatile capitalization rates than a U.S.-only portfolio.

Perhaps the most important argument for adding foreign properties to an all-U.S. portfolio is the impact upon total returns. Again, examining a global portfolio that includes New York, London, Paris, Frankfurt, and Sydney office buildings, it was demonstrated that the global portfolio generated a higher and more stable return over the 1979–89 period than most of the individual markets included in the global portfolio (Figure 8–5). This result is the logical conclusion one would expect after noting that global portfolio vacancy rates, rental levels, and capitalization rates were all more stable than a U.S.-only portfolio.

While the above comments provide a clear financially based diversification justification for global real estate investment, several additional

FIGURE 8–3
Percent Change in Rent Levels in Five Cities and in a Global Portfolio of Equally Weighted Investment in Each City, 1977–1991

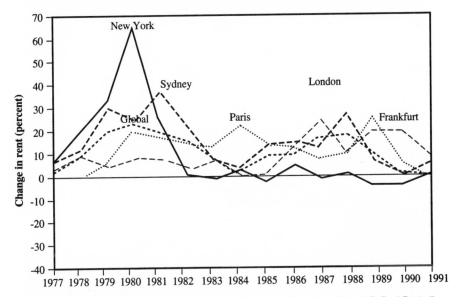

Source: Reprinted with permission from Charles H. Wurtzebach, "Looking at Non-U.S. Real Estate," *Real Estate Review*, Spring 1991, published by Warren Gorham Lamont, a division of Research Institute of America Inc., Boston; Copyright 1991 Research Institute of America.

nonperformance reasons have led U.S. investors to explore the attractiveness of developing global real estate portfolios. These include the recent weakness in the U.S. real estate market and the relatively strong long-term economic outlook in non-U.S. markets that is expected to result in attractive real estate investment opportunities.

The recent weakness in the U.S. real estate market has caused institutional investors difficulty in achieving their targeted real estate allocation levels. A typical pension fund's targeted real estate investment allocation level ranges from 10 percent to 15 percent, with the average pension fund's real estate assets representing between 4 percent and 5 percent of its total portfolio. This has led some to suggest that U.S. pension plans have not been successful in reaching their targeted real estate allocations. In an effort to achieve their policy level asset allocation targets and the associated performance, the acceptable definition of an institutional real estate investment has been broadened by many funds to include property types

FIGURE 8–4

Capitalization Rates in Five Cities in the U.S. East Coast and in a Global Portfolio (1978–1990)

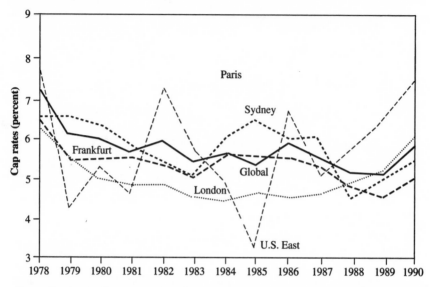

Source: Reprinted with permission from Charles H. Wurtzebach, "Looking at Non-U.S. Real Estate," *Real Estate Review*, Spring 1991, published by Warren Gorham Lamont, a division of Research Institute of America Inc., Boston; Copyright 1991 Research Institute of America.

such as apartments. Many of these investors are also broadening their range of acceptable locations by adding international investment in real estate.

The attractive long-term economic outlook for European economies is directly related to the emergence of increased economic cooperation and a reduction in the barriers to trade. Furthermore, Europe has about 320 million people, while the United States is comprised of approximately 250 million. Predictions for overall economic growth suggest that during this decade, Europe will surpass the United States in total gross domestic product (GDP). Though there will clearly be real estate market cycles to contend with, as the recent decline in the London office market attests, expected underlying economic growth should bode well for the long-term fundamentals of commercial real estate performance.

This strong economic outlook suggests significant growth and increasing real estate investment opportunities. Most major multinational

FIGURE 8–5
Comparison of Volatility of Office Returns (Total Annual Return 1979–1989)

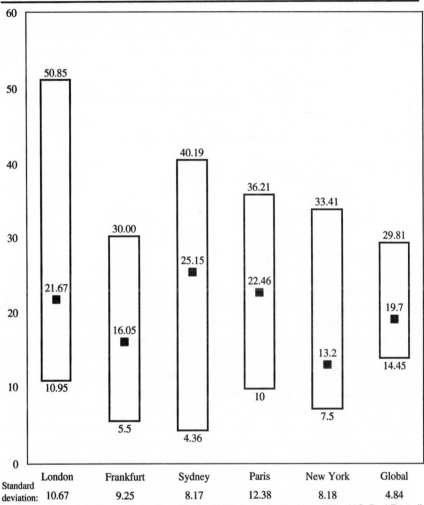

Source: Reprinted with permission from Charles H. Wurtzebach, "Looking at Non-U.S. Real Estate," *Real Estate Review*, Spring 1991, published by Warren Gorham Lamont, a division of Research Institute of America Inc., Boston; Copyright 1991 Research Institute of America.

corporations are expanding their European operations in anticipation of increased trade opportunities. In addition, over the next few years the opening of Eastern Europe will have a positive impact on real estate demand in the long term.

RISKS ASSOCIATED WITH NON-U.S. REAL ESTATE: U.S. PENSION PLANS

However, as is true in all investment fields, there are important unique risks associated with investing in non-U.S. real estate markets. These risks must be carefully evaluated by potential investors in terms of how they are different from U.S. real estate risk and how they can be mitigated. For some investors, evaluation of these risks will lead to a decision not to invest in non-U.S. real estate markets, for others, these risks can be effectively managed. These special risks include:

- Lack of local knowledge.
- Political risk.
- Currency risks.
- Small-scale markets.

Lack of Local Knowledge

Although most U.S. pension plans that consider investments in foreign real estate markets are large and sophisticated, few are experienced global real estate investors. There are a host of formal and informal differences between U.S. and non-U.S. real estate markets. Formal differences include differences in land ownership and tax laws. Informal differences include an array of important cultural differences that affect all investors, plus real estate specific differences such as lease terms and negotiation practices. Consequently, the very way that business is conducted in international real estate markets can add risk to the investment process. This risk can be mitigated by investors that create investment-manager joint ventures with reputable foreign real estate firms and/or by co-investing with experienced non-U.S. investors in their local markets.

Political Risk

The U.S. investors evaluating foreign real estate markets must consider the existence of two kinds of political risk: global and local. Global political risks include the risk that foreign governments may nationalize markets, close borders, create new borders, or restrict capital flows. In certain markets, the risk of armed conflict can be real, as recent conflicts in Eastern Europe vividly demonstrate. Local political risks involve the difficulty of gaining access to local government services. A developer that cannot obtain the required permits soon finds itself in trouble. Political stability at both the national and local levels contributes to the general stability of real estate performance.

Currency Risks

Any investment in nondollar-denominated assets exposes the U.S. investor to currency risks. Investors in some asset categories can utilize hedging strategies to protect themselves from unanticipated changes in currency exchange rates. However, for long-term investors such as those in real estate, currency risk can represent a significant challenge. Investors who wish to protect the periodic cash flows generated by tenant rental payments from unexpected declines in local currency exchange rates may be able, in the short term, to efficiently hedge local currency liabilities. However, it can be difficult and expensive to hedge long-term capital appreciation that is expected to be realized in 10 to 15 years. Given the long-term holding period associated with real estate investment, many investors in non-U.S. real estate do not attempt to hedge the capital appreciation portion of real estate returns. They subscribe to the theory that, in the long run, currency markets reach equilibrium.

Small-Scale Markets

Many non-U.S. markets have size characteristics different than those of the U.S. markets in which U.S. pension funds typically invest. Generally, non-U.S. markets are not as large or as diversified as markets in the United States. Except for a few markets such as London, Paris, and Frankfurt, most non-U.S. markets are relatively small and contain fewer huge office towers and regional malls. The smaller scale of non-U.S. markets reduces the actual number of investment opportunities available and increases the risk of becoming overexposed in an individual market.

On the other hand, one of the great advantages of non-U.S. markets, especially those of industrialized Western Europe, is that they tend to be densely populated. This means that they are usually not surrounded by vast expanses of undeveloped land, and suburban sprawl is not a prevalent phenomenon.

RATIONALE FOR DOMESTIC REAL ESTATE:
U.K. INSTITUTIONS

In terms of real estate investment, the most important U.K. institutions are life assurance companies, followed by pension funds and general insurance companies. The U.K. institutions became major players in the U.K. property market in the 1970s. Through a combination of investing, developing, funding developers, and improving existing assets, as Table 8–2 indicates, property portfolios reached nearly 20 percent of total assets in 1980. This exposure far exceeded the 4 percent–5 percent reached on average by U.S. institutional investors.

By 1989, the average property weighting in U.K. institutional portfolios had fallen to around 10 percent. However, it is not clear whether this is the result of a well-developed portfolio strategy to disinvest, or whether it is simply the result of the strong stock market performance in the 1980s. Even at this lower allocation level, property investment by U.K. institutions far exceeds that of their U.S. contemporaries. Nonetheless, current forecasts suggest property weighting may fall to 8 percent for U.K. institutions by the year 2000.

In a recent survey of institutional property fund managers covering a range of funds of between £10 million to £10 billion, the following motivations for investing in U.K. real estate were established.[2] Several of

TABLE 8–2
Global Asset Allocation: Estimated Weights (percent)

SS	1980	1989	2000
UK equities	45	53	40
Overseas equities	9	21	35
Bonds	21	8	10
Index linked	0	2	2
Property	20	10	8
Cash	4	6	5

Source: World Markets Company, Yamaichi.

[2]A. Baum, and A. Schofield, *Property as a Global Asset* (Berkshire, Eng.: University of Reading Centre for European Property Research, 1991).

the identified motivations paralleled those of U.S. institutions. These include:

1. Attractive performance compared with U.K. stocks and bonds.
2. Property was regarded as an inflation hedge.
3. Property investment allows managers to match assets and liabilities.
4. Opportunity to outperform competing fund managers.
5. Property represents a major asset class.

Attractive Performance Compared with U.K. Stocks and Bonds

The level of returns on U.K. property has been lower than equities over the last two decades but higher than gilts (U.K. bonds). However, since the risk on equities, as measured by the standard deviation of returns, is higher than on property and gilts, risk-adjusted property performance has been attractive. Property provided an attractive level of returns accompanied with lower variability, thus providing a stabilizing influence on portfolio performance. Going forward, however, the illiquidity of property along with the likelihood of an increase in the volatility of future property returns may have the effect of increasing the risk on property to a level comparable to that on equities.

In addition to lower return variability over the period from 1968 to 1990, U.K. property returns appear to be uncorrelated with the returns on other U.K. assets. This means property provided multiasset portfolio diversification benefits.

U.K. Property Regarded As an Inflation Hedge

The purpose of an inflation hedge is to protect the portfolio from an inflation-induced reduction in purchasing power. An asset can be viewed as an inflation hedge if its nominal returns vary positively with the rate of inflation. Property and equities should be a hedge against inflation because the expected real income stream from both property and equities is independent of the rate of inflation. Most forecasts of U.K. rental growth and dividend growth are undertaken in real terms and depend upon the real growth of the economy. Therefore, property investment has generally provided investors with an effective inflation hedge.

Property Investment Allows Managers to Match Assets and Liabilities

Since most institutions carry long-term liabilities, the long-term nature of real estate investment facilitates liquidity matching. If the liabilities are denominated in real terms, an increase in interest rates which might be expected to accompany an increase in inflation increases the cash flows required to meet higher liability payouts. The long-term investment horizon of real estate and its inflation hedging capabilities enhance its investment attractiveness.

Opportunity to Outperform Competing Fund Managers

The performance of U.K. fund managers, to a greater extent than their U.S. colleagues, is evaluated via comparisons to investment performance benchmarks. Benchmarks are indicators of results produced by the asset allocations of investment managers. The major factor determining the importance of benchmarks to investors is the degree to which the organization is in competition with other similar organizations. Some institutions may not be in direct competition, but expect their fund managers to be measured against other fund managers on a regular, at least, annual basis.

Property Represents a Major Asset Class

In a 1991 survey by the London Business School, investable commercial real estate in the United Kingdom was found to have a value of roughly 55 percent of the total U.K. stock market, leading to an argument for a neutral weighting of around 30 percent in real estate. This is much greater than actual allocations and acts as a significant encouragement toward higher allocations to real estate.

The objective of many U.K. institutional investors is primarily to outperform competitors without risking significant underperformance. This is particularly true when the client (the fund trustee) has the ability to switch from one manager to another in an attempt to achieve higher returns.

Many managers are judged either directly against their competitors, or against an index. Failure to perform against that index (often in the short term) will affect their reputation and rewards. Ideally this should not significantly affect the asset allocation procedure, but a 1991 survey[3] indicated that this is a major consideration for most fund managers.

RATIONALE FOR NONDOMESTIC REAL ESTATE: U.K. INSTITUTIONS

Information regarding international property exposure by U.K. institutions is not generally available. Recent surveys suggest that a majority of U.K. pension funds hold more than 15 percent of their property assets overseas. Insurance companies hold much less, and even the largest nondomestic investors appear to hold less than 7 percent or 8 percent. More U.K. institutions hold property in North America than in any other region, including Europe.

In a 1989 survey[4] the main reasons for holding overseas property were stated by these institutions to be diversification and the potential for better performance. For the largest investors in Europe, there is in addition a great shortage of available domestic real estate investment product. Most funds expect to increase their levels of overseas property investment, particularly in the European Community.

Swedish and Japanese investors have been particularly prominent in European real estate markets in the late 1980s and early 1990s. It is estimated that over 50 percent of U.K. property investment transactions featured investors from these countries over that period. Their likely motivations are similar, as restrictions on nondomestic investment by institutions were recently lifted at the same time as domestic markets appeared overheated and lacked in choice of available product.

Attractive Historical Absolute Returns

At any time, capitalization rate (or yields, in the United Kingdom) will differ from market to market. This means that higher initial income returns may be available outside domestic markets. In addition, both

---

[3]*Ibid.*

[4]G. Browning, *Overseas Property Investment Strategy: Do UK Institutions Have One?* (London, Eng.: Department of Property Valuation and Management, The City University, 1989).

rental values and capitalization rates vary from market to market, delivering high returns in some markets and low returns in others.

Table 8–3 shows how capitalization rates have moved in the major European markets from 1985 to 1991. The yields quoted for 1991 are May/June; others are for November/December. For each market, the yield is the initial return receivable from a prime investment property in the prime location, fully let to a first-class covenant at an open-market rent and based on the income receivable and the capital value calculated gross of taxes and other fees. Higher returns have been delivered in the Paris and Frankfurt office markets than in London, but not over identical periods. These varying returns suggest that international real estate investment can offer higher returns when compared to a U.K.-only investment strategy.

Future return potential through rental income will be driven by demand, generated by economic activity, and supply. For example, in European markets, GDP gowth is expected to be lowest in the United Kingdom and in Germany. This is shown in Table 8–4, which demonstrates the attractions of nondomestic European property to U.K. institutions and may explain the yield differentials reported across the major European markets (Table 8–3).

Property Risk

Understanding risk is as important as understanding return. Institutional investors now have a good knowledge of the theory of risk and return and in particular of portfolio theory. They appreciate the theoretical role of property within the portfolio, with particular reference to its risk-return and covariance with other assets. The contribution of an asset to the risk of the portfolio depends upon the expected standard deviation of returns and the correlation of the return on the asset with that of other assets within the portfolio. For example, if an asset were expected to be negatively correlated with other assets then a lower risk premium would be required.

Tables 8–5 and 8–6 show the relevant U.K. data. This shows that over the last two decades equities have outperformed gilts and property, but the returns in both real and nominal terms have been far more volatile. Meanwhile, property has shown considerably more return than gilts and also less volatility. Without examining the correlation between assets, this evidence would suggest that a portfolio containing property in the place of gilts would have delivered greater return with lower risk than one excluding property.

TABLE 8–3
Office Capitalization Rates

Year	London	Paris	Frankfurt
1985	6.20	6.00	5.25
1986	6.30	5.50	5.00
1987	6.00	5.00	5.00
1988	5.90	5.00	4.75
1989	5.90	4.50	5.00
1990	7.00	4.80	5.00
1991	7.60	4.80	4.50

Sources: Hillier Parker and Jones Lang Wooton, *Real Estate Strategy.*

TABLE 8–4
Average Annual GDP Growth

	United Kingdom	Germany	France	Spain
1960–90	2.5	3.1	3.7	4.6
1980–90	2.8	2.4	2.1	3.0
1991–95	1.8	1.8	2.7	2.9

Source: Business Strategies Ltd., *Real Estate Strategy.*

For other European property markets, some historic data is available to estimate the historic volatility of property returns. However, there is little reason to believe that previous volatility across markets will be repeated in the future or is likely to be significantly different across markets.

Property Investment and Portfolio Diversification

Table 8–6 shows the correlation between returns on equities, gilts, and property between 1968 and 1990. The historic correlation of property returns with returns on other assets is low, while the correlation of returns on equities and gilts is relatively high. Property would appear to offer good diversification opportunities.

Table 8–7 presents the correlation coefficient between property, equities, and gilts from 1968 to 1990. After remaining relatively stable

TABLE 8–5
Annual Return and Risk, U.K., 1968 to 1990 (percent)

	Property	Gilts	Equities
Nominal return	15.4	10.0	18.7
Nominal risk	10.2	12.5	22.0
Real return	5.6	0.6	8.7
Real risk	11.0	12.6	21.7

Source: Jones Lang Wooton, *Real Estate Strategy*.

TABLE 8–6
Correlations of Nominal Returns, U.K., 1968 to 1990 (percent)

	Property	Gilts	Equities
Property	100		
Gilts	14	100	
Equities	15	64	100

Source: Jones Lang Wooton, *Real Estate Strategy*.

and positive when estimated between 1968 and 1990, and 1974 and 1990, the correlation of property and equities, and property and gilts suddenly becomes very negative and around 40 percent, after the positive contribution of 1974 is lost. This suggests that over recent time periods the contribution of property performance to multiasset diversification has increased.

Baum and Schofield (1991)[5] suggest that depending upon the time period chosen, a correlation coefficient of between plus 50 and minus 40 percent between returns on property and returns on gilts and equities is attainable. This suggests that while the correlation values are unstable over varying periods of time, property does provide portfolio diversification characteristics.

---

[5]Baum and Schofield, *Property as a Global Asset* (1991).

TABLE 8–7
Correlations of Nominal Returns, U.K., 1968 to 1990 (%)

| Start | 1968 | 1969 | 1970 | 1971 | 1972 | 1973 | 1974 | 1975 | 1976 | 1977 |
End	1990	1990	1990	1990	1990	1990	1990	1990	1990	1990
Property and equity	15	16	17	16	13	12	25	−43	−40	−40
Property and gilt	14	15	16	16	15	16	30	−25	−21	−21
Equity and gilt	64	79	77	78	79	80	79	59	57	57

Source: Jones Lang Wooton, *Real Estate Strategy*.

The varying correlations between equities and property and gilts and property arise from differences in the measurement period and valuation methodologies. Returns on gilts and equities are reported on the basis of current transactions. By contrast, property returns are based on subjective valuations. The comparative method of valuation may result in valuations being based on information that was obtained in the market some time ago. This implies that there may be a systematic delay in the reporting of property returns, which may cause the low correlations.

Table 8–8 reports correlation coefficients between property returns and equity and gilt returns six months before and a year before. The correlation coefficient between property and equities and property and gilts is higher when using equity and gilt returns lagged a year.

In the United Kingdom and the United States, both the volatility of property market performance measures and the relevant correlation coefficients are understated by the smoothing of appraisal valuations. Historic estimates of delivered returns may therefore be poor proxies for expected future volatility.

In markets where historic returns are not available, the correlation of rental growth is often used as a proxy for return. This analysis is likely to produce highly misleading results. A more appropriate analysis is to assess the behavior of economies under different assumptions about the world economy. For example, the impact of the Gulf Crisis on expectations of the European economies was different. Forecasts of the U.K. economy were revised upward because the United Kingdom is a net exporter of oil. By contrast, the forecasts of many European economies were revised downward.

If these revisions to economic forecasts had been incorporated into the pricing of European property, then it is likely that there would have been a positive impact upon U.K. property at the cost of a negative impact

TABLE 8–8
Correlations Coefficients with Nominal Property Returns, Current, Six-Month Lag, and One-Year Lag

	Current	Six-Month	One-Year
Equities	15	23	25
Gilts	14	11	20

Source: Jones Lang Wooton, *Real Estate Strategy.*

in Europe. There would have been negative correlation between the U.K. and European markets, which stems from the difference in the structure of the U.K. economy compared to the European economy. Examining fundamentals in this way is likely to be rewarding.

ADVANTAGES OF NONDOMESTIC REAL ESTATE INVESTMENT

Lease Structures

The structure of leases in the United Kingdom is such that they run for long periods (typically 25 years) and the rent is subject to upward-only rent reviews every 5 years. This generates a certainty of nominal income from property which is not evident in the European markets, where leases are typically shorter and often index linked. In addition, 25-year leases can reduce default risk for a significant period. These differences have several effects.

First, there are differences in the riskiness of different real estate markets through the leasing structure. Second, the delivery of return differs between markets. For example, where leases are index linked the impact of inflation will be vital in determining nominal returns, and the impact of different rent review periods will also affect the expected cash flow from a building and its value to an investor. For the same reason there will be differences in the inflation-hedging quality of different real estate markets.

Vacancy

The London market, for example, has traditionally been regarded as supply constrained because of planning controls. However, a loosening of planning regulations in the 1980s damaged this protection, and the very high availability of finance in the middle and late 1980s has helped to create a building boom which has produced unprecedented high-vacancy rates. This will reverse as planning controls gain more strength from recent legislation, but significant damage has been done. This illustrates the need to identify markets which are supply constrained alongside the factors that can erode that protection.

Marketing

For competitive financial services groups, international property management offers further advantages in terms of promotion of products and staff development. More pertinent is the education that a manager can gain in overseas markets that will contribute to domestic business development and even to enhanced returns.

Taxation

There are major differences in corporate income and capital tax rates in different countries. It is possible for investors to restructure in such a way as to minimize tax liability, but this may be costly. Investors' interest in various international investments will be greatly influenced by their anticipated after-tax returns and by the certainty of the tax regulations.

Liquidity

Little evidence has been collected to confirm differential degrees of liquidity across the different markets, but it is possible (for example) that the tax levied on the purchaser of a secondhand building in Paris, or the lack of an active foreign investment community in Stockholm, will each have a significant impact on the liquidity of real estate investments in these markets. Illiquidity constrains the freedom of investors to switch to more attractive assets and is a serious problem: markets should therefore be avoided if illiquidity is high and unrewarded.

Lumpiness

Property is also a highly lumpy asset class, meaning that efficient, well-diversified portfolios can only be constructed if at least a minimum allocation of resources is made to the real estate asset class. Reasonable diversification within the United Kingdom, for example, will require 20–30 properties, which usually implies a commitment of close to £50,000. Unless property weight is to exceed historic highs, this requires a total fund size of at least £200,000, considerably in excess of the mean size of U.K. pension funds. The result is that a great number of small funds holds no direct property.

Holding nondomestic property as a diversified asset will be even more difficult for all but the largest investors, and specific risk will have to be accepted. For a very large U.K. investor with (say) £5 billion allocated to real estate, it is currently unlikely that more than 20 percent of that money would find its way to nondomestic real estate. Average investment sizes in institutional grade nondomestic property will be much higher than in domestic markets and might average £25 million to £50 million.

Following a strategy of building portfolios in North America and Europe will allow between 12 and 25 buildings in each global zone. If these are spread across market sectors (retail, office, hotel, for example) the holdings are most unlikely to diversify away the specific risk of the assets in the context of these markets, and the advantages of global diversification will have to be balanced against the riskiness of the nondomestic portfolios. The importance of establishing the investor's objectives cannot be too highly stated.

Information

The fundamental problem in all of the European markets outside the United Kingdom is the availability and reliability of market information. The investment and letting markets are less highly developed than in the United Kingdom. Statistical indexes are in their infancy and are prone to inaccuracy.

Given that the investment markets are less mature than in the United Kingdom, evidence of transactions is often limited. Prime investment properties in most European cities are currently scarce and so yield information may not be up to date. In Madrid, owner occupation is still common and in Frankfurt much of the prime office property is owner occupied by the German banks.

Again, accurate representations of likely future supply are difficult to obtain. Unsophisticated market information is not routinely gathered and held in a readily accessible form. From a poor information base, it is difficult to assess and understand development attitudes. However, as with rents and yields, information is apt to become more widely available and increasingly reliable as more international agents establish local offices in these markets.

Transaction Costs

The yields in all markets reflect gross income receivable and a gross price. Typically, landlords' operating costs are passed on to the tenants. Transaction costs include transfer taxes and agents' and legal fees. Agents' and legal fees are reasonably similar across all markets.

However, transfer taxes vary considerably. The purchaser of property in the United Kingdom is subject only to stamp duty at 1 percent and in Germany to a transfer tax of 2 percent on the value of the property. In Spain, the purchaser of new property or property under development is liable to stamp duty of 1 percent plus VAT of 5 percent on purchase. The purchaser of a secondhand building, however, must pay a nonrecoverable transfer tax of 5 percent plus the stamp duty.

This dual market is even more pronounced in Paris and particular caution is required when considering the Paris office yield data. Developers or purchasers of a new property or property under development are not liable for transfer tax but must pay VAT of 18.6 percent. This is recoverable as long as the building is sold within five years. However, the purchaser of a secondhand building or new building that is not sold within five years must pay a nonrecoverable transfer tax amounting to nearly 19 percent.

CONCLUSION

In the United Kingdom, pension funds will become increasingly mature as the age structure of the U.K. population changes to include a greater concentration of pensioners. Pension funds will continue to disinvest in direct property and only the largest funds in stable or growing industries will maintain significant percentages of their total assets in property.

On the other hand, the insurance business will continue to grow, with insurance companies outstripping pension funds as the largest investor group. Personal pensions managed by insurance companies and life-associated savings plans will increase in importance. This trend is well understood by the insurance sector. After the current downturn has run its course and when the supply crisis is seen to have been brought under control, life funds will increase their property exposure.

While the 1980s was a decade of debt, with relatively little new equity issue, the 1990s will see a swing back to equity as the corporate sector attempts to wind down its debt and as overseas institutional investors provide a source of equity finance. This is dependent upon prices, and equity prices may soon fall to a level at which they appear cheap to overseas investors. The U.K. equity market will recover before the U.K. property market turns, but the returns of the 1980s will not be seen in the 1990s.

The impact of globalization upon the investment behavior of the U.K. institutional investor will be considerable. Nondomestic property is attractive in terms of risk, return, and diversification. Those investors with overseas liabilities will use overseas securities as the main liability match but may build overseas portfolios of property for similar reasons. As competitors increase overseas portfolios, benchmarks will change and increased exposure for those in competitive businesses will become necessary.

However, overseas property is one of several sources of competition for the institutional funds which might otherwise be directed at U.K. property. Other drains on funds will include overseas securities, which will take up to 50 percent of all U.K. institutional assets by the end of the decade.

Innovations will be essential if the global property markets are to retain the interest of investors. These are likely to include a form of syndication/securitization and swaps and joint ventures between investors of different domiciles and between institutional and corporate sectors.

Lack of liquidity in property is a particular problem for institutional investors who habitually use tactical moves in and out of sectors to attempt to boost performance in the short term. Tactical asset allocation is impossible to achieve in property because of a lack of liquidity, specifically the lack of an identifiable secondary market. If this were to be achieved through some form of securitization then the attractiveness of property may increase considerably. The effect on the market will be to improve efficiency and increase the amount of trading, but will also increase the volatility of property. Despite this, low-risk international real estate investment will become more and more possible.

BIBLIOGRAPHY

Achour, Dominique, and Robert L. Brown. "The Performance of Real Estate Related Investments: A Re-Evaluation." *The Real Estate Appraiser and Analyst* 49, no. 4 (Winter 1983), pp. 64–69.

Aldrich, Eastman, and Waltch, L.P. "Why Real Estate?"Aldrich, Eastman, and Waltch, L.P., April 1991.

Ambrose, Brent W., and Hugh O. Nourse. "Factors Influencing Capitalization Rates." Working Paper, 1991.

Ballard, Claude M., and Brian J. Strum. "Pension Funds in Real Estate: New Challenges/Opportunities for Professionals." *The Appraisal Journal* 46, no. 4 (October 1978), pp. 551–69.

Brueggeman, William B.; A.H. Chen; and T.G. Thibodeau. "Real Estate Funds: Performance and Portfolio Considerations." *AREUEA Journal** 12, no. 3 (Fall 1984), pp. 333–54.

Brueggeman, William B.; Jeffrey D. Fisher; and David M. Porter. "Rethinking Corporate Real Estate." *Journal of Applied Corporate Finance* 3, no. 1 (Spring 1990), pp. 30–50.

Burns, William L., and Donald R. Epley. "The Performance of Portfolios of REITs and Stocks." *The Journal of Portfolio Management* 8, no. 3 (Spring 1982), pp. 37–41.

California Housing Advisors. "The Role of Single Family Home-building in an Institutional Investment Portfolio." California Housing Advisors, 1991.

Cambon, Barbara R. "Measurement of the Performance of Real Estate." *Real Estate: Valuation Techniques and Portfolio Management,* Institute of Chartered Financial Analysts, 1989, pp. 63–68.

Capozza, Dennis R., and Gregory M. Schwann. "The Value of Risk in Real Estate Markets." *Journal of Real Estate Finance and Economics* (June 1990), pp. 117–40.

---

*AREUEA Journal—American Real Estate and Urban Economics Association Journal.
Note: A valued source for this bibliography was: Jeffrey Fisher and C.F. Sirmans, *Real Estate in Pension Fund Portfolios: An Annotated Bibliography* (Pension Fund Real Estate Association; Glastonbury, CT, Summer 1991).

Chadwick, William J., and Lawrence J. Haas. "Diversification of Pension Fund Real Estate Investments." Pension Briefings, June 1986, pp. 1–18.

Chan, K.C.; Patric H. Hendershott; and Anthony B. Sanders. "Risk and Return in Real Estate: Evidence from Equity REITs." *AREUEA JOURNAL* 18, no. 4 (Winter 1990), pp. 431–52.

Cole, Rebel; David Guilkey; and Mike Miles. "Toward an Assessment of the Reliability of Commercial Appraisals." *The Appraisal Journal* 54, no. 2 (July 1986), pp. 422–32.

Cooperman, Leon G.; Steven G. Einhorn; and Meyer Melnikoff. "Our Expanding Universe: The Case for Pension Fund Investment in Property." Goldman Sachs, New York.

Corgel, John B., and Michael L. Oliphant. "One or More Commingled Real Estate Funds?" *Journal of Portfolio Management* 17, no. 4 (Summer 1991), pp. 69–72.

Curcio, Richard J., and James P. Gaines. "Real Estate Portfolio Revision." *AREUEA Journal* 5, no. 4 (Winter 1977), pp. 399–410.

Davidson, Harold A., and Jeffrey E. Palmer. "A Comparison of the Investment Performance of Common Stocks, Homebuilding Firms, and Equity REITs." *The Real Estate Appraiser and Analyst* 44, no. 4 (July/August 1978), pp. 35–39.

Dokko, Yoon; Robert H. Edelstein; Marshall Pomer; and E. Scott Urdang. "Determinants of the Rate of Return for Nonresidential Real Estate: Inflation Expectations and Market Adjustment Lags." *AREUEA Journal* 19, no. 1 (Spring 1991), pp. 52–69.

Draper, Dennis M., and M. Chapman Findlay. "Capital Asset Pricing and Real Estate Valuation." *AREUEA Journal* 10, no. 2 (Summer 1982), pp. 152–83.

Ennis, Richard M., and Paul Burik. "Pension Fund Real Estate Investment under a Simple Equilibrium Pricing Model." *Financial Analysts Journal* 47, no. 3 (May–June 1991), pp. 20–30.

Ennis, Richard M., and Paul Burik. "The Influence of Non-Risk Factors on Real Estate Holdings of Pension Funds." *Financial Analysts Journal* 47, no. 4 (November–December 1991), pp. 1–15.

Fama, Eugene F., and G. William Schwert. "Assets Returns and Inflation." *Journal of Financial Economics* 5, no. 1 (1977), pp. 115–46.

Findlay, M. Chapman, III.; Carl W. Hamilton; Stephen D. Messner; and Jonathan S. Yorkman. "Optimal Real Estate Portfolios." *AREUEA Journal* 7, no. 3 (Fall 1979), pp. 298–317.

Firstenberg, Paul M.; Stephen A. Ross; and Randall C. Zisler. "Real Estate: The Whole Story." *The Journal of Portfolio Management*. 14, no. 3 (Spring 1988), pp. 22–34.

Firstenberg, Paul M., and Charles H. Wurtzebach. "Managing Portfolio Risk and Return." *Real Estate Review* 19, no. 2 (Summer 1989), pp. 61–65.

Fisher, Jeffrey; David Geltner; and R. Brian Webb. "Historical Value Indices of Commercial Real Estate." Working Paper, Indiana University Center for Real Estate Studies, July 1991, pp. 1–17.

Fisher, Jeffrey D.; Susan Hudson-Wilson; and Charles H. Wurtzebach. "Equilibrium in Real Estate Markets." *The Journal of Portfolio Management,* Summer 1993.

Folger, H. Russell. "20% in Real Estate, Can Theory Justify It?" *The Journal of Portfolio Management* 10, no. 2 (Winter 1984), pp. 6–13.

Folger, Russell H.; Michael R. Granito; and Laurence R. Smith. "A Theoretical Analysis of Real Estate Returns." *Journal of Finance* 40, no. 3 (July 1985), pp. 711–19.

Follain, James R. "Comments on 'Inferring an Investment Return Series for Real Estate from Observations on Sales'." *AREUEA Journal* 17, no. 2 (Summer 1989), pp. 231–34.

Friedman, Harris C. "Real Estate Investment and Portfolio Theory." *Journal of Financial and Quantitative Analysis* 6, no. 2 (March 1971), pp. 861–74.

Froland, Charles. "What Determines Cap Rates on Real Estate?" *The Journal of Portfolio Management* 13, no. 4 (Summer 1987), pp. 77–82.

Froland, Charles; Robert Gorlow; and Richard Sampson. "The Market Risk of Real Estate." *The Journal of Portfolio Management* 12, no. 3 (Spring 1986), pp. 12–19.

Gau, George W. "Weak Form Tests of the Efficiency of Real Estate Investment Markets." *Financial Review* 19, no. 4 (November 1984), pp. 301–20.

Gau, George W., "Efficient Real Estate Markets: Paradox or Paradigm?" *AREUEA Journal* 13, no. 4 (Summer 1987), pp. 1–12.

Gau, George W., and Ko Wang. "A Further Examination of Appraisal Data and the Potential Bias in Real Estate Return Indexes." *AREUEA Journal* 18, no. 1 (Spring 1990), pp. 40–48.

Geltner, David. "Bias in Appraisal-Based Returns." *AREUEA Journal* 17, no. 3 (Fall 1989), pp. 338–52.

Geltner, David. "Estimating Real Estate's Systematic Risk from Aggregate Level Appraisal-Based Returns." *AREUEA Journal* 17, no. 4 (Winter 1989), pp. 463–81.

Geltner, David. "Return Risk and Cash Flow Risk with Long-Term Riskless Leases in Commercial Real Estate." *AREUEA Journal* 18, 4 (Winter 1990), pp. 377–402.

Geltner, David. "A Further Examination of Appraisal Data and the Potential Bias in Real Estate Return Indexes: Comment and Clarification." *AREUEA Journal* 19, no. 1 (Spring 1991), pp. 102–12.

Geltner, David. "Temporal Aggregation in Real Estate Return Indices." Working Paper, 1991.

Giliberto, S. Michael. "A Note on the Use of Appraisal Indexes of Performance Measurement." *AREUEA Journal* 16, no. 1 (Spring 1988), pp. 77–83.

Giliberto, S. Michael. "Real Estate vs. Financial Assets—An Updated Comparison of Returns in the U.S. and the U.K." Salomon Brothers, New York, February 16, 1989.

Giliberto, S. Michael. "Thinking about Real Estate Risk." Salomon Brothers, New York, May 26, 1989.

Giliberto, S. Michael. "Equity Real Estate Investment Trusts and Real Estate Returns." *The Journal of Real Estate Research* 5, no. 2 (Summer 1990), pp. 259–63.

Giliberto, S. Michael. "Real Estate in the Portfolio: Then and Now." Salomon Brothers, New York, July 8, 1991.

Giliberto, S. Michael, and Robert E. Hopkins. "Metropolitan Employment Trends: Analysis and Portfolio Considerations." Salomon Brothers, New York, May 14, 1990.

Goetzman, William N., and Roger G. Ibbotson. "The Performance of Real Estate as an Asset Class." *Journal of Applied Corporate Finance* 13, no. 1 (Spring 1990), pp. 65–76.

Gold, Ronald A. "Real Estate: Can Institutional Portfolios Be Efficiently Diversified without It?" JMB Institutional Realty Corporation, June 1986.

Goldberg, Sandon J. "Toward an Indexed Portfolio of Real Estate. Part III: Industrial Buildings." Salomon Brothers, New York, June 19, 1989.

Gordon, Jacques N. "The Diversification Potential of International Property Investments." *The Real Estate Finance Journal* 7, no. 2 (Fall 1991), pp. 42–48.

Graff, Richard A., and Daniel M. Cashdan, Jr. "Some New Ideas in Real Estate Finance." *Journal of Applied Corporate Finance* 3, no. 1 (Spring 1990), pp. 77–89.

Grissom, Terry V.; David J. Hartzell; and Crocker H. Liu. "An Approach to Industrial Real Estate Market Segmentation and Valuation Using the Arbitrage Pricing Paradigm." *AREUEA Journal* 15, no. 3 (Fall 1987), pp. 199–219.

Grissom, Terry V.; James L. Kuhle; and Carl H. Waither. "Diversification Works in Real Estate, Too." *The Journal of Portfolio Management* 13, no. 2 (Winter 1987), pp. 66–71.

Guilkey, David; Mike Miles; and Rebel Cole. "The Motivation for Institutional Real Estate Sales and Implications for Asset Class Returns." *AREUEA Journal* 17, no. 1 (Spring 1989), pp. 70–86.

Guntermann, Karl L., and Richard L. Smith. "Derivation of Cost of Capital and Equity Rates from Market Data." *AREUEA Journal* 15, no. 2 (Summer 1987), pp. 98–109.

Gyourko, Joseph, and Donald Keim. "Risk and Returns of Investing in Real Estate: Evidence from a Real Estate Stock Index." Working Paper, The Wharton School, University of Pennsylvania, September 27, 1992.

Gyourko, Joseph, and Peter Linneman. "Owner-Occupied Homes, Income-Producing Properties, and REITs as Inflation Hedges: Empirical Findings." *Journal of Real Estate Finance and Economics* 1, no. 4 (December 1988), pp. 347–72.

Hallengren, Howard E. "How Different Investments Fare during Inflationary Cycles." *The Commercial and Financial Chronicle* 219, no. 7415 (June 3, 1974), pp. 3–9.

Hartzell, David J. "Real Estate in the Portfolio." Salomon Brothers, New York, August 27, 1986.

Hartzell, David J. "Real Estate Risks and Returns: Results of a Survey." Salomon Brothers, New York, March 23, 1989.

Hartzell, David J., and S. Michael Giliberto. Expectation for Risks and Returns for Real Estate and Financial Assets." Salomon Brothers, New York, April 20, 1990.

Hartzell, David J.; John S. Hekman; and Mike Miles. "Diversification Categories in Investment Real Estate." *AREUEA Journal* 14, no. 2 (Summer 1986), pp. 230–54.

Hartzell, David J.; John S. Hekman; and Mike Miles. "Real Estate Returns and Inflation." *AREUEA Journal* 15, no. 1 (Spring 1987), pp. 617–37.

Hartzell, David J., and David Shulman. "Real Estate Risks and Returns: A Survey." Salomon Brothers, New York, February 12, 1988.

Hartzell, David J.; David Shulman; Terence C. Langetieg; and Martin L. Leibowitz. "A Look at Real Estate Duration." *The Journal of Portfolio Management* 15, no. 1 (Fall 1988), pp. 16–24.

Hartzell, David J.; David Shulman, and Charles H. Wurtzebach. "Refining the Analysis of Regional Diversification for Income-Producing Real Estate." *The Journal of Real Estate Research* 2, no. 2 (Winter 1987), pp. 85–95.

Hoag, James W. "Towards Indices of Real Estate Value and Returns." *Journal of Finance* 35, no. 2 (May 1980), pp. 569–80.

Hopkins, Robert E., and David Shulman. "Toward an Indexed Portfolio of Real Estate. Part II: Recent Construction." Salomon Brothers, New York, January 3, 1989.

Hopkins, Robert E., and Bernadette A. Testa. "Economic Diversification in Real Estate Portfolios II." Salomon Brothers, November 15, 1990.

Hopkins, Robert E., and Bernadette A. Testa. "Economic Diversification in the Real Estate Portfolio: Recent Industrial Trends." Salomon Brothers, New York, March 1, 1991.

Hudson-Wilson, Susan. "New Trends in Portfolio Theory." *The Journal of Property Management* 55, no. 3 (May/June 1990), pp. 57–58.

Hudson-Wilson, Susan, and Katrina Sherrerd, eds. *CFA Readings in Real Estate.* Institute of Chartered Financial Analysts: Charlottesville, VA, 1990.

Hudson-Wilson, Susan. "Are Measures of Real Estate Returns Wrong?" *Pensions & Investments Age,* March 1990.

Ibbotson, Roger G., and Carol L. Fall. "The U.S. Market Wealth Portfolio." *The Journal of Portfolio Management* 5, no. 1 (Fall 1979), pp. 82-92.

Ibbotson, Roger G., and Laurence B. Siegel. "The World Market Wealth Portfolio." *The Journal of Portfolio Management* 9, no. 2 (Winter 1983), pp. 5–17.

Ibbotson, Roger G., and Laurence B. Siegel. "Real Estate Returns: A Comparison with Other Investments." *AREUEA Journal* 12, no. 3 (Fall 1984), pp. 219–42.

Ibbotson, Roger G.; Laurence B. Siegel; and Kathryn S. Lowe. "World Wealth: Market Values and Returns." *The Journal of Portfolio Management* 12, no. 1 (Fall 1986), pp. 4–23.

Kaplan, Howard M. "Farmland as a Portfolio Investment." *The Journal of Portfolio Management* 11, no. 2 (Winter 1985), pp. 73–78.

Kostin, David J. "An Initial Benchmark for Global Office Building Investments." Salomon Brothers, New York, October 4, 1989.

Kostin, David J. "Toward an Indexed Portfolio of Real Estate. Part IV: Regional Shopping Centers." Salomon Brothers, New York, October 4, 1989.

Liu, Crocker H.; Terry V. Grissom; and David J. Hartzell. "The Impact of Market Imperfections on Real Estate Returns and Optimal Investor Portfolios." *AREUEA Journal* 18, no. 4 (Winter 1990), pp. 453–78.

Liu, Crocker H.; David J. Hartzell; Wylie Greig; and Terry V. Grissom. "The Integration of the Real Estate Market and the Stock Market: Some Preliminary Evidence." *Journal of Real Estate Finance and Economics* 3, no. 3 (September 1990), pp. 261–82.

Liu, Crocker H.; David Hartzell; Terry V. Grissom; and Wylie Greig. "The Composition of the Market Portfolio and Real Estate Investment Performance." *AREUEA Journal* 18, no. 1 (Spring 1990), pp. 49–75.

Liu, Crocker H., and Jianping Mei. "The Predictability of Returns on Equity REITs and Their Co-Movement with Other Assets." Working Paper, 1991.

Lusht, Kenneth M. "Inflation and Real Estate Investment Value." *AREUEA Journal* 6, no. 1 (Spring 1978), pp. 37–49.

Miles, Mike. "What Is the Value of U.S. Real Estate?" *Real Estate Review*, 20, no. 2 (Summer 1990), pp. 69–77.

Miles, Mike; Rebel Cole; and David Guilkey. "A Different Look at Commercial Real Estate Returns." *AREUEA Journal* 18, no. 4 (Winter 1990), pp. 403–30.

Miles, Mike, and Arthur Esty. "How Well Do Commingled Real Estate Funds Perform?" *The Journal of Portfolio Management* 8, no. 2 (Winter 1982), pp. 62–68.

Miles, Mike, and Tom McCue. "Historic Returns and Institutional Real Estate Portfolios." *AREUEA Journal* 10, no. 2 (Summer 1982), pp. 184–99.

Miles, Mike, and Tom McCue. "Diversification in the Real Estate Portfolio." *The Journal of Real Estate Research* 7, no. 1 (Spring 1984), pp. 17–28.

Miles, Mike, and Tom McCue. "Commercial Real Estate Returns." *AREUEA Journal* 12, no. 3 (Fall 1984), pp. 355–77.

Miles, Mike, and Michael Rice. "Towards a More Complete Investigation of the Correlation of Real Estate Investment Yield to the Rate Evidenced in the Money and Capital Markets: The Individual Investor's Perspective." *The Real Estate Appraiser and Analyst* 44, no. 6 (November–December 1978), pp. 8–19.

Miles, Mike; R. Brian Webb; and David Guilkey. "On the Nature of Systematic Risk in Commercial Real Estate." Working Paper, July 1991, pp. 1–33.

Park, Jeong Yun; Donald J. Mullineaux; and It-Keong Chew. "Are REITs Inflation Hedges?" *Journal of Real Estate Finance and Economics* 3, no. 1 (March 1990), pp. 91–103.

Phyrr, Stephen A.; Waldo L. Born; and James R. Webb. "Development of a Dynamic Investment Strategy under Alternative Inflation Cycle Scenarios." *The Journal of Real Estate Research* 5, no. 2 (Summer 1990), pp. 177–93.

Quan, Daniel C., and John M. Quigley. "Inferring an Investment Return Series for Real Estate from Observations on Sales." *AREUEA Journal* 17, no. 2 (Summer 1989), pp. 218–30.

Quan, Daniel C., and John M. Quigley. "Price Formation and the Appraisal Function in Real Estate Markets." *Journal of Real Estate Finance and Economics* 4, no. 2 (June 1991), pp. 127–46.

Robichek, Alexander A.; Richard A. Cohn; and John J. Pringle. "Returns on Alternative Investment Media and Implications for Portfolio Construction." *Journal of Business* 55, no. 3 (July 1972), pp. 427–43.

Ross, Stephen A., and Randall C. Zisler. "Risk and Return in Real Estate." *Journal of Real Estate Finance and Economics* 4, no. 2 (June 1991), pp. 175–90.

Roulac, Stephen E. "Can Real Estate Returns Outperform Common Stocks?" *The Journal of Portfolio Management* 2, no. 2 (Winter 1976), pp. 26–43.

Roulac, Stephen E. "Influence of Capital Market Theory on Real Estate Returns and the Value of Economic Analysis." *The Real Estate Appraiser and Analyst* 44, no. 6 (November–December 1978), pp. 62–71.

Rubens, Jack H.; Michael T. Bond; and James R. Webb. "The Inflation-Hedging Effectiveness of Real Estate." *The Journal of Real Estate Research* 4, no. 2 (1989), pp. 45–55.

Shulman, David. "Inflation in Real Estate: Will this Time Be Different?" Salomon Brothers, New York, March 6, 1989.

Shulman, David; Sandon J. Goldberg; David J. Hartzell; and Robert E. Hopkins. "Toward an Indexed Portfolio of Real Estate. Part I: Office Buildings." Salomon Brothers, New York, June 2, 1988.

Shulman, David, and Robert E. Hopkins. "Economic Diversification in Real Estate Portfolios." Salomon Brothers, New York, November 1988.

Sirmans, C.F., and James R. Webb. "Expected Equity Returns on Real Estate Financed with Life Insurance Company Loans: 1967–1977." *AREUEA Journal* 8, no. 2 (Summer 1980), pp. 218–28.

Sirmans, G. Stacy, and C.F. Sirmans. "The Historical Perspective of Real Estate Returns." *The Journal of Portfolio Management* 13, no. 3 (Spring 1987), pp. 22–31.

Statman, Meir. "Discussion of 'A Theoretical Analysis of Real Estate Returns'." *Journal of Finance* 40, no. 3 (July 1985), pp. 719–21.

Titman, Sheridan, and Arthur Warga. "Risk and the Performance of Real Estate Investment Trusts: A Multiple Index Approach." *AREUEA Journal* 14, no. 3 (Fall 1986), pp. 414–31.

Walker, J. Raymond. "Real Estate as a Pension Fund Investment." Southern California Edison Company, May 27, 1975.

Walker, J. Raymond. "Performance Measurement for Real Estate in the Portfolio Context." Working Paper, 1991.

Webb, James R. "On the Exclusion of Real Estate from the Market Portfolio." *The Journal of Portfolio Management* 16, no. 1 (Fall 1990), pp. 78-84.

Webb, James R.; Richard J. Curcio; and Jack H. Rubens. "Diversification Gains from Including Real Estate in Mixed-Asset Portfolios." *Decision Sciences* 19, no. 2 (Spring 1988), pp. 434–52.

Webb, James R., and Jack H. Rubens. "Portfolio Considerations in the Valuation of Real Estate." *AREUEA Journal* 14, no. 3 (Fall 1986), pp. 465–95.

Webb, James R., and Jack H. Rubens. "How Much in Real Estate? A Surprising Answer." *The Journal of Portfolio Management* 13, no. 3 (Spring 1987), pp. 10–14.

Webb, James R., and Jack H. Rubens. "The Effect of Alternative Return Measures on Restricted Mixed-Asset Portfolios." *AREUEA Journal* 16, no. 2 (Summer 1988), pp. 123–37.

Webb, James R., and C.F. Sirmans. "Yields for Selected Types of Real Estate vs. the Money and Capital Markets." *The Appraisal Journal* 50, no. 2 (April 1982), pp. 228–42.

West, David A. "Recent Institutionalization of Real Estate Investments." *Business and Society,* 1987, pp. 45–52.

Wheaton, William C., and Raymond G. Torto. "Income and Appraised Values: A Reexamination of the FRC Returns Data." *AREUEA Journal* 17, no. 4 (Winter 1989), pp. 439–49.

Wurtzebach, Charles H. "Assembling an Equity Real Estate Portfolio." *Investing,* Fall 1989, pp. 87–91.

Wurtzebach, Charles H. "Looking at Non-United States Real Estate." *Real Estate Review* 21, no. 1 (Spring 1991), pp. 48–54.

Wurtzebach, Charles H.; Glenn R. Mueller; and Donna Machi. "The Impact of Inflation and Vacancy on Real Estate Returns." *The Journal of Real Estate Research,* 1991.

Young, Michael S. "Comparative Investment Performance: Common Stock versus Real Estate." *Real Estate Issues* 2, no. 1 (Summer 1977), pp. 30–46.

Zerbst, Robert H., and Barbara R. Cambon. "Historical Returns on Real Estate Investment." *The Journal of Portfolio Management* 10, no. 3 (Spring 1984), pp. 5–20.

INDEX